"In simple, eloquent, and compellir̶ ̶ ̶ ̶ ̶ ̶ ̶ ̶ ̶ ̶ account of how God's law, understoo̶ ̶ ̶ ̶ ̶ ̶ ̶ ̶ ̶ the grace released in Jesus Christ, is the best guide we could find. Barrs shows us the biblical path to a sane and balanced worldview, avoiding the pitfalls of utopian theocracy, libertarian naïveté, and cultural indifference. More than a guide, this book is an invitation to see God as our only comfort in life and in death. *Delighting in the Law of the Lord* is simply delightful!"

William Edgar, Professor of Apologetics, Westminster Theological Seminary, Philadelphia

"We live in morally confusing times—confusing for the culture, confusing for the church. We've lost the compass, and, truth be told, when it comes to personal or societal issues, most of us Christians simply don't think of the law of God as providing much guidance. 'Think again!' says Jerram Barrs. In his winsome across-the-kitchen-table style, Barrs explains why we need to retrieve afresh one of God's greatest gifts. Churches will love this resource!"

Nicholas Perrin, Dean, Wheaton College Graduate School

"Jerram characteristically begins with a relevant piece of cultural analysis, honed from his decades of outreach to unbelievers, in which he traces the declension in Western culture from deism to postmodernism. But God has not delivered his people from the hopelessness of secularism and relativism to have them render the joyless obedience of moralism and legalism. Jerram expounds the true nature and purpose of God's law from the Psalms, which extol God's law in light of the Bible story of creation and redemption, and he draws primarily on the Gospels for stories to illustrate how this perspective on God's law works out in practice. All will find this book challenging and helpful, but I recommend it especially to those engaged in communication of the truth that is in Jesus, particularly preachers, Bible study groups, parents, and Christian schools."

David Clyde Jones, Professor Emeritus of Systematic Theology and Ethics, Covenant Theological Seminary; author, *Biblical Christian Ethics*

"Equally committed to the graciousness of God, the goodness of his law, and the calling of human beings to embody God's moral character in all that we do, Jerram Barrs gently but decisively charts a course that falls into neither the ditch of meaningless moral relativism nor the choking grip of Christian legalism. He convincingly shows the biblical importance of the law as an essential guide to Christian discipleship, service, and happiness, both personally and within the larger realities of the church and society. Immersed in Scripture, theologically sound, and pastorally driven, Barrs writes from a lifetime of ministry that is both insightful and pastorally engaging. This catechesis of the way of the Lord should be in every ministry toolbox and is an absolute must-read by every Christian who wants to find greater integrity of life and deeper relationship with Christ, our fellow human beings, and God's good creation."

Michael D. Williams, Professor of Systematic Theology, Covenant Theological Seminary

DELIGHTING *in the* LAW *of the* LORD

Other Crossway Books by Jerram Barrs

Echoes of Eden: Reflections on Christianity, Literature, and the Arts

Learning Evangelism from Jesus

The Heart of Evangelism

Through His Eyes: God's Perspective on Women in the Bible

DELIGHTING
in the LAW *of the* LORD

GOD'S ALTERNATIVE
to LEGALISM AND MORALISM

JERRAM BARRS

CROSSWAY

WHEATON, ILLINOIS

Trade paperback ISBN: 978-1-4335-3713-4
Mobipocket ISBN: 978-1-4335-3715-8
PDF ISBN: 978-1-4335-3714-1
ePub ISBN: 978-1-4335-3716-5

Library of Congress Cataloging-in-Publication Data

Barrs, Jerram.
　　Delighting in the law of the Lord : God's alternative to legalism and moralism / Jerram Barrs.
　　　　pages cm
　　Includes bibliographical references and index.
　　ISBN 978-1-4335-3713-4 (tp)
　　1. Bible and law. 2. Law and gospel—Biblical teaching. 3. Law (Theology)—Biblical teaching. I. Title.
BS680.L33B37　　　　2013
241'.2—dc23　　　　　　　　　　　　　　　　　2013014375

Crossway is a publishing ministry of Good News Publishers.

VP		23	22	21	20	19	18	17	16	15	14	13
15	14	13	12	11	10	9	8	7	6	5	4	3	2	1

I dedicate this book to my much-loved father-in-law,
my "Dad" since my own beloved father's death in 1972.
Dad, you were a beautiful model of a man who loved the
Lord and who delighted in his law. Your service of firstfruits
has been an inspiration to people all over this world. Now with
full assurance, you know the Lord's delight in you, and you,
I am confident, gladly cast your crown at his feet every day,
knowing that apart from Jesus all your labors would have
been in vain. You lived out Psalm 1 every day of your life
as you gave yourself to loving the Lord and following
his commandments. Of you it could truly be said:

Blessed is the man
who walks not in the counsel of the wicked,
nor stands in the way of sinners,
nor sits in the seat of scoffers;
but his delight is in the law of the LORD,
and on his law he meditates day and night.

He is like a tree
planted by streams of water
that yields its fruit in its season,
and its leaf does not wither.
In all that he does, he prospers.

Contents

1 The Good Life (1): Do We Need God's Laws Today?   11

2 The Good Life (2): Found in Christianity or Postmodernism?   27

3 The Source of Law: Humanity or God?   42

4 The Beauty of the Law   60

5 The Giving of the Law at Sinai   73

6 Law and the Image of God (1)   87

7 Law and the Image of God (2)   99

8 The Spirit of the Law   113

9 Jesus Expounds the Law   124

10 Jesus Fulfills the Law   135

11 Jesus Overcomes the Curse of the Law   147

12 How Substantial Is the Healing We Can Expect?   160

13 How Have Different Traditions Understood the Law?   172

14 Jesus Challenges Additions to God's Law   186

15 Jesus's Attack on Legalism   199

16 Rules for the Family and Church?   212

17 Jesus Applies the Law   226

18 Jesus Shows Amazing Grace   239

19 Lessons from Jesus's Two Approaches   252

20 To Whom Ought We to Show and Tell the Law?   265

21 The Law of God and Our Secular Society   281

22 Living as Salt and Light in and for the World   295

23 Old Testament Law: How Should We View It?   308

24 The New Covenant and the Law   327

General Index   331

Scripture Index   341

1

The Good Life (1)

Do We Need God's Laws Today?

How do you think about the law of God? Many of God's commandments were written down around thirty-five hundred years ago during the life of Moses; others come from the time of Jesus and his apostles, almost two thousand years ago. Do you sometimes think, "I personally don't need laws written thousands of years ago to direct my life; I am quite capable of reflecting on the challenges I face each day and making up my own mind about what is right for me"? Or do you perhaps assume that the culture in which we live today knows better about how we should live than people from such distant times and different cultures? After all, we might reason, our scientific knowledge has advanced so much in terms of our understanding of the individual and society that it is no longer necessary for us to obey a moral code written in a time of comparative ignorance about human life.

In this first chapter, my plan is to begin to challenge such views. Our first challenge will be to set before us a brief passage from one of the psalms of David, for in this psalm we see David setting out his passionate belief that he needs God to teach him through God's laws how he, David, ought to live. I suggest that the reader consider making these words of David a personal prayer, both for the reading of this book and, more importantly, for daily life.

Make me to know your ways, O Lord;
   teach me your paths.
Lead me in your truth and teach me,
   for you are the God of my salvation;
   for you I wait all the day long.

Remember your mercy, O Lord, and your steadfast love,
   for they have been from of old.
Remember not the sins of my youth or my transgressions;
   according to your steadfast love remember me,
   for the sake of your goodness, O Lord!

Good and upright is the Lord;
   therefore he instructs sinners in the way.
He leads the humble in what is right,
   and teaches the humble his way.
All the paths of the Lord are steadfast love and faithfulness,
   for those who keep his covenant and his testimonies.

For your name's sake, O Lord,
   pardon my guilt, for it is great.[1]

There are many beautiful things in this excerpt from Psalm 25. A repeated refrain is David's longing to be taught by "the Lord." Notice how, in the above text and in your Bible, capital letters are used for the name "Lord" to remind us that David is using God's personal name, *Yahweh*, the name that refers to God's everlasting faithfulness to his promises. David knows that he needs "the Lord" to show him how to live, for he understands that he is a sinner and that, therefore, he cannot be trusted to know what is right; so he humbles himself to ask the Lord to teach him. The Word of God teaches us that humility before the Lord is essential for each one of us as we come to reflect on how we are to live today, and tomorrow, and every other day of life in this world. Do I trust myself? Do I think I am wise enough to know how I should live? Or am I prepared to humble myself and ask my heavenly Father to teach me?

Notice, too, how David describes what he wants to learn about the right way to live: the right way to live is the way of the Lord. David

---

[1] Psalm 25:4–11.

desires to understand the paths in which the Lord walks, for David knows that there is no one else in the universe whose life is fully characterized by moral goodness. No one, except the Lord himself, lives the truly good life. David wants to be like God, to follow in the steps of love, mercy, and faithfulness that describe the way the Lord lives.

A third point to note here is that as soon as David reflects on the character of God, he cannot help but think about his own failure to be like God, his inability to walk steadfastly in the ways of the Lord. Because he realizes this inability and failure, David confesses his guilt. The more clearly he thinks about the character and pattern of the life of the Lord, the greater David's sin seems to him. For us today, just as with David, any careful study of the law of God is going to have this uncomfortable element of revealing our sin and humbling us. The more we reflect on the ways of the Lord, the more our sins are exposed. So be prepared to see yourself in new and discomfiting ways!

We should also observe that the aspects of God's character that David focuses on here are the love and gracious mercy of God, for these are central to any meditation on the ways of the Lord. As David says, "All the paths of the LORD are steadfast love and faithfulness" toward us. Another way to express this is to think about the great commandments as Jesus summarizes them for us: "You shall love the Lord your God with all your heart and with all your soul and with all your mind. This is the great and first commandment. And a second is like it: You shall love your neighbor as yourself. On these two commandments depend all the Law and the Prophets."[2]

Just as with us, so it is with the Lord. The summary of all the law for us, of all the teaching of God's Word, is that we are to love God and our neighbor. The reason for this is that all the paths of the Lord are steadfast love and faithfulness. He desires that we be like him. David desires that he be like the Lord; he desires that all his thoughts, words, and actions be filled with steadfast love and faithfulness. The apostle Paul expresses the same idea this way: "Love is the fulfilling of the law."[3]

Do we agree with David's prayer? Do we believe that we need to humble ourselves before God and to ask him to teach us the way he

---

[2] Matthew 22:37–40.
[3] Romans 13:10.

walks, that we ought to desire to know God's law so well that we will be convicted of our sins and led to confession? Before we try to answer these questions, perhaps it would be helpful for us to think about just why we might be tempted to believe that we know better as to how we should live than the laws in the Bible do, why we might feel that our culture today possesses greater knowledge of human behavior than the writers of God's Word could possibly have had. To understand our own reactions, we need to think about our cultural setting. This is necessary, for all of us are deeply shaped by the society in which we live. Hear Paul's words:

> I appeal to you therefore, brothers [and sisters], by the mercies of God, to present your bodies as a living sacrifice, holy and acceptable to God, which is your spiritual worship. Do not be conformed to this world, but be transformed by the renewal of your mind, that by testing you may discern what is the will of God, what is good and acceptable and perfect.[4]

If we desire to understand what God's good and acceptable and perfect will is for us, that is, his law, then we first need to reflect on the culture in which we live and on the ways it shapes us. Only then will our minds be renewed and our lives transformed. Without this cultural awareness we will be unconscious imitators of the patterns of life around us rather than people who walk in the ways of the Lord. And we will doubt that we need moral instruction from the distant past and from such different cultural settings.

Consider some examples from the recent past. First, I am sure that many readers of this book were aware of the riots happening in August 2011 in London, and in many other parts of the United Kingdom. What was most troubling about the wanton damage and theft that accompanied these riots was the apparent absence of moral guilt or shame among many of the perpetrators of these crimes. I read interviews in which young people spoke proudly and defiantly about the destruction they had caused and the goods they had stolen from the stores that were broken into and looted. These young people came across as having no conscience about the people who were hurt, or even killed,

---

[4] Romans 12:1–2 (see ESV footnote 1).

or about the personal and financial damage done to those who had property stolen or ruined.

Or, for a different kind of example, consider typical court cases on matters of obscenity, like the prosecution arising from the exhibition of Robert Mapplethorpe's photographs in Cincinnati, Ohio, some years ago:

> Mapplethorpe's X Portfolio series sparked national attention in the early 1990s when it was included in *The Perfect Moment*, a traveling exhibition funded by National Endowment for the Arts. The portfolio includes some of Mapplethorpe's most explicit imagery, including a self-portrait with a bullwhip inserted in his anus. Though his work had been regularly displayed in publicly funded exhibitions, conservative and religious organizations, such as the American Family Association, seized on this exhibition to vocally oppose government support for what they called "nothing more than the sensational presentation of potentially obscene material." As a result, Mapplethorpe became something of a cause célèbre for both sides of the American culture war. The installation of *The Perfect Moment* in Cincinnati resulted in the unsuccessful prosecution of the Contemporary Arts Center of Cincinnati and its director, Dennis Barrie, on charges of "pandering obscenity."[5]

Another example is the various prosecutions and acquittals arising from the music and lyrics of the group 2 Live Crew:

> In 1989, the group released their album, *As Nasty As They Wanna Be*, which also became the group's most successful album. A large part of its success was due to the single "Me So Horny," which was popular despite little radio rotation. The American Family Association (AFA) did not think the presence of a "Parental Advisory" sticker was enough to adequately warn listeners of what was inside the case. Jack Thompson, a lawyer affiliated with the AFA, met with Florida Governor Bob Martinez and convinced him to look into the album to see if it met the legal classification of obscenity. In 1990 action was taken at the local level and Nick Navarro, Broward County sheriff, received a

---

[5]"Robert Mapplethorpe," accessed May 21, 2013, http://en.wikipedia.org/wiki/Robert_Mapplethorpe. I would not usually quote a Wikipedia article, unless it had extensive and authoritative referencing (which the article on Mapplethorpe does have). In addition, in this case, the Wikipedia article simply summarizes what was widely reported at the time in the media.

ruling from County Circuit Court judge Mel Grossman that probable cause for obscenity violations existed. In response, Luther Campbell maintained that people should focus on issues relating to hunger and poverty rather than on the lyrical content of their music.

Navarro warned record store owners that selling the album might be prosecutable. The 2 Live Crew then filed a suit against Navarro. That June, U.S. district court Judge Jose Gonzalez ruled the album obscene and illegal to sell. Charles Freeman, a local retailer, was arrested two days later, after selling a copy to an undercover police officer. This was followed by the arrest of three members of The 2 Live Crew after they performed some material from the album at a nightclub. They were acquitted soon after, as professor Henry Louis Gates, Jr. testified at their trial in defense of their lyrics. Freeman's conviction was overturned on appeal as well.[6]

In both of these cases jury members were interviewed after the acquittals. Many of them said something like this: "I think that these photographs (or these lyrics) are obscene. I do not want to see them (hear them); and I do not want my children to see them (hear them). But who am I to say that no one else should be able to see them (hear them) if they so wish? This is only my personal opinion. It is not my place to declare these photos (or these lyrics) objectively obscene."

A fourth example comes from the visit of Pope John Paul II to St. Louis, Missouri, in January 1999. Those who live in the St. Louis area especially will remember how rapturously he was received in this city. His visit was the biggest event in the history of St. Louis, with up to a hundred thousand people turning out to hear him speak. He spoke with great passion about two moral issues in particular: sexual chastity and fidelity, and the sacredness of human life and the great moral evil of abortion. These talks were received with lengthy standing ovations.

However, one has to note with sadness that many of those who applauded him so fervently appear to have had no serious intention of putting his words into practice in their own personal lives. I do not say this to attack Roman Catholics in particular, for the same problems exist among the members of almost all churches.

---

[6] "2 Live Crew," accessed May 21, 2013, http://en.wikipedia.org/wiki/2_Live_Crew. Again, the Wikipedia article is both well footnoted and a clear and helpful summary of what was commonly reported at the time.

I serve as the pastor officiating the ceremony in several weddings each year, and I am afraid I have come to assume that it is a rare couple who are not already having sexual intercourse before marriage. In the 1970s, when I was first ordained and began to take wedding services, I could be confident that eight out of ten couples who had grown up in Christian homes would be sexually chaste, though it was already rare at that time to find a young man or woman from a non-Christian home who had not been sexually active. Today, my sorrowful estimate is that it will only be one or two out of ten young couples, of whatever background, who have remained chaste until marriage.

A fifth example comes from a Christian student I heard interviewed on public radio about abortion. The student, clearly an evangelical believer, said, "I believe that abortion is the murder of an innocent human life." She went on to say, "I also believe that abortion is a matter of personal choice and that, therefore, we ought not to have laws against abortion." I hear many Christians who think and speak in a similar manner about abortion, and about many other moral issues, concerning which the historical church has taken an unequivocal stand, not only for the individual Christian's life, but also for the life of society.

A sixth example comes from my own conversations with young people about Hitler and the Holocaust. Many are not prepared to condemn as absolute evil the slaughter of six million Jews and of many Gypsies, Christians, and mentally and physically disabled people, and countless others in the death camps of Nazi Germany. It is the same with the murders by Islamic terrorists. I hear many people expressing themselves with views like this: "I personally think the terrorist killings are wicked. But I have to recognize that, from their perspective, these are not crimes, but rather legitimate acts of protest against corrupt and evil regimes. So it all depends on one's perspective as to whether one decides their acts are evil."

How have we come to this, that people around us, including our fellow Christians, find it so difficult to make objective or absolute moral judgments? We need to go back some distance in time to understand our path to this present dilemma. We will begin with some brief reflections on what is often referred to as modernism, looking first at deism, then at secular humanism. Then we will turn to postmodernism.

MODERNISM (1):
DEISM OR NATURAL RELIGION, A NEW PATH

In Psalm 25 David wrote about the path of the Lord. Deism may be described as a new path in religion that some began to take during the early 1600s. Deism arose in the context of an understandable reaction to the religious wars and the persecutions that followed the period of the Reformation. Many, both inside and outside the church, reacted to these shocking departures from the gospel of Christ (such as taking up arms against fellow Christians or putting them on trial and burning them to death as heretics). Others went much further and also rejected the institutional churches, their claims to authority, and their doctrines.

One of the leaders of this rejection of the Christian churches was Lord Herbert of Cherbury, who is known as the "father of deism." He argued that churches are always fighting over beliefs and practices, and that, therefore, it is necessary for all people of sense and good will to get back to the basics of true Christianity. He declared that all beliefs about God, and all the ways of life that arise from those belief systems, are the same at their roots. Therefore, he argued, it is right for us to find the common notions that are present in all religious beliefs, and to discern what we consider to be true in the religions and churches that we find around us. He rejected the authority of churches and Scriptures and argued, instead, that in ourselves we have two means of judging that are perfectly adequate to enable us to come to notions of truth and goodness, and to live the good life.

1. Our reason: we will evaluate religious claims for ourselves.
2. Our conscience: we can ask what seems right about God to us.

Herbert came up with a kind of common-denominator religion, one he thought all people of good will would believe and follow. He removed all the distinctive doctrines of Christianity (the Trinity, the divinity of Christ, Jesus's incarnation, his substitutionary death) and taught that the true religion, which every person of sense and moral virtue could acknowledge, consists of honor for God and moral behavior to our fellow humans.

Herbert's ideas were very influential, and over the following 150 years there was a flourishing of deist thought and writing. One very significant example is Matthew Tindal, who wrote *Christianity as Old as Creation*, published in 1730 in England. Its subtitle is *The Gospel, a Republication of the Religion of Nature*. He was called "the great apostle of deism," and his book, "the Bible of deism." He made the following basic points:

1. God is fair, so all peoples must know the truth about God, and all religions must lead to God.
2. All religions teach us to honor God.
3. All religions teach us to do what is right—God's moral commandments are self-evidently good.
4. There will be an afterlife with rewards and punishments.
5. Our personal calling is the pursuit of our individual happiness.
6. It is obvious that we should all work for the common good.

Many deists in Tindal's day, in the eighteenth century, continued to attend church. The same is true in our day. And like today, many pastors and churches became deist rather than genuinely Christian in any biblical sense, though they continued to call themselves Christian. "Our religion," they said, "is the true Christianity." What was once thought of as Christian came to be considered narrow, rigid, doctrinaire, harsh, intolerant, and unloving, far removed from the true spirit of Jesus.

In deist settings, then as today, the Bible was still respected as containing much that is good and true, and there remained some sense of accountability to God. However, the final authority became the individual's conscience and reason; and the final goal of life became the pursuit of personal happiness, the pursuit of one's own definition of the good life.

For churchgoers and for some outside the church (though in declining numbers) the Bible was still seen as a source to be considered for moral direction. However, in our day the individual has become increasingly the final source of moral authority over such questions as sexual fidelity, homosexuality, human life issues like abortion and euthanasia, truth telling, theft, and so forth. This is so for present-day deists in a way that would have been unthinkable for the eighteenth-century deist, who regarded such moral issues as crystal clear. One might say that in the eighteenth century, deists simply assumed that what the Bible taught was self-evident moral truth. This is no longer the case for deists today; and often it is no longer the case even for those who think of themselves as Bible-believing Christians.

Modernism (2): Secular Humanism, the Next Step

The next step along the path away from Christianity was the declaration that it is not just the churches that are the problem, but religions in general and the Christian religion in particular. The secular humanists developed a more consistent modernism and proclaimed: "We do not need any traditional religion. Why should we humans bother with God at all?" For the secular humanist this world is simply material. There is only the natural world, and we humans are a part of this natural world. Time and chance, and the process of evolution working on matter and energy, are a sufficient source and explanation of everything that exists.

Humanism's basic thrust is deep optimism about reason and human nature. What will be our guide along the path of life? Secular humanists set out their answer in the following beliefs:

1. We must put our trust in reason. There is no need for revelation (the Bible) at all. In place of revelation from some imagined god, human reason will lead us into all the truth and answer all our questions.
2. The application of the scientific method as we use our reason in the scientific endeavor will enable us to understand the world around us and to control the forces of nature, thereby creating a better world. Science will also enable us to understand and to control the human person and to solve our problems. This later application of reason and science in order to understand and solve the problems of individuals and societies began to develop in new and powerful ways at the beginning of the twentieth century.
3. Human nature is basically good. We just need education and the right laws and social structures to create a new world order, an enduring citadel of peace, prosperity, and happiness here on earth.
4. We as humans can figure out what is good for ourselves. Ethics does not need religion or God. The enlightened individual knows what is best for himself or herself and is able to live a moral,

happy, and productive life without any need for divine revelation
or intervention.

Most ordinary Americans would not identify themselves with
these basic beliefs of secular humanism. Most have not completely
lost some kind of belief in God or some sense of the afterlife. But in
truth, all of us, whether we have ever thought about it or not, whether
we recognize it or not, are impacted by these convictions of deism and
secular humanism.

Modernism has had the effect of seriously undermining any claims
to religious, doctrinal, or moral authority, whether of God, of Christ,
of creeds, of churches, or of church leaders. The deep conviction of
people around us, and of each one of us, is this: "I can think things
through for myself and come to my own conclusions about God, doctrine, and morals." Modernism also undermines all our sense of accountability to God. We create a god in our own image, a god who will
not hold us accountable and who would never dream of judging us.

POSTMODERNISM: EXISTENTIALISM, A DEAD END

With existentialism or postmodernism, the new road taken by modernism loses its way, and has, perhaps, come to a dead end.[7] The path
to the good life peters out, disappearing in the woods of skepticism and
irrationality. Existentialism is simply a consistent atheism. The existentialist recognizes that without God, everything changes. In Europe,
the way people thought was deeply influenced by the World Wars. In
the United States, the Vietnam War had something of the same effect.
Postmodernism comes to several bleak conclusions:

1. Reason is inadequate to find objective or absolute truth. Because
   we are finite, truth is forever beyond us.
2. Science is not our savior, for technology produces not only good
   but evil. Scientific research has created weapons of mass destruction for modern warfare: nuclear arsenals and biological and chemical weapons with unimaginable consequences. Our technological
   society has had such an impact on the world of nature that, rather

---

[7] No one yet knows what will follow postmodernism. The prayer of the Christian must be that the Lord
will have mercy on us and that he will grant to us, to our churches, and to our cultures a renewal,
restoration, and reformation of faith and life.

than bringing about a glorious future, it offers instead environmental disasters that could threaten and destroy human life. Technology controls and dehumanizes us even in the ways it reaches into our homes through television and the Internet.

3. There are a deep loss of optimism about human nature and a growing recognition that humans can do terrible evil.
4. There are no sure grounds for hope about the future. We are alone in the universe, with nothing to cling to or to trust in.
5. There is no sure and certain morality, for everything is ultimately relative.

For most ordinary Americans, and for a much smaller number of Europeans, such a vision is too stark and too bleak. Especially in the United States, there is still a strong strain of modernist optimism among people. However, the postmodern skeptical way of seeing human life has a deep impact on the alienation of many young people. We see this in movies like *The Deer Hunter*, *Apocalypse Now*, *Blade Runner*, many of the films of Woody Allen, *American Beauty*, or the sci-fi series *The Matrix*. The first *Matrix* movie was hailed by many Christians because it appeared to have a glimpse of possible redemption. Later, however, deep pessimism about the human condition became evident. We also see this bleakness in many television shows and in much music listened to by younger generations.

This postmodern way of thinking impacts everyone by increasing our doubts about finding truth, by causing us to question the value of reason, and by making us cynical about respect for authority; at odds with truth, reason, and authority is postmodernism's passionate emphasis on the centrality of the individual. What is the effect of this skepticism on ordinary people? We may summarize the consequences with the following simple though desperately destructive statements:

1. There is no objective truth.
2. There is no absolute truth.
3. There is only personal truth.
4. You have your truth; I have mine.

Adding to this uncertainty about knowing truth is the fact that we live in an increasingly pluralistic society. We have, in the United

States today, the most religiously diverse society the world has ever seen. What does this pluralism of belief have to do with the growth of cynicism? Postmodernism teaches that this pluralism of belief is the way it ought to be, for it insists that there is no one truth which describes reality; that our finite grasp on reality is so tenuous that there can be nothing but the belief systems of individuals or cultural groups; and that none of these can claim either the status of *truth* or even superiority over any of the others. Anyone who claims to speak truth is greeted with skepticism. Sometimes this skepticism is polite, but frequently it is bitter, mocking, and abusive.

In addition, postmodernism stresses that in knowing, I am never free. I always come to every issue with prejudices, with beliefs, with a background—and these "glasses" determine what I see. Some postmodernists emphasize the "shared knowledge" (or prejudices) of various communities, while others stress the isolation of the individual knower. But whichever of these approaches is espoused, the overall result is an increasing skepticism about any kind of truth claim.

So reason is a weak tool and can never lead us to true knowledge, for it is constrained by our prejudices. Reason and the claim to possess knowledge are weapons used by the powerful to maintain their power and interests at the expense of the powerless. Knowledge becomes a weapon in the culture wars for various groups to reinforce their already held positions, and to use against each other. This recognition that knowledge is sometimes used as a weapon to suppress others and their views feeds the drift to cynicism and the questioning of people's motives.

The consequence of this loss of confidence in reason, and the accompanying loss of confidence in there being truth, is that Western societies have raised a generation of skeptics and cynics. Consider the dwarves in C. S. Lewis's *Last Battle*. Lewis writes that they were so reluctant to be taken in, they could no longer be taken out of their skeptical and cynical attitude. Hope was now impossible for them. In Europe this problem is far more advanced; the cynicism of Lewis's dwarves is almost universal in France, Britain, and in most European countries.

Young people, in particular, are deeply pessimistic and cynical about what life holds for them. The deeper philosophical skepticism that is at the heart of our culture is made worse by the social and familial settings in which great numbers of young people spend their early years. Many grow up in homes where they receive no moral direction from their parents; and if no teacher, church member, or friend reaches out to lead them to the Lord and his paths, we find a generation without any moral compass. Some grow up in settings with little practical hope of escaping problems of poverty, unemployment, poor education, and social deprivation of every kind. Many more, from every social class, have the added burden of being raised in families where there are such betrayal of trust, such failure of commitment and parenting, such wounding of hope and love, that deep alienation and a suspicious attitude toward all people are no surprise.

So, what are the consequences of our intellectual and social climate for vast numbers of people?

1. *Loss of belief in truth.* There is nothing that can make sense of the human condition, so the conclusion is, "meaningless, meaningless, everything is meaningless."
2. *Loss of hope, both for this world and for one's own life.* There is no story that gives us ground for hope for our solar system, our planet, the human race, or my own future, so there is no alternative but cynicism and apathy.
3. *Loss of respect for authority.* There is no one and no thing that deserves my trust or obedience, so there is no one to whom I may turn with the confidence that they will give me answers or meaning.
4. *Loss of respect for everything sacred.* Religions, like all other claims to truth, are simply power games, and anything or anyone that any group has held to be sacred or precious should be scorned and held up for ridicule; consequently there is a delight in shocking the viewer or listener. (I hardly need to give you examples here, for we see them repeatedly in our cultural setting.)
5. *Loss of moral certainty.* There are no transcendent moral commandments; there is no "you shall" or "you shall not." There are no commandments that come from above for this generation. No one individual, no group, no authority, no religion, no sacred book, no god, has the right to tell anyone else how they ought to live. In such a society there is inevitably cynicism about claims to moral certainty.

You may reply, "This does not affect me, or many of the people I know." I want to challenge that claim. Cynicism is corrosive—it works like a cancer, taking over all that is healthy and hopeful, and we are all affected by it.

Now that we see something of what has shaped the attitudes of our hearts and minds, perhaps we can turn back to Psalm 25 and pray that the Lord would enable us to make the words of David our own heartfelt cry, our own prayer that the Lord will be gracious to us, and that he will teach us his paths, in order that we may walk in the ways of the Lord, and so may live his good life.

> Make me to know your ways, O Lord;
>   teach me your paths.
> Lead me in your truth and teach me,
>   for you are the God of my salvation;
>   for you I wait all the day long.
>
> Remember your mercy, O Lord, and your steadfast love,
>   for they have been from of old.
> Remember not the sins of my youth or my transgressions;
>   according to your steadfast love remember me,
>   for the sake of your goodness, O Lord!
>
> Good and upright is the Lord;
>   therefore he instructs sinners in the way.
> He leads the humble in what is right,
>   and teaches the humble his way.
> All the paths of the Lord are steadfast love and faithfulness,
>   for those who keep his covenant and his testimonies.
>
> For your name's sake, O Lord,
>   pardon my guilt, for it is great.

Questions for Personal Reflection and Group Discussion

1. Read Psalm 25:4–11 and set down for yourself what in particular you pray for as you ask the Lord to teach you to walk in his paths.

2. Do you see any aspects of our postmodern culture that you consider to be helpful to us as Christian believers, aspects for which we ought to be thankful? This may seem a strange question after the challenging things that I have

written about the loss of truth and of moral certainty in our postmodern setting. However, Scripture charges us always to be ready to discern what is good and helpful in any human setting. If you reflect on this question with care, you will soon see that there are many very lovely aspects of our postmodern cultural context.

3. What are some aspects of our postmodern culture that you consider to be most challenging for Christians? Which two make teaching a difficult calling? Almost all of us teach in some setting, whether it is one-on-one with a friend or a more formal situation teaching children, teenagers, or adults in a school, in a Sunday school class, or in a Bible study. What makes people reluctant to hear you and to accept any challenges you might bring to their lives?

4. What are two aspects of our postmodern culture that create problems for you in your own personal life as someone seeking to be faithful to the Lord?

5. What two aspects of our postmodern culture bring pressures on you as a parent as you commit yourself to raising godly children in our contemporary setting? (Or if you do not have children, try to imagine the challenges of being a parent in our postmodern times.)

2

The Good Life (2)

Found in Christianity
or Postmodernism?

In the first chapter we followed in the steps of deism, secular humanism, and postmodernism to find where these schools of thinking might lead us, and to see whether they would fulfill their initial promise of the good life, a life of moral beauty without any input from the Christian faith or the Christian God. Should we draw from that brief and discouraging survey the conclusion that all our neighbors are thoroughly postmodern in their thinking and lifestyle, that they are all committed atheists, or that they have no solid moral convictions and no sense of guilt or shame when they do wrong? That is not the conclusion I wish to draw, for it would not be accurate.

This past century witnessed a loss of biblical content to people's views of God, of truth, and of moral convictions. As we have seen, this loss is far more advanced in Europe than in the United States. However, there are no people who are thoroughly consistent in holding to postmodern skepticism about truth or about moral law. No one is a moral relativist all the time. Indeed, anyone who does have complete doubt about the possibility of knowing anything truly will go rapidly insane. Extreme skepticism rarely happens (thank God!), though occasionally uncertainty about finding truth can have devastating consequences. I have met people who have become mentally and emotionally paralyzed by their deep doubts and their suspicion that life is ultimately absurd.[1]

In such situations the three great needs are: first, prayer for the work of God in the person's heart; second, believers living a life that is characterized by meaning and hope; and third, a strong, committed love for the individual who has become trapped in the pit of despair. Only when such a person is deeply loved and is able to observe a meaningful and hopeful life firsthand can he or she begin to think clearly again about questions of truth and moral order. The Lord can and does deliver people who come to such desperate places. That is the theme of Psalm 107, a psalm that describes God's unfailing love for those who lose their way in life.

> Some wandered in desert wastes,
>> finding no way to a city to dwell in;
> hungry and thirsty,
>> their soul fainted within them.
> Then they cried to the LORD in their trouble,
>> and he delivered them from their distress.
> He led them by a straight way
>> till they reached a city to dwell in.
>
> Some sat in darkness and in the shadow of death,
>> prisoners in affliction and irons,
> for they had rebelled against the words of God,
>> and spurned the counsel of the Most High.
> So he bowed their hearts down with hard labor;
>> they fell down, with none to help.
> Then they cried to the LORD in their trouble,
>> and he delivered them from their distress.
> He brought them out of darkness and the shadow of death,
>> and burst their bonds apart.
>
> Some were fools through their sinful ways,
>> and because of their iniquities suffered affliction;
> they loathed any kind of food,
>> and they drew near to the gates of death.

---

[1] This was my own situation. I became suicidal from doubt that life had any ultimate meaning. See chapter 3 for an account of my experience, and of the Lord's delivering me from the pit of despair.

Then they cried to the LORD in their trouble,
    and he delivered them from their distress.
He sent out his word and healed them,
    and delivered them from their destruction.[2]

Scripture encourages us never to give up on the Lord, no matter how desperate a person's life seems; and never to give up on praying for people, on living faithfully, and on being full of hope before them and loving them. Psalm 107 finishes:

Whoever is wise, let him attend to these things;
    let them consider the steadfast love of the LORD.[3]

Thankfully, of course, most people do not come to this extremity of distress as they strive to live in our postmodern setting—a setting that undermines truth and meaning, hope and moral order. Instead, both within and outside the churches, most people are in two minds, living in a state of confusion about whether certainty of truth and certainty of objective moral standards are possible.

In big questions of truth, questions concerning God and ultimate meaning, people are deeply in doubt. In poll after poll, George Barna has found that approximately two-thirds of Americans agree with statements such as the following: "There is no such thing as absolute truth. People can define truth in different ways and still be correct." Among people under thirty, the numbers rise to around 80 percent. Many opinion polls confirm this widespread skepticism as to whether truth is possible. Our personal observations also confirm this trend when we watch television, listen to the radio, read the press, or have conversations with neighbors, coworkers, or classmates.

And yet, when it comes to matters of truth with regard to everyday life, everybody operates as if truth can be known with complete confidence. Everyone knows which side of the road to drive on, and all are aware of the necessity of stopping at red lights—except when they are ill, drunk, or being criminally foolish. Everyone knows that the sun will rise each morning and that the universe has a rational

---

[2] Psalm 107:4–20.
[3] Verse 43.

and trustworthy order to it—unless they are insane or, in very rare cases, become so troubled by postmodern skepticism that they can no longer function. Everyone knows that all human relationships depend on truthfulness in what is communicated, and on trusting the truthfulness of others—except, again, when people are mentally impaired through illness or through drink or drugs, or they are being hypocritical or purposefully misleading. We live, and we have to live each day, in the confidence that truth can be known. There is honor even among thieves; they have to be able to know when truth is being spoken in order to carry out a robbery or to dispose of stolen goods.

The same situation holds when we think about matters of moral order, or moral law. We have to know that some things are right and others are wrong. Just as with issues of truth, we find that people are pulled in two directions. They express doubt about ultimate moral certainty and about particular moral choices. All around us we find two views struggling with each other: the one we might label traditional or, more properly, Christian; the other, skeptical, relative, or postmodern. People do not think clearly, and this is true of almost all, whether claiming to be Christian or non-Christian. If we listen to people, even to ourselves, we find expressions of now one, now the other of these two ways of seeing our world.

This confusion and lack of clarity are revealed in the ways people respond to different questions. If asked regarding absolute truth or absolute moral standards—unalterable laws of right and wrong in human behavior—most people will answer in ways that show their commitment to relativism. The same is true if they are asked concerning a woman's right to choose regarding abortion, or about people's sexual freedom. As we saw in several of our examples in the first chapter, people may have strong views themselves against abortion, or pornography, or lyrics encouraging sexual violence against women, or unfaithfulness in marriage; but when they are asked whether everyone should have the same views, they claim no right to make such statements or "impose" their personal views on others; in other words, they express moral relativism.

However, if asked about the rise in crime or about lawlessness in their cities related to drugs and gang warfare, most people, though not all, will insist that we need stronger laws, harsher sentences, more police enforcement, and the like. If we ask about the sexual molestation of children,[4] or about those who prey on the elderly to steal their money, or about other such acts against the defenseless, almost everyone will declare such behavior wicked and abominable. People respond passionately about such matters, believing with complete confidence that there is objective (nonrelative) evil done, that there is true guilt, and that there must be punishment.

To help us understand these confused responses, we will look more carefully at the two views that vie for our allegiance.

A Christian (Traditional) View

In a Christian or traditional view, morality and law are fixed and eternal. This firm belief in a universal moral law carries with it several other convictions that bear on the moral consciousness of all people.

First, there is a belief that all people are accountable to God, or to objective standards or principles of truth, justice, equity, and goodness. At the time of the founding of our nation, the views of almost everyone were shaped by a Judeo-Christian understanding, even among those who were not Christians. This was true of deists like Jefferson, and even of rationalists like Benjamin Franklin, as well as of people who professed Christian faith, such as John Witherspoon or George Washington. Today it is rather different. While over 90 percent of Americans say, "I believe in God," there is not much content to that belief, and for many of us there is only a hazy relationship between the existence of God and ultimate moral law in the universe. Yet, when pushed on issues like child molestation, almost all Americans will affirm absolute notions of moral law.

Second, there is a widely held belief that morality and good laws express people's responsibilities to one another. People recognize that

---

[4] In the St. Louis area there was a particularly shocking example of this. An eleven-year-old boy disappeared on his way home from school on his bicycle. Thankfully, an observant friend of the boy, who is very knowledgeable about automobiles, noticed a white pickup in the area that he had not seen before. A few days later a neighbor who was talking to a policeman noticed a pickup that matched the friend's description, and a warrant was used to enter the apartment of the owner of the vehicle. Inside were found the missing boy and another who had been missing for five years, all that time a prisoner of the man who had taken him. I doubt that anyone in the whole St. Louis area would have spoken in a morally relativistic manner about this crime.

we live in community and that, therefore, objective moral standards, and also society's laws, must be applied to our relationships with our neighbors. Most Americans live this way and are deeply offended when individuals, businesses, or political figures act against these laws and responsibilities.

I cannot imagine anyone defending dairy producers who watered down their milk, then added melamine to it to increase the levels of protein, and then marketed this mixture as dried milk powder for babies. People are sickened by such appalling greed, and by the accompanying failure to reflect on the damage to the health of the babies who were given this milk to drink: malnutrition, kidney stones, kidney failure, severe illness, and in several cases, infant death. What is more horrifying is that those who perpetrated such wickedness did so in full awareness that great numbers of cats and dogs had become sick and died a year earlier when melamine was added to pet food for the same purpose of increasing measurable levels of protein.

Even those who espouse relativism in principle and who teach that morals are relative will take a passionately "traditional" view in actual cases, and they will do this without realizing the inconsistency and contradiction in what they are communicating. An example is my wife's teacher at a university in the St. Louis area, where Vicki was taking courses toward a Master of Arts in French and education. One of the professors teaching an education course was a passionate relativist. One evening, he spent four hours of lecture time insisting that his class of present and would-be teachers should never impose their own moral values on their students in school—whether they were teaching at the primary, secondary, or tertiary level. He used examples about sexuality, homosexuality, pornography, human life, and other issues of personal moral choice.

The very next week he spent much of the four hours inveighing against the loss of truthfulness among students, the growing disrespect for authority, the widespread cheating on exams, and the casual practice of plagiarism when pupils download material from the Internet and paste it into their papers without attribution. It never seemed to occur to him that he was being grossly inconsistent. When it came to issues that mattered to him as a teacher, he had a firm set of objective moral standards and laws, and a strong sense of the moral responsibility of his students.

Third, despite what many have been taught (that humans are born basically good), there is still a widespread recognition that human beings are sinful from the heart and that we all need to be restrained by moral teaching in schools and churches, and by laws and law officers. Benjamin Franklin insisted that people need to be taught morality and law—even though he appears to have had no Christian belief himself. He thought such instruction was necessary to train people in what is right and to help restrain the human tendency to selfishness and evil. About a month before his death Franklin wrote to a friend, Ezra Stiles, the president of Yale University, in reply to Stiles's inquiry about Franklin's views on religion:

> As to Jesus of Nazareth, my opinion of whom you particularly desire, I think the system of Morals and his Religion, as he left them to us, the best the World ever saw or is likely to see; but I apprehend it has received various corrupt changes, and I have, with most of the present Dissenters in England, some doubts as to his divinity; though it is a question I do not dogmatize upon, having never studied it, and think it needless to busy myself with it, when I expect soon an opportunity of knowing the Truth with less trouble.[5]

Today, even though many people would not state the issues in the same manner as Franklin did, yet most of our neighbors realize that children need discipline and instruction. Even those who do not provide moral instruction and discipline for their own children somehow believe that it is the responsibility of the schools or the government to do something about these matters. That was my mother's experience as a teacher of first- through third-grade children in a small country school in the south of England. The parents expected that she would teach their children reading, writing, and math; but they also expected her to teach them manners and morals.

We should note here that this is one of the areas where people become open to the gospel of Christ, because God's image and God's

---

[5] Benjamin Franklin, letter to Ezra Stiles, quoted in Carl Van Doren, *Benjamin Franklin* (New York: Viking, 1938), 777–78.

moral wisdom—both present in all human beings—act as a goad on their consciences when they find themselves in positions of responsibility for their children. Many people become open to attending church and thinking about the Christian faith when they start their families. They recognize that their sons and daughters are not morally perfect, that they have struggles with self-centeredness, pride, resistance to authority, and many other issues. New parents look out at the surrounding culture and realize that it is not giving much moral direction to their sons and daughters. They feel inadequately prepared to instruct their children themselves, and so they send (if not bring) them to church in the hope that they will get assistance in this task.

This sense of responsibility in parents is a wonderful quality, for it is one of those areas where the Holy Spirit brings his testimony to bear on people's hearts and draws them toward the truth. Such areas of the Spirit's witness are always present in people's lives, as Paul declares to the pagans in Lystra: "He has not left himself without testimony: He has shown kindness by giving you rain from heaven and crops in their seasons; he provides you with plenty of food and fills your hearts with joy."[6]

One of the most powerful means of witness is the need for moral order and for mutual moral obligation between people, what some call natural law. While such an expression is, in a sense, appropriate because this is a constant human reality, the Bible does not refer to this reality as natural law, but rather it credits God as the author of these laws known by all peoples on the earth. He is the true source of this moral wisdom and the law on the human heart; and he gives both of these generously to all people.[7]

This universal reality of moral wisdom and law is one of the primary reasons that C. S. Lewis's books *Mere Christianity*, *The Abolition of Man*, and the Narnia stories and science fiction trilogy have been so greatly used by God to draw people to faith in Christ. This is also true of the apologetic work of Francis Schaeffer,[8] and of the preaching and books of Tim Keller, such as *The Reason for God*.

---

[6] Acts 14:17, NIV.
[7] See Proverbs 8:1–4, 15–16; Romans 2:14–15.
[8] See, as examples of Francis Schaeffer's writing on these issues, *The God Who Is There*, *Escape from Reason*, *He Is There and He Is Not Silent*, *Death in the City*, *How Should We Then Live?*, and *Whatever Happened to the Human Race?*

Our task is to pray for wisdom in order to be sensitive to these areas of the Spirit's testimony in a person's heart or in a particular human culture, and then cooperate with God's work by sharing the good news of who the true God is, and that he is the author and giver of moral law. In such a case, where we experience a sense of our obligation to others, we may pray (to adapt Psalm 119:18),

> Open my [their] eyes, that I [they] may behold
>   wondrous things out of your law.

Fourth, there is also the general recognition that there is objective guilt when this moral order and the obligations between people inscribed in law are broken. Very few people will deny such objective guilt in cases like the capture of children for molestation, or the selling of children and women into slavery. One of the primary areas of slavery in the United States today, and also in western Europe, is prostitution slavery. Women from Asia, South America, and eastern Europe are captured directly by slavers, or are sold by their parents to slavers, or are induced by false promises of marriage or of good employment by slavers. These women, and even young girls, are then brought to the United States (or to western Europe), their passports are stolen, and they are forced into prostitution for the enrichment of their slavers. Almost all Americans will insist that there is true guilt in such cases and that there needs to be just and severe punishment. It is difficult to imagine even the most committed moral relativist insisting that such enslavement of women is simply a matter of personal choice or of varying cultural norms about the treatment of women, or that there should be no punishment for such practices.[9]

Fifth, it was once universally believed, both in the United States and in western Europe, that much of the law given by God and upheld by the state in our societies exists to provide protection for the ordinary man and woman from those who are powerful and ruthless. This is a major theme of Old Testament law, as we shall see later in our studies. This was one of the fundamental convictions behind the development of what is called common law in Britain in the Middle Ages.

---

[9] One of the most powerful attacks on prostitution slavery that I have found is the outstanding Jack Reacher novel by Lee Child, *Worth Dying For*.

This heritage of common law to protect vulnerable citizens against those with status, money, and power is the source of many of our laws here in the United States.

This common-law element of what I am calling a Christian or traditional understanding of law is forgotten by many today, so much so that large numbers of evangelicals are suspicious of attempts to restrain the abuse of power by business executives and others with money and social clout, fearing that such attempts at restraint arise from a socialist or Marxist understanding of economics, or are unwarranted restrictions on the freedom of the market. But such a response neglects our own history and is a profound misunderstanding of the teaching of Scripture.

Sixth, it was also almost universally believed that there is a sacred framework for the life of society. Responsibility to one's neighbors, upholding God's law, and respect for the laws of the land were, and should be, fostered by home, by church, and by schools teaching young people love for God and love for neighbor. This sixth element of a Christian or traditional view of law has now been radically undermined and is almost totally neglected in the upbringing and education of most children.

However, despite this loss of these last two parts, the fifth and sixth convictions of a traditional approach to moral law, it is evident that almost everyone around us is still deeply shaped by a Christian approach to moral practice and to the laws of the land.

A POSTMODERN VIEW

At the same time, postmodernism vies for our allegiance. According to this view, morality and law are constantly open to change. We may also call this view moral relativism, or moral skepticism. Like the traditional or Christian view, this view comes with several other convictions about the nature of reality and of human societies.

First, law is not based on objective standards, but is simply the expression of a culture's habits and customs. Morality changes from generation to generation and from culture to culture. Such an approach reigns in many university anthropology and sociology departments, and also in much popular entertainment. Think of examples you have heard in school or seen in a movie or television show.

Second, law and objective morality are opposed to freedom. Traditional values, law enforcement, and society's laws all hinder personal liberty. There is a constant pressure for law to be pushed back to give more freedom to individuals and to corporations. Where individual freedom is concerned, this is true for much of the political left in our nation and for many liberal judges. We should note that this is also true for the far right of our political spectrum where a thinker such as Ayn Rand and her ideas continue to have a strong influence. She believed that all true human achievement comes from individual effort, genius, and accomplishment, and she was passionately opposed to Judeo-Christian moral laws as an unnecessary restraint on personal freedom; she also opposed any government interference with the free choices of the individual. Here are two brief quotes from her work:

> A government is the most dangerous threat to man's rights: it holds a legal monopoly on the use of physical force against legally disarmed victims.[10]

> Civilization is the progress toward a society of privacy. The savage's whole existence is public, ruled by the laws of his tribe. Civilization is the process of setting man free from men.[11]

Because of these convictions about complete freedom, Rand also believed that total laissez-faire capitalism is the only good way for a society to function well economically and to grow. In her thinking, selfishness and self-interest are virtues, and altruism, is a weakness. She attacked all forms of meekness, service, altruism, and self-sacrifice as unworthy of the dignity of human beings. Nietzsche had similar views and considered Jesus to be the one who, above all others, emasculated the human race by his emphasis on living for others to the point of laying down one's life. A precursor to Nietzsche's thought, the English poet Swinburne, expressed such hatred of Jesus this way: "Thou hast conquered, O pale Galilean; the world has grown grey from thy breath."[12]

Such a philosophy of life is a very far cry from what was taught and lived by the Lord Jesus Christ, and from what the faithful church

---

[10] Ayn Rand, *The Virtue of Selfishness: A New Concept of Egoism* (New York: New American Library, 1964), 103.
[11] Ayn Rand, *The Fountainhead* (New York: Dutton, 1996), 669. To explore her views, see also *Atlas Shrugged*.
[12] Algernon Charles Swinburne, "Hymn to Proserpine," 1866.

has espoused throughout its history. However, if you listen to some of our politicians, it is not difficult to hear ideas that are very similar to those of Ayn Rand. What is most troubling about this development is the way in which many Christians have taken on board a similar view of freedom, of the virtue of self-interest, of rejecting the need for laws in our society (especially with regard to business); they have at the same time ignored what God's law has to say about the need for restraints on freedom, about the centrality of moral obligation to one's neighbors in business practice and in all economic—indeed, in all human—activity. Aleksandr Solzhenitsyn had some very helpful words about this shift in thinking away from a Christian understanding. And, as he said so forcefully at Harvard University, no one could accuse him of sympathizing with socialism.

> However, in early democracies, as in American democracy at the time of its birth, all individual human rights were granted because man is God's creature. That is, freedom was given to the individual conditionally, in the assumption of his constant religious responsibility. Such was the heritage of the preceding thousand years. Two hundred or even fifty years ago, it would have seemed quite impossible, in America, that an individual could be granted boundless freedom simply for the satisfaction of his instincts or whims. Subsequently, however, all such limitations were discarded everywhere in the West; a total liberation occurred from the moral heritage of Christian centuries with their great reserves of mercy and sacrifice.[13]

Third, law is understood in the postmodern view to be simply about rights rather than responsibilities. People ask, "What can I get out of the law?" or, "How can I use the law for my advantage?" rather than, "Where should my way of life be governed by the law?" Consequently there is constant litigation, for the law is seen as a tool for the individual's benefit. Our courts are choked with cases that reveal this kind of approach to the law. One very personal example is of a friend of mine who was recently divorced. Her husband was greedy and fought vigorously to avoid sharing his wealth (*their* wealth) and to minimize his financial responsibility for his wife or his children. He lied to the

---

[13] Aleksandr Solzhenitsyn, "A World Split Apart" (commencement address delivered at Harvard University, June 8, 1978).

court repeatedly, slandered his wife's character, hid his own assets, and exaggerated her situation and her resources. It became a terrible burden to keep trying to fight for what was right. I am confident that every person reading this has his or her own examples of such misuse of the law to lament and share.

Fourth, all that matters is legalistic righteousness, being right according to the letter of the law. The law is pushed to its limits. Who is concerned for the spirit of the law? Solzhenitsyn spoke to this problem in his wonderful address at Harvard:

> The defense of individual rights has reached such extremes as to make society as a whole defenseless against certain individuals. It is time, in the West, to defend not so much human rights as human obligations.
>
> Destructive and irresponsible freedom has been granted boundless space. Society appears to have little defense against the abyss of human decadence, such as, for example, misuse of liberty for moral violence against young people, motion pictures full of pornography, crime and horror. It is considered to be part of freedom and theoretically counter-balanced by the young people's right not to look or not to accept. Life organized legalistically has thus shown its inability to defend itself against the corrosion of evil.[14]

Fifth, law is open to manipulation by pressure groups that see the legal system as a means of getting their will inscribed in law, regardless of morality or the public good. I hardly need to give examples of this problem as all senators and congressional representatives are constantly lobbied by powerful interest groups and are subject to the temptation of bribery in the form of financial support in exchange for their serving the interests of the lobbyist rather than the people they represent. This problem exists on college campuses as well. For example, one of my sons applied to be a dorm monitor at his university. One of the requirements for the position was that he sit and watch a video of gay sex and not be offended. He refused and, because of this, had to find other work.

Sixth, there is a reluctance to talk about guilt, except in the most obvious cases of clear evil that offends almost everyone. Even in these

---

[14] Ibid.

cases, we see a drift away from the notion that evil behavior is an of-fense against objective moral standards. I will never forget reading an article by a British columnist about the subject of pedophilia, in which she at first expressed her abhorrence and then said something like this: "I have no doubt, that within ten years time, I and my liberal friends may well come to accept that sex with children is not abominable but rather an appropriate expression of personal freedom."[15]

Seventh, punishment becomes rehabilitation or education, rather than the retribution of society against crime. I would commend for your reading on this subject C. S. Lewis's excellent essay "The Humani-tarian Theory of Punishment," published in the volume *God in the Dock* and in other collections of his writings.

Eighth, there is a loss of the Judeo-Christian framework for moral reflection and for teaching moral order, law, and responsibility to our children. Moral education becomes simply helping a child to come to his or her own notions about what he or she thinks is right and wrong, rather than teaching children a set of objective moral standards that arise within a sacred canopy, a universe created and governed by the giver of the law.

All of us are impacted personally as well as surrounded by others who are shaped by both of these ways of thinking: the Christian or traditional view and the postmodern, relativist view. Most of us are confused. We all resonate with the idea that law restricts liberty and that everything should be a matter of personal choice. Yet, at the same time, we all feel that much that is legal is an offense against common decency and good sense.

In our next chapter we will begin to build a biblical response to this dilemma. My prayer is that these first two chapters will create in us all a hunger for seeing "wonderful things" in God's law.

Questions for Personal Reflection and Group Discussion

1. I quoted a Barna poll that found two-thirds of Americans agreeing with the following: "There is no such thing as absolute truth. People can define truth in different ways and still be correct." What examples can you think of

---

[15] I will refrain from mentioning the name of the columnist, in the hope and prayer that she might have changed her views.

that reveal how this relativism with regard to truth affects peoples' views of morality and law?

2. Many schools have taught values clarification to children rather than objective and clear moral standards. Have you had experience of this, and what do you think are the consequences of such an approach to moral education on the children who are taught this?

3. The vast majority of Americans believe that human beings are basically good. What do you think about this belief, and what do you see to be some of its consequences?

4. Jean-Paul Sartre, the French existentialist philosopher, wrote: "Man is condemned to be free."[16] What do you think he meant by this?

5. Why do you think that the society in which we live is so litigious, that people are willing to sue one another so readily? Do you know of local examples of this?

6. Once God as the source of law and the notion of the universe as a "sacred canopy" are lost, the only real alternative is that humanity becomes the sole source of moral values and law. If we put ourselves in the position of those who hold such a view, then what are the possible ways we might create values and laws for our society?

---

[16] Jean-Paul Sartre, *Existentialism and Human Emotions* (New York: Philosophical Library, 1957), 23.

3

THE SOURCE OF LAW

Humanity or God?

In our second chapter we thought about the confusion there is in the United States, and indeed all over the Western world, about the nature of morality and law, a confusion that infects both Christian believers and unbelievers. I suggested that there are two views vying for our allegiance:

1. The Christian or traditional view: morality and law are fixed and eternal.
2. The postmodern or relativist view: morality and law are constantly open to change.

The first view, a Judeo-Christian worldview, declares that there is a universal moral law arising from the character of the Creator. Along with this belief come several other convictions:

- accountability to God, or at least to objective standards or principles of truth, justice, equity, and goodness;
- belief that morality and good laws express people's responsibilities to one another;
- a widespread recognition that human beings are sinful from the heart and that we all need to be restrained by moral teaching in schools and churches, and by laws and law officers;
- the recognition that there is objective guilt when this moral order and legal obligations between people are broken;

- the realization that laws exist to provide protection for the ordinary man and woman from those who are powerful and ruthless—the common law tradition;
- the almost universal conviction that there is a sacred framework for the life of society.

The second, fundamentally relativistic, worldview also carries with it several convictions about the nature of reality and human societies:

- law is not based on objective standards, but is simply the expression of a culture's habits and customs;
- law and objective morality are opposed to personal freedom;
- law is simply about my rights, rather than my responsibilities;
- all that matters is legalistic righteousness, being right according to the letter of the law;
- law is open to manipulation by pressure groups that see the legal system as a means of getting their will inscribed in law;
- there is a reluctance to talk about objective guilt, except in the most obvious cases of clear evil that offend almost everyone;
- punishment becomes rehabilitation or education, rather than retribution;
- we do not need a Judeo-Christian framework for moral reflection and for teaching moral order, law, and responsibility to ourselves, our children, and society.

Obviously, this picture of our situation is something of an over-simplification to give us a handle on understanding what is happening around us and in our own lives. But there can be no doubt that at the heart of our culture there is a steady drift from seeing law and morality as God's gifts to us. Instead, law and morality are seen as having their origins here on earth, as arising from human reflection about the nature of our lives and about how we should live. To the passionate secularist this is a cause for rejoicing, as can be seen in this excerpt from a secular humanist perspective:

> Ethics is an autonomous field of inquiry, . . . ethical judgments can be formulated independently of revealed religion, ... human beings can cultivate practical reason and wisdom and, by its application, achieve lives of virtue and excellence. . . . For secular humanists,

ethical conduct is, or should be, judged by critical reason, and their goal is to develop autonomous and responsible individuals, capable of making their own choices in life based upon an understanding of human behavior.[1]

TURNING FROM GOD: WHAT OPTIONS REMAIN?

When humans turn from God as the source of moral order and law and see themselves as the source, there are, in the end, only four options available to a society. We can see all four of these options constantly at work in the world around us.

Option 1: The Individual Decides for Himself or Herself

The French thinker Jean-Paul Sartre expressed his insistence that the individual stands alone to make his or her own personal moral choices in a dramatic way:

> The existentialist, on the contrary, thinks it very distressing that God does not exist, because all possibility of finding values in a heaven of ideas disappears along with Him; there can no longer be an *a priori* Good, since there is no infinite and perfect consciousness to think it. Nowhere is it written that the Good exists, that we must be honest, that we must not lie; because the fact is we are on a plane where there are only men. . . . Man is condemned to be free. . . . to invent man.[2]

This might be fine if people were completely good and if there were no corruption in our human nature. However, that is not the reality with which we all live. I was not born in innocence. I am not, nor have I been for a single day of my life, completely good. I do not do the good things I wish to do; and there are many bad things that I do not want to think or do or say, but find myself thinking, saying, and doing every day of my life.[3]

Yet, despite our knowledge of our imperfections, there has been a passionate embracing of the notion that we are free to choose our own values. The widespread emphasis on the freedom of the individual

---

[1] "A Secular Humanist Declaration," the Council for Democratic and Secular Humanism, 1980, accessed at http://www.secularhumanism.org/index.php?page=declaration&section=main.
[2] Jean-Paul Sartre, *Existentialism and Human Emotions* (New York: Philosophical Library, 1957), 22–23.
[3] See the apostle Paul on this issue of our inability to do what we know to be right, Romans 7:14–24.

has created a situation in our society much like that in the day of the Judges, where "everyone did as he saw fit."[4] Consider what evil may be done in the name of free choice!

We might think of human life issues, like abortion, where the emphasis on personal choice leads every day to the killing of thousands of little babies (approximately one million a year within the United States). Just recently a senior judge ruled that a state cannot require a woman considering abortion to be shown images of the baby developing in her womb, or to listen to an account of the stage of life and growth her child has reached, or to read material that will give her this information. The judge ruled that requiring a woman to be given such true knowledge would interfere with her personal freedom.

Or we might consider matters of sexuality. Some 80 percent of high school students are engaged in sexual relationships, and the figures for college students are well over 90 percent. Even at the junior high level the figures for sexual activity appear to be around 50 percent. Many aspects of these figures are tragic: sexual involvement without personal or even physical maturity; the increase of sexually transmitted diseases among young people; the hardening of the conscience; the damage that young men and women do to themselves and each other emotionally and psychologically; the filling of the mind with images and memories of sexual encounters that cannot be erased when the person does eventually commit himself or herself to another person in marriage; and above all, the separation of sexual involvement from deep personal commitment.

In addition, all of us know people whose spouses have abandoned them and their children because of the refusal to say no to sexual temptation and desire. Similarly, readers will remember the politician who abandoned his sacred vows and his wife and children with the statement, "My truth is that I am a gay American." That expression "my truth is" captures the very heart of the issue of the freedom to define life for myself and to make whatever choices I wish when it comes to matters of personal morality.

Of course, it is impossible to keep this "freedom of choice" bound

---

[4] Judges 21:25, NIV.

only to matters of sexuality and human life. The past thirty years have seen many examples of this demand for freedom invading financial and business issues. Famous financial institutions and business leaders, both male and female, have been found to be making choices to enrich themselves at the expense of others without respect for the laws of the land or ethical considerations. Indeed, after such perpetrators of financial crimes have served their prison sentences, they are invited, for enormous fees, to give lectures in which they teach others how to make money by insider trading, or by bending the laws, or by finding loopholes in the laws. Several years ago the Harvard Business School felt constrained to add a new course in business ethics because of the widespread flouting of the laws and of traditional moral standards in contemporary business practice. The problem was this: why should a man or woman in the financial world obey the law or observe traditional business ethics if he or she proved to be clever enough to get away with illegal or unethical behavior?

For a final example of self-made standards, consider the lyrics of songs that encourage brutal violence toward women. Under current laws there can be no successful prosecutions of songwriters and singers for such lyrics because of what is considered the absolute right of freedom of expression. As we saw earlier, juries are reluctant to convict people in such cases because no matter how much they are appalled by the words of a song, they find themselves unable to set any limitation on someone else's freedom either to sing such songs or to listen to them.

The personal autonomy of the individual to do whatever he or she wishes—this is the greatest idol of our culture, and our most serious problem. We are only at the beginning of seeing the devastating consequences of the view that people are free to do whatever makes them happy. Consider again the young people who rioted in Britain in August 2011. They are a generation whose only moral education has been, "Do whatever you wish."

Option 2: The Majority Decides for Us All
The novelist William Golding is said to have commented, "If God is dead and man is the highest, is his own creator, then good and evil

is decided by majority vote."[5] These words capture the problem with what we may call sociological law, that is, society making its own laws. Or we may refer to this simply as democracy—the rule of the people. Sadly, this is how many Americans do understand democracy. Even judges on the Supreme Court look to the opinion of the majority when they rule on laws. The consequence of this is that the law in the United States, as well as other Western societies, increasingly follows the popular consensus. We see this expressed in the way many states have referenda on such matters as euthanasia or embryo experimentation. We will have many more referenda on moral issues as this view becomes more dominant in our society. We see this also when politicians or judges abandon their own moral convictions and change them to reflect the views of the majority. But the majority can never tell us what is right and good.

Consider what evil may be done in the name of the majority! Think of the wickedness of the slave trade, or of the setting aside of almost every treaty ever made by our national and state governments with Native Americans. This ignoring of solemn treaties arose simply because of pressures from the majority population. Think of ethnic cleansing in Bosnia or Kosovo, where hundreds of thousands of people had their homes and property stolen, women were raped, and great numbers of people murdered, all at the will of politicians serving the majority. Think, again, of abortion, another kind of ethnic cleansing, but not acknowledged as such, because the victims are unseen and have no voice to raise a protest or to make their case.

No majority can turn brutality and wickedness into ethical behavior, but such evil is the consequence of our postmodern rejection of moral order and our refusal to submit to a transcendent source of law.

Option 3: Those in Power Decide, or "Might Makes Right"

Some believe that those in power have the right to determine what is moral. The powerful may be dictators with guns. In Uganda, Idi Amin had his Christian chief justice gunned down in his courtroom because

---

[5] Many years ago, in the early 1970s, I came across this remarkable statement attributed to Golding. I apologize if he was not responsible for these words. They express very powerfully an implication of sociological law.

he was resisting Amin's tyrannical rule. Adolf Hitler and his Nazi regime decided that Jews, Gypsies, the physically and mentally disabled, and anyone who resisted the Third Reich should be put to death.[6] Or think of Saddam Hussein and his brutal reign with the killing of the Marsh Arabs, the chemical ruining of their home region in the marshlands, and the despoliation of that extraordinary environment, with its vast numbers of waterbirds and other creatures. The abominable decision to spray poisonous chemicals over the marshes there in southern Iraq ended a millennia-old civilization.

But it is not only violent dictators who illustrate this third option of those in power deciding what the law will be. In the United States, powerful elites impose their views on the many through the courts, through the congress, through the media, through wealthy business interests, or even through the executive office. Consider how our culture has become subject to powerful groups with money to give to our political representatives; then think of the access to power and decision making that comes along with that money. Such powerful groups sometimes do evil to the majority in the name of their own cause, often to further their own self-interest.

For example, agricultural subsidies become a means of bankrolling the most wealthy landowners at the taxpayers' expense. This happens because these landowners have bought political support from both Democrat and Republican senators and congressional representatives. Lest you think this is an exaggeration, let me tell a personal story. My wife and I were invited to dinner at the home of a friend. Also invited was one of the biggest landowners in Missouri, who farmed millions of acres. In the early part of our dinner he complained bitterly about the "lazy poor" who demand unemployment benefits and who insist on their healthcare being subsidized at the cost of hardworking taxpayers, like himself.

A little later in the meal the subject turned to farming subsidies. He boasted of how he was receiving millions of dollars every year not to farm great tracts of land, thereby preventing overproduction of rice and other crops and keeping the price of those crops higher. Farm subsidies were originally designed to help small farmers, but today

---

[6] If you have not seen the film *Sophie Scholl: The Final Days*, I would encourage you to buy or rent it.

they have become the means of subsidizing some of the wealthiest members of our society—at the taxpayers' expense.

Option 4: Someone's Ideology Decides

If there is no respect for the individual or for the majority, then an ideology will become the means of bringing people to power, an ideology that imposes its vision for the world on the populace of a land. Marxism or radical Islam are the obvious examples of such ideologies. Both radical Islam and Marxism promise to create the ideal society. Committed Marxists and radical Muslims have one thing in common. Both of them believe that they know what is best for everyone. They have a vision in their minds of how society ought to function. They alone know how everyone else should live, how everything should be organized. In addition, both of these political ideologies have no doctrine of original sin. They have no room in their worldview for the conviction that they might be wrong, that they might be fallible once they come to power. Because of this, there is an utterly unrealistic idealism about their vision of the world, about how society should function, and, above all, about their own use and abuse of power. The consequence is very great evil, done in the name of their supposed good.

Consider the words of David Aikman in a *Time* magazine article written about Kampuchea (Cambodia). Aikman was reporting on the terrible atrocities that had happened under the Khmer Rouge, the army of committed Marxists under the leadership of Pol Pot that took power in Cambodia. They killed over one third of the population of 7.5 million. Cities were destroyed to end the old corrupt society and make a completely new beginning. What happened in Cambodia were some of the greatest acts of wickedness by any government anywhere in the history of our world—and all for an ideology. Aikman commented:

> Where the insane reversal of values lies is in the belief that notions like "purity" or "corruption" can have any meaning outside an absolute system of values: one that is resistant to the tinkering at will by governments or revolutionary groups. The Cambodian revolution, in its own degraded "purity," has demonstrated what happens when the Marxian denial of moral absolutes is taken with total seriousness by

its adherents. Pol Pot and his friends decide what good is, what bad is, and how many corpses must pile up before the rapacious demon of "purity" is appeased.

In the West today, there is a pervasive consent to the notion of moral relativism, a reluctance to admit that absolute evil can and does exist. This makes it especially difficult for some to accept the fact that the Cambodian experience is something far worse than a revolutionary aberration. Rather, it is the deadly logical consequence of an atheistic, man-centered system of values, enforced by fallible human beings with total power, who believe, with Marx, that morality is whatever the powerful define it to be and, with Mao, that power grows from gun barrels.[7]

The more confident one is that humanity is the only source of law and of the knowledge of good and evil, then the more readily evil will be done. This is true even when a group claims to be instituting the will of God but uses that claim as a cloak and cover for its own ideology.

Turning to God: Restoring Order and Beauty

What will we as Christians put forward against these options? We have to heed Jeremiah's warning:

My people have committed two evils:
they have forsaken me,
　the fountain of living waters,
and hewed out cisterns for themselves,
　broken cisterns that can hold no waters.[8]

We can only find a true fountain for the good life for ourselves and our societies if we turn back to God himself. He is the fountain of order and beauty in both the physical and moral senses. He is the Creator of this ordered physical universe—a universe that reflects his own character of consistency and trustworthiness. God the Son is the same yesterday, today, and forever.[9] His character never changes, for he, his Father, and the Spirit are pure and filled with integrity. James writes of the "Father of lights with whom there is no variation or shadow

---

[7] David Aikman, "Cambodia: An Experiment in Genocide," *Time*, July 31, 1978, 39–40.
[8] Jeremiah 2:13.
[9] Hebrews 13:8.

due to change."[10] Through God the Son "all things were created . . . . And he is before all things, and in him all things hold together."[11] He "upholds the universe by the word of his power."[12]

We take the rational and ordered structure of the physical universe for granted—but this is only because we live in a culture that has its view of the nature of reality rooted in a Judeo-Christian worldview.[13] Animist and Hindu societies have no such confidence in the orderly nature of the universe. Instead, for the animist, the world is an abode of spirits who rule in unpredictable and even malevolent ways. For the Hindu, this physical world is ultimately Maya, illusory, and such a worldview will never lead to science or to technology.[14] But we know that the universe was made by the God who is faithful and consistent, who holds to his word, and who never is capricious or malevolent. So we gladly join in with the psalmist who praises God as the Creator in Psalm 148:

> Praise him, sun and moon,
>> praise him, all you shining stars!
> Praise him, you highest heavens,
>> and you waters above the heavens!
>
> Let them praise the name of the LORD!
>> For he commanded and they were created.
> And he established them forever and ever;
>> he gave a decree, and it shall not pass away.[15]

For a fuller exposition of this recognition of the wonderful structures of this universe, read Psalm 104 or Job 38–41. Psalm 19, which C. S. Lewis described as "the greatest poem in the Psalter and one of the greatest lyrics in the world,"[16] exults in this beautiful order of creation and declares that, because it is so lovely and so consistent, it reveals very clearly the nature of its Creator:

---

[10] James 1:17.
[11] Colossians 1:16–17.
[12] Hebrews 1:3.
[13] For a careful reflection on this, see Charles B. Thaxton and Nancy R. Pearcey, *The Soul of Science: Christian Faith and Natural Philosophy* (Wheaton, IL: Crossway, 1994).
[14] See Vishal Mangalwadi, *The Book That Made Your World: How the Bible Created the Soul of Western Civilization* (Nashville: Thomas Nelson, 2011).
[15] Psalm 148:3–6.
[16] C. S. Lewis, *Reflections on the Psalms* (New York: Harcourt, 1958), 63.

The heavens declare the glory of God,
  and the sky above proclaims his handiwork.
Day to day pours out speech,
  and night to night reveals knowledge.
There is no speech, nor are there words,
    whose voice is not heard.
Their measuring line goes out through all the earth,
  and their words to the end of the world.[17]

Notice here how the psalmist refers to the speech and knowledge revealed by the creation. No random world could possibly reveal knowledge and speech, but only a world with consistent and trustworthy order. It is indeed on this foundation of the universe reflecting the integrity and trustworthiness of God himself that all the laws of science are built. We might even say that the discovery of any physical law is simply a discovery of the rational and trustworthy manner in which God has created the universe, and the way he governs the universe as one who is utterly faithful. Nature is not chaotic, but predictable. Without this, science would be impossible; and human life, or any other life, would not exist.

Just as the character of God is the foundation for physical laws, so his character is the foundation of moral law. The one true God defines in his own being what is holy, good, just, merciful, and right. Behind the laws that God gives to the human race stands the character of the triune God: Father, Son, and Holy Spirit. How does Scripture speak about the character of God? God is presented to us as the Holy One, the one who is perfect in righteousness. In his presence the cherubim and seraphim cry continually,

Holy, holy, holy is the LORD of hosts;
  the whole earth is full of his glory![18]

The Lord who gives us his commandments is the righteous, awesome, and transcendent God. At the time that the law is made known at Sinai, God reveals himself in terrifying majesty and holiness. The people are warned to consecrate themselves in preparation for the Lord's coming

---

[17] Psalm 19:1–4 (see ESV footnote 2).
[18] Isaiah 6:3.

down on Mount Sinai "in the sight of all the people." When he comes there is a storm theophany (an appearance of God) that is seen in the rest of Scripture as foundational to the knowledge of God:

> On the morning of the third day there were thunders and lightnings and a thick cloud on the mountain and a very loud trumpet blast, so that all the people in the camp trembled. . . . Mount Sinai was wrapped in smoke because the LORD had descended on it in fire. The smoke of it went up like the smoke of a kiln, and the whole mountain trembled greatly. . . . The sound of the trumpet grew louder and louder.[19]

The writer of Hebrews refers back to this revelation and to its terrifying nature. But he does not do this to teach us that there was law at Sinai, and in contrast there is now grace in Christ.[20] Instead, he teaches us that the words given to us by Christ come with an even greater obligation to listen and to obey because Christ is the one who has come from heaven to speak, whereas the law was given at a mountain here on this earth.[21] Hebrews warns that we will not escape judgment if we fail to listen, and then the writer finishes with these words: "Let us offer to God acceptable worship, with reverence and awe, for our God is a consuming fire."[22]

This description of the revelation of God's holiness from Exodus 19 also appears repeatedly at the very end of the Bible, in the book of Revelation. Indeed, John alludes more frequently to this Exodus passage than to any other Old Testament text; so the Mount Sinai revelation with its thunder, lightning, smoke, fire, trumpet sounds, and loud voice returns again and again. Elements of the Sinai theophany appear in John's vision of the heavenly throne[23] and at the climax of each series of judgments: the seals,[24] the trumpets,[25] and the bowls.[26]

The deeply significant issue here is that the holiness and fearful majesty of God revealed at Sinai are a true representation of what John

---

[19] Exodus 19:16–19; see also 20:18.
[20] Many people have understood the Hebrews text in this way: "At Sinai there was law and judgment and fear; now in Jesus there is grace and mercy and love." But this is not the point the writer is making, as should be clear above.
[21] Hebrews 12:18–29; see also John 3:13.
[22] Hebrews 12:28–29.
[23] Revelation 4:5.
[24] Revelation 8:5.
[25] Revelation 11:19.
[26] Revelation 16:17–18.

sees in heaven, and a true representation of what will be displayed on this earth in a far greater way at the end of this age; for then "the Lord Jesus is revealed from heaven with his mighty angels in flaming fire."[27] Awesome holiness and terrifying justice are not some aspects of God's revelation of himself that have been left behind at Sinai— they are eternally constant realities of who God is, realities that will never change.

We might respond, "But such perfect holiness is a problem, a terrifying problem for us!" Indeed it is; and that of course is why Jesus has come to save us from the judgment that should justly be ours. However, lest we flee to wishing that God were somehow less than perfect, so that we would not need to fear him, we need to think about the beauty of such holiness. Moral perfection is God's nature, and so his character is the basis for affirming that this is a moral universe, a universe in which there is a distinction between good and evil, kindness and cruelty, justice and injustice. Without this doctrine of the perfect holiness of God, I would not be a Christian today.

WHAT TURNED ME TO GOD

There were three big questions with which I wrestled as an unbeliever.

1. What does it mean to be human? Am I just a part of the physical universe, related ultimately to the molecule, the amoeba, the tree rat, and the whale, or is there some solid foundation for all the aspects of our human life that seem so different from other creatures in this world? How can I affirm the significance of the joys that I, and all others, experience? Is there any ultimate foundation to assure me that my life has any meaning, or am I simply an accident of time and chance in an ultimately meaningless universe?

2. Is there a foundation for distinguishing between good and evil? Does it really make any final difference whether one lives one's life seeking to do what seems right, or are such distinctions meaningless because chance and death happen to everyone, to the good as well as the evil?

3. Is there an explanation for, and resolution to, suffering? Is there any meaningful account of the sorrows, the troubles, the evils of life

---

[27] 2 Thessalonians 1:7–8.

in this world: or, again, is this all ultimately absurd? Will there ever be any overcoming of the suffering endured, any resolution to our sorrows, any wiping away of the tears that sometimes overwhelm us?

I came to the conclusion that there were no answers to these questions and became suicidal. Why bother to live if life is indeed absurd; if there is no foundation for human uniqueness; if there is no reason to distinguish right from wrong, so that it does not matter what I do; if there is no satisfactory explanation for suffering that will justify our tears; if there is no final victory over grief and death?

I had read much literature which told me that life without meaning was indeed the human condition: books by Thomas Hardy, Jean-Paul Sartre, Albert Camus, and Ernest Hemingway; plays by Henrik Ibsen, Samuel Beckett, and Eugène Ionesco. I listened to music that gave me the same message: Richard Strauss's opera *Elektra*; music by Bob Dylan, the Rolling Stones, and many other singers and groups. In the mid-sixties a whole series of movies came out that insisted that there are no answers to these questions, and, to my undoing, I watched many of those movies: films by Bergman, Antonioni, Fellini, and Roman Polanski. (*The Silence, Wild Strawberries, Blow-Up, Juliet of the Spirits*, and *Repulsion* are some of the films I saw at that time.) Already in the 1960s in Britain and in all of Europe much of both intellectual and popular culture had a deep vein of despair and nihilism running through it. There seemed to be no answers to my questions—and in particular the second of these questions began to haunt me.

I read enough of Hindu scriptures to discover that no answer could be found there. In the Bhagavad-Gita there is a discussion between Lord Krishna and the man Arjuna. Arjuna asks the god whether he should fight for what is good and against the evil. The god replies that in the end there is no difference between the two, but that here in this world it might be needful for humans to strive for what appears good. This was not a satisfactory answer to my burning question. It affirmed my conviction that religion would not help my search for meaning. I did not at that time know the difference that the existence of the personal and infinite God would make.

What I had found was that in Hindu pantheism there is no ultimate distinction between light and darkness, good and evil, kindness and cruelty, justice and injustice. Joseph Campbell, a passionate exponent of such views, said this:

> "God" is an ambiguous word in our language because it appears to refer to something that is known. But the transcendent is unknowable and unknown. God is transcendent, finally, of anything like the name "God." God is beyond names and forms. Meister Eckhart said that the ultimate and highest leave-taking is leaving God for God, leaving your notion of God for an experience of that which transcends all notions.
>
> The mystery of life is beyond all human conception. Everything we know is within the terminology of the concepts of being and not being, many and single, true and untrue. We always think in terms of opposites. But God, the ultimate, is beyond the pairs of opposites, that is all there is to it. . . .
>
> Heraclitus said that for God all things are good and right and just, but for man some things are right and others are not. When you are a man, you are in the field of time and decisions. One of the problems of life is to live with the realization of both terms, to say, "I know the center, and I know that good and evil are simply temporal aberrations and that, in God's view, there is no difference."
>
> . . . Since in Hindu thinking everything in the universe is a manifestation of divinity itself, how should we say no to anything in the world? How should we say no to brutality, to stupidity, to vulgarity, to thoughtlessness?
>
> . . . For you and for me—the way is to say yes.[28]

My conclusion was not to say yes to brutality, thoughtlessness, and evil, but to end my life. If this was indeed the nature of reality, then I no longer wished to be part of it. I left the university one day with the intention of throwing myself over a cliff. There, one step from eternity, I was held back by the order and beauty of the natural world around me. It was January, cold and with a harsh wind, but it was sunny and the skies were clear and blue. The trees were bare, but they still had beauty; there were no flowers, but the grass was green and alive. Titmice and nuthatches flitted through the dark branches or patrolled the trunks for insect larva. Though it was midwinter, it was glorious; and above all, it was not chaotic but, rather, full of patterns and consistency.

---

[28]Joseph Campbell, with Bill Moyers, *The Power of Myth*, ed. Betty Sue Flowers (New York: Random House, 1991), 56–57, 82, 84.

This ordered structure of the natural world gave me the hope that I must keep on searching. If there could be such beauty, such order, even in winter, surely there had to be some other answer than meaningless-ness to my questions. I walked back to the bus stop and returned to the university determined to keep looking. Though I did not know it at the time, I had experienced what David describes in Psalm 19:

> The heavens declare the glory of God,
>   and the sky above proclaims his handiwork.
> Day to day pours out speech,
>   and night to night reveals knowledge.
> There is no speech, nor are there words,
>   whose voice is not heard.
> Their measuring line goes out through all the earth,
>   and their words to the end of the world.[29]

A few days later I was introduced to a Christian named Michael, who was prepared to take my questions and sense of absurdity as is-sues that needed addressing and answering with compassion, love, and careful reflection. I had met other Christians, but this was the first time one had taken my questions seriously and given the time to show that there were answers. My first serious introduction to the Bible was a study Michael did on the book of Ecclesiastes. He began by reading the first two chapters, which includes:

> Vanity of vanities, says the Preacher,
>   vanity of vanities! All is vanity.[30]

He went on to show how the book of Ecclesiastes says that if there is no holy God, if there is no judgment that separates good from evil, then life is absurd and one might as well despair of living. This was very shortly after I met Michael. He did not, at that time, know that I was struggling with the very question he addressed that evening. It was the first time in my life that I thought, "Maybe, there is a God, if he can lead one of his followers to speak about the very issue that had almost driven me to kill myself."

---

[29] Psalm 19:1–4 (see ESV footnote 2).
[30] Ecclesiastes 1:2, RSV.

Ecclesiastes points to the answer to the question about good and evil that so haunted me. There is indeed a personal and infinite God with a character of perfect holiness who will call all of us to account for our actions, our words, and our thoughts. On the judgment day it will be revealed, despite all protests, that good is good and that evil is evil, for "there is no variation or shadow due to change" in God.[31]

His law, revealed in Scripture, and to the human conscience, is an expression of his holy character and demonstrates to us the ultimate reality of a moral universe. Just as there are physical laws that we can trust, and on the basis of which we can live our daily lives without fear of chaos, so there are moral laws that are just as fixed, just as inviolable. We live in a world where there is a constant accountability to the unchangeable character of God. This is beautiful, for without this, life would be impossible. This fixed moral reality gives us the confidence to face each day knowing that our lives have eternal significance. In every moral choice we make, we are casting stones into a pool and making ripples that go on forever.[32]

Questions for Personal Reflection and Group Discussion

1. If humanity is the only source of moral values and law, can you think of any possible ways we might create values and laws for our society other than the four mentioned in this chapter: the individual, the majority, the powerful, or some ideology? We might take an opinion poll or vote in a referendum to get the majority view. Or we might ask Congress or the Supreme Court to decide for us. Do you see any problems with these various options?

2. Jean-Paul Sartre wrote, "Man is condemned to be free. . . . condemned every moment to invent man."[33] What do you think he meant by this? Would you be comfortable with having to invent what it means to be human each moment of your life?

3. Would it make you uncomfortable if you believed that you had to take the whole weight on your own back of deciding what is good and what is evil, not only for yourself, but also for everyone else? How well do you think you might do?

---

[31] James 1:17.
[32] This image of casting stones into a pool and making eternal ripples is one that Francis Schaeffer used repeatedly in his teaching.
[33] Sartre, Existentialism and Human Emotions, 23.

4. What is your response to the emphasis of this chapter on God's character standing behind the physical laws of this world? Is this a new way of thinking for you? Do you find this comforting?

5. Have you understood the connection between God's law and God's character? Or have you sometimes thought of God's law as arbitrary and as simply an expression of his urge to tell us what to do? Have you ever been afraid that God might be a sort of heavenly tyrant, imposing arbitrary and despotic rules on us?

6. Have you, at any point in your life, struggled with the thought that life is absurd and that it ultimately makes no difference what we do? What caused you to wrestle with this issue? What has comforted you if you have had such thoughts?

7. Do you find God's perfect holiness only fearful because of the prospect of judgment that awaits us? Or do you find it wonderful that this aspect of God's character makes a sure foundation for affirming the significance of human choices and actions?

4

The Beauty
of the Law

After reading chapter 3, many readers might wonder, "But, isn't Christianity an ideology, like Marxism or radical Islam?" This is a significant question, and one that every Christian needs to be ready to answer, because this is how any unbeliever will think about committed believers in Jesus.

So, what is an ideology? The following are two dictionary definitions:[1]

> a systematic body of concepts especially about human life or culture
> . . . the integrated assertions, theories and aims that constitute a sociopolitical program

Clearly, inasmuch as the Christian faith expresses a body of concepts that give an account of human life in this world and of the way we are to live, then we may agree that Christianity is an ideology. However, we believe that the Christian faith is not a sociopolitical program or agenda of human ideas; rather, our convictions arise from God's revelation about our world, about our human condition, and about God's resolution to our problems.

So, in talking with a non-Christian, we will need to show that the Christian faith is the true ideology—the ideology that gives the only accurate and faithful account of our world and of our life here in

---

[1] *Merriam-Webster's Collegiate Dictionary*, 11th ed. (Springfield, MA: 2008), senses 2a and 2c.

this world; in addition, the Christian faith gives the only satisfactory resolution to the tragedy of the human condition. This resolution is revealed in the Bible's record of God's intervention to deliver us from our sorrows. Also, in communicating our faith to an unbeliever, we will try to show why any other ideology is inaccurate in its account of reality, unable to give an answer to the problem of suffering, and inadequate in its prescriptions for human life.

One simple example here may demonstrate the inadequacy of Marxism and radical Islam and show them to be human inventions rather than God's truth, human-made ideologies rather than the one answer revealed from above. As we saw in the last chapter, both radical Islam and Marxism promise to create the ideal society. One reason for this is that neither of them acknowledges the problem of original sin. Neither of these worldviews recognizes that human beings are fundamentally flawed. The fall is not a doctrine of orthodox Islam. Islam urges people to submit to Allah and believes that perfect submission to him is possible, and that entire obedience to Allah will bring about an ideal society. Marxism does not admit that humans are corrupted in their very being. Instead, Marxism insists that at the basis of all human problems are particular economic structures.

This denial of original sin leaves both Marxists and radical Islamists with no sense of their own sin or fallibility, and therefore of the inadequacy of their plans for resolving human problems. It is because of this utopian vision of a perfect society—a new world order coming about as a result of their plans of social, economic, and political action—that many abominably wicked things are done. We could say that the more idealistic and utopian the ideology, the more disastrous will be its recipe for change when it is put into action. It is so sure it is right that it sees no need to put any restraint on its leaders as they implement their vision. Think again of Cambodia and the Khmer Rouge, or of the Taliban in Afghanistan.

Christianity is very different. There is no conviction that we have a blueprint for an ideal society; we know that we are sinful and that all our human plans and actions will be flawed. We recognize, therefore, that there need to be restraints on the power and the vision of those who lead us. We know there will be no perfect society till Jesus comes.

It is Christianity that has insisted on restraints on those in power; and Christianity has demanded that there be checks and balances in our political systems so that we can deal rigorously with sin.

This conviction that humans are sinful has been one of the most liberating doctrines in political history. It is only when Christians have made the mistake of departing from Scripture that they have become idealistic and felt they have a template for creating an ideal world. Examples of this in the history of the church are few and minor, but there are many major examples of the disastrous consequences of both Marxism and radical Islam.

To return to the foundational point made in chapter 3, all biblical study of the law begins with the conviction that God's own character stands behind the moral order of this world and behind the commandments that he gives to us his creatures. This is the fundamental reason why the Scriptures speak so positively about the law.

Praising a set of commandments is an alien notion in our cultural context, but that is where the biblical view begins: with praise and thanksgiving for the law. Psalm 19 is an example of this high view of the law of God. It is also one of the best-known and best-loved of all the psalms, "the greatest poem in the Psalter," according to C. S. Lewis.[2] Another commentator puts it this way: "The psalm combines the most beautiful poetry with some of the most profound of biblical theology."[3]

The psalm divides into three obvious sections, both in its poetical structure and in its content. The first part provides a backdrop for the second, on the law, which will be our main focus.

PART 1: PSALM 19:1—6

> The heavens declare the glory of God;
>> the skies proclaim the work of his hands.
> Day after day they pour forth speech;
>> night after night they display knowledge.
> There is no speech or language
>> where their voice is not heard.
> Their voice goes out into all the earth,
>> their words to the ends of the world.

---

[2] C. S. Lewis, *Reflections on the Psalms* (New York: Harcourt, 1958), 63.
[3] Peter C. Craigie, *Word Biblical Commentary*, vol. 19, *Psalms 1–50* (Waco, TX: Word, 1983), 183.

In the heavens he has pitched a tent for the sun,
  which is like a bridegroom coming forth from his pavilion,
  like a champion rejoicing to run his course.
It rises at one end of the heavens
  and makes its circuit to the other;
  nothing is hidden from its heat. (NIV)

David opens the psalm with an affirmation of the heavens declaring God's glory, followed by the parallel affirmation that the skies "proclaim" the work of his hands. If we follow David's urging and look up at the sky, we see there the clearest possible declaration that we live in a created universe. And we see that the Creator is worthy of praise, for it is so evident that what he has made is glorious. As the apostle Paul says, "His invisible attributes, namely, his eternal power and divine nature, have been clearly perceived, ever since the creation of the world, in the things that have been made."[4] Whenever my wife, Vicki, and I spend time on the Gulf Coast in Naples, Florida, we see many thousands of people heading for the beach every evening to watch the sun setting. But it is not only on the Gulf Coast that people feel constrained to lift their eyes to look up at the sky; all over the earth we find this sense of the extraordinary beauty of creation.

In verse 2 David declares that this revelation is not occasional, obscure, or sporadic but, rather, continuous. Day after day, night after night, there is an ever-present display and proclamation of God's creative power and glory. Whether we see the sun shining, or the clouds refracting its light in an array of shades and colors, or a moonlit or starry night, there is a constant revelation of God. David is clearly thinking of the progression of the sun, moon, and stars across the sky. He does not have our twenty-first-century astronomical knowledge, but he does not need such knowledge to observe that there is regularity in the movement of the heavenly bodies, a regularity that governs our days and seasons and years, and that these patterns point to their great designer.

In verses 3–4 David tells us that this revelation is universal. People may not understand each other across the barriers of different

---
[4] Romans 1:20.

tongues, but there is one language that is understood by every nation and language group, and that is the language spoken by the heavens. Of course, there are no literal words spoken by the sun, moon, and stars, but they are universally "heard" and universally understood.

This is why Paul argues in Romans 1 that all human beings are inexcusable for failing to worship God. There is no one who may say that he or she is ignorant of his existence, his power, and his glory. Vicki and I live in Missouri, where every spring and every fall are simply lovely and our hearts are filled with gladness. God has set us in a place here on this earth where it would be inexcusable if we did not give him honor and glory and praise, for we see him revealed so clearly, especially in those seasons, but indeed in every season of the year.

From the end of verse 4 through verse 6 David reflects on the particular glory of the sun. He uses the beautiful image of the heavens as a "tent" or "pavilion" in which the sun dwells. These verses personify the sun, but unlike all other poetry from the ancient world extolling the sun, they do not deify the sun or offer it worship (think of the wonderful Greek stories of the chariot of the sun). Here in this poem the intent of the personification is to point to the majesty and goodness of God, who is the provider of the gift of the sun and the Creator of its glory. The image shifts to speak of the sun as a "bridegroom" coming forth from the wedding chamber as he rises in the morning in the vigor of life and joy—like one newly married!

Then the image shifts again to a "champion," that is, a warrior or hero who delights in displaying his strength and speed. As I reflected on this I thought of the words of Eric Liddell in the movie *Chariots of Fire*, "God . . . made me fast. When I run I feel his pleasure." All of us understand this image of the champion, for there is something full of joy and power in seeing someone like Michael Phelps, the swimmer, or one of the Olympic gymnasts, or any other great athlete at the Olympic Games, exercising their extraordinary abilities. Just so it is with the sun, says David: there is an expression of God's delight and glory as we daily see its rise in the east and then follow its course across the sky. The sun is visible everywhere and nothing is hidden from its heat. So too, God's glory is evident everywhere, and the clarity and power of this revelation call us all to acknowledge him. No one can say that God is hidden from them, or that the knowledge of the Creator is obscure.

PART 2: PSALM 19:7–11

Suddenly the subject changes! From the first section of the psalm, glorying in the light of God's revelation of himself in creation, David turns to the light of God's revelation of himself in his law:

> The law of the LORD is perfect,
>   reviving the soul.
> The statutes of the LORD are trustworthy,
>   making wise the simple.
> The precepts of the LORD are right,
>   giving joy to the heart.
> The commands of the LORD are radiant,
>   giving light to the eyes.
> The fear of the LORD is pure,
>   enduring forever.
> The ordinances of the LORD are sure
>   and altogether righteous.
> They are more precious than gold,
>   than much pure gold;
> they are sweeter than honey,
>   than honey from the comb.
> By them is your servant warned;
>   in keeping them is great reward. (NIV)

Readers of the psalm sometimes wonder whether these two sections of the poem fit together. "Aren't these two sections really two separate psalms?" "Were these separate ideas and poems just thrown into the same psalm?" "What has the sun got to do with the written commands of God in the Bible?" I often get asked such questions. As I begin to address these questions here, we should notice first that the statement about the sun's shining everywhere ties the two sections of the psalm together. The sun gives its light and heat, bringing life to the world and revealing its Creator. The law has the same nature as the sun, giving light and life everywhere and even burning itself into the conscience, thus revealing its Creator. As with the sun, so with the law—nothing is hidden from its light or heat.

Structure

But there is more that ties these two sections together than this double image of light. As we begin to reflect on this second section of Psalm 19, it might be helpful for to us to look very briefly at how the psalm was structured by David.

Notice the length of the lines in the first section: they are longer and more measured and stately as they tell of God's glory revealed in the heavens. The second section, verses 7–11, delights in the law of God as it reveals his purposes for our lives. The law of God is the second great light of God's revelation of himself. Again, notice the length of the lines: the lines of these verses are shorter and have a quicker tempo, like the rising and falling of waves, as David expresses his love for the law. He is consciously changing the music and rhythm of the poetry as he moves from one source of God's light to the other.

We should note too that the name of God changes from the first to the second section of the psalm. He is *Elohim*, that is, God, the Almighty, in the first section, where he is revealed as Creator by the heavens. He is *Yahweh*, the "LORD," the faithful, covenant-keeping, redeeming, and gloriously personal God in the second section, for this is how the law reveals him. Creation tells us something about who God is as the powerful and majestic one. The law tells us far more about his holy, loving, and gracious character. These brief reflections on the poetic structure may help us to understand why we love this psalm so much.

Verses 7–9

David turns to the law and gives us six affirmations about its beauty and glory, each affirmation being followed by a statement of its benefits to us.

Before we look at these six affirmations, we need to ask what David means by "the law." It is important to ask this question because we live in a time when people want to be a law unto themselves, to do what is right in their own eyes. The idea that there is a set of rules or commandments that *dictate* to everyone how he or she should live is not popular in our culture today, even in the church! The law is one of the most neglected aspects of God's Word in many of our churches, largely because of this cultural setting.

So what does David mean? By "the law," or *Torah*, David means the law of Moses: God's moral commandments. The law also contains wonderful promises and the revelation of God's grace and mercy, as well as demands. The Ten Commandments, that marvelous summary of the law, begin with the statement, "I am the LORD your God, who brought you out of the land of Egypt, out of the house of slavery."[5]

The law also contains the ceremonies and sacrifices to provide atonement for the inevitable failures to keep the commandments, atonement that portrays so wonderfully the mercy of God and the hope of ultimate sacrifice to be made by God's Son. But David certainly has in view the commandments that God has given us to direct our lives. The law should be seen as God's gracious provision for his people, even in its moral demands, for these moral demands set out for us the way of life that God himself observes—and his way of life is altogether lovely!

Six Affirmations about the Law

1. In verse 7 David tells us that "the law of the LORD is perfect"; it is without blemish, and therefore it gives new life to the soul, "reviving" it over and over again. This word "reviving" (or "restoring") is the same word used in Psalm 23. Just as the Lord, my shepherd, leads me beside still waters and restores my soul, so his law is a spiritual restorative because of its spiritual beauty. I am to keep returning to it, that I might be refreshed, just as each day needs the life-giving light of the sun. Do you keep turning to the law for new life, to be refreshed in your understanding of how you may live in righteousness, of how your life might become lovely like the Lord's?

2. "The statutes of the LORD [or "the testimony of the LORD"—ESV] are trustworthy" or sure; that is, they are faithful and beyond any doubt. God himself has testified to us what true virtue is, both in his *acts* of justice, mercy, and faithfulness revealed in history and in his

---

[5] Exodus 20:2.

words of wisdom about genuine righteousness. Therefore, his words enable us to become wise, for in our sinful and rebellious hearts we are "simple," that is, prone to instability and easily led astray morally. What about you? Do you turn to God's statutes each day to be made wise in knowing what is faithful and true in all your work and relationships?

3. "The precepts of the LORD [God's declarations of our moral obligations] are right," that is, they are clearly morally beautiful and upright, for they reflect God's own goodness; and so they bring joy to the heart of the one who gives his or her life to observing them. Are they beautiful to you? Do you seek to understand what goodness God desires for you to live in, so that your life might be attractive to him, attractive to your family and to others around you, and a joy to your own heart?

4. "The commands of the LORD are radiant," that is, they are like a lamp to show light along our way, so that we can see which way to walk (again, here we see the parallel to the sun). If we follow God's laws, we will always have light to direct our lives each day. Are you walking in that light? Are you eager to know from God's commands what is holy, what is kind, what is compassionate and merciful as you live in this world, so that you will walk constantly in the light of his way?

5. "The fear of the LORD is pure." Here David refers to the way of life that expresses reverence for the Lord. God's way is pure and wholesome, and it will endure forever. True righteousness is always in style; it does not change from culture to culture, or from one moment of history to another, or from one situation to another. Is your life pure and wholesome? Is that how others see you, and can you honestly say that this is your desire, with regard to your appearance, for example, or your attitude toward your home and your possessions? Do you set a guard before your eyes and over your heart so that you may live in purity, chastity, fidelity, and contentment in the fear of the Lord?

6. "The ordinances of the LORD are sure"; that is, the declarations of the Lord as to what it means to live justly and faithfully are right and good. When you see them being observed in business or in the political sphere, you should rejoice for they are "altogether righteous." What about your sphere of work? Do people observe your life and find a sure and certain integrity and trustworthiness?

Verses 10—11

In verses 10—11 David teaches us to treasure the laws of God more highly than any wealth or physical comfort or pleasure. We are to live not for money or possessions or security, or in anxiety about our pension fund or savings (even if they have been reduced to half their size by a worldwide financial crisis); rather, we are to live "by every word that comes from the mouth of God."[6] Our food and drink should be to delight in doing the will of our heavenly Father, just as Jesus did. Our wealth should be to commit ourselves to walk in the ways of the Lord. Who or what do you serve? What is your delight? What is your treasure? These are David's questions for us.

He adds in verse 11 that God's laws warn us. Indeed they do, for they show us so clearly where we are sinful, and there is always plenty of failure and disobedience to be exposed! Yet, at the same time, David urges us to enjoy the rewards that God delights in giving us, his children, whenever we make any step forward in keeping the commandments.

PART 3: PSALM 19:12—14

In the final section of the psalm we see David turning to examine his own heart and life. He has gloried in God's revelation of himself in creation; he has delighted in the Lord's revelation of himself in his law. Now he asks, in effect, "What about me? Is there any revelation of God in my life?"

> Who can discern his errors?
>   Forgive my hidden faults.
> Keep your servant also from willful sins;
>   may they not rule over me.
> Then will I be blameless,
>   innocent of great transgression.
>
> May the words of my mouth and the meditation of my heart
>   be pleasing in your sight,
>   O Lord, my Rock and my Redeemer. (NIV)

---

[6] Matthew 4:4.

Lest we think that David imagines himself righteous and morally flawless (this would be to misunderstand completely what he has been saying about the law), David acknowledges his sin to the Lord. He knows that he cannot see all his own faults and failures to keep the law. He knows that his heart is deceitful and that it contains many hidden sins, so he cries out for forgiveness.

But we may wonder, how does this final part of the psalm follow from David's words of delight in the law? The answer is that nothing is hidden from the burning light of the law. Like the sun, the law exposes us by the beauty and clarity of its light, as well as enabling us to see and giving us direction. So in reflecting on the law, David is led to reflect on his sin. Any proper meditation on the law will have this effect, for while we delight in the beautiful way of life set out in the law, and while we rejoice in the moral integrity that any obedience brings, yet the more surely we see the light of the law, and the more clearly we see ourselves by the light of the law, the more too we will see our failures and our falling short. So David prays for the Lord's mercy and forgiveness not only for the sins of which he is aware, but also for the far greater number of his hidden sins.

Having prayed for forgiveness in verse 12, David prays in verse 13 that the Lord will help him to become holy. He knows that he cannot make himself pure or free from sin; he knows that he is powerless to do this; so he prays that the Lord will keep him from willful sins, from being dominated by sin. This needs to be the prayer of us all. Like David, we are to pray that the Lord will make us "innocent" or acquitted of "great transgression." Like David, I need acquittal. Like David, I need protection from great sins. How about you? Where do you need the acquittal of the Lord at this particular time in your life? Cry out to him like David!

In verse 14 the psalm ends with a prayer that David's own words and thoughts might reflect the loveliness of the Lord, just as the heavens speak out God's glory and the law unveils the beauty of his Redeemer's character. And how beautiful indeed is our Redeemer as we see his life described for us in every line of the Gospels! The beauty of his righteous life is more glorious than the beauty of the heavens.

David desires that he might be a third light making God known.

David longs that he too might reveal God in his thoughts and "words" (the same Hebrew term used for the "words" of the heavens in verse 4 is used here in verse 14). This final verse of the psalm, where David expresses his longing to make God known in his own life, names the Lord "my Rock and my Redeemer," for David knows that the Lord loves him, that the Lord has forgiven him, and that the Lord will enable him to walk in the ways of his law. This is so for us today—God has redeemed us through the grace of his Son. Christ has acquitted us, declaring us innocent. And Christ will enable us to walk in his light, equipping us to reveal his beauty in our lives as we commit ourselves to obeying his commandments out of gratitude for his great love.

What place do these three lights have in our lives? Do we glory daily in the light of creation? Do we delight in walking in the light of the law? Are our lives a light to the world? That is the Lord's desire for each of us. If we ask him, he will gladly make this our reality!

Questions for Personal Reflection and Group Discussion

1. Do my words about the significance of the doctrine of sin make sense to you, and do they help your understanding of why such evil can be done by people with a visionary ideology like Marxism or radical Islam? Have you thought before about the politically liberating value of the biblical doctrine of original sin?

2. In what ways do you think this Christian doctrine of sin has shaped our political system? Do you think this biblical understanding is under threat in our society today?

3. Is beginning our thinking about God's commandments with the acknowledgment of the beauty of the law a new idea to you?

4. Had you wondered about whether Psalm 19 holds together as one poem? Were you persuaded by this chapter's exposition that it is indeed one poem?

5. What are some of the most special experiences you have had of being overwhelmed by the loveliness of creation?

6. Was it a new idea to you that the law reveals far more about who God is than does the creation, because the law teaches us about God's character and not simply his power and his creativity?

7. What parts of the law do you personally see as most beautiful?

8. Why is it a good thing, rather than a problem, to come to the law to have your sins exposed?

9. Where in particular does your life need to become lovelier than it is now? Or to put the question another way, in what ways do you think you need to be made wiser by the law?

5

THE GIVING OF
THE LAW AT SINAI

In chapter 4 we looked at Psalm 19 to see how David praises God for the way he has revealed his glory in creation, and for the even greater clarity and beauty of his self-revelation in his law. We will return to this issue of the beauty of the law many times, for this is one of the most significant truths to realize: God's law is beautiful because it reveals God's character. This is the most basic reason why we should love the law. Our delight should be to meditate on the law day and night, as the Psalms teach us:

> Oh how I love your law!
>   It is my meditation all the day.[1]

This issue of loving the law of God is so important that, to understand more fully why we should love the law, we turn in this chapter to the giving of the law at Mount Sinai.

THE CONTEXT IN WHICH THE LAW IS GIVEN

God gave the law in the context of the covenant he had already initiated centuries before. This covenant is set out in detail in the promises God made to Abraham. Abram and Sarai were the original names of this couple whom God called to himself. They and their ancestors had lived for many generations in Mesopotamia, the land between the rivers

---

[1] Psalm 119:97.

Tigris and Euphrates (in present-day Iraq). Judging by the names Abram and Sarai, and also by the results of archaeological excavation in the cities of that area, they appear to have been a people who worshipped the moon god. Abram and Sarai lived the first part of their lives in a city called Ur of the Chaldees and then moved north to another city, Haran.

Then their history took a completely new direction. The Lord God, Creator of heaven and earth, came to them and revealed himself to them. God called Abram and Sarai to leave their ancestral gods, to leave their native country, to leave their family, and to travel to a new land, a land he would show them. When God called them to worship and to serve him, he made a series of remarkable promises to them.

He promised them that they would have innumerable descendants, even though they were childless in their old age because Sarai was barren. He promised to raise up a nation from this couple and from their descendants, and to make that nation great. He promised to bless them with personal fellowship with him, that he would be their God, and that he would be the God of their descendants in the generations to come. He promised that they and their descendants would be his own beloved people. He promised that he would make them a blessing to all the nations of the world. He promised that one day one of their descendants (their seed) would be a very particular blessing to the whole world.[2]

God confirmed his covenant promises with Abraham and Sarah (the new names he gave them), and with the following generations of Isaac and Jacob and their families, and also with their descendants. It was from these ancestors that the tribes came which would be formed into the nation of Israel at the time of the exodus from Egypt. *Yahweh*, "the LORD," committed himself to Abraham, Isaac, and Jacob and to his people, Israel. He declared to them: "I am the LORD your God," and he made his covenant with them.

It is within this context of the Lord's covenant with Abraham, his son, and his grandson that, several generations later, the Lord comes to Moses in Egypt. When God appears to Moses at the burning bush, he reveals himself to Moses as the "LORD, the God of your fathers, the God of Abraham, the God of Isaac, and the God of Jacob."[3]

---

[2]Genesis 12:1–3; this covenant is expressed in much greater detail in Genesis 15 and 17, and repeated in summary in several places, most especially in Genesis 22:15–18.
[3]Exodus 3:6, 15.

The Creator of this earth, and of the whole vast universe, selected a people for himself who were to be his treasured possession out of all the nations of the earth.[4] He began this election process with Abraham and Sarah. His purpose was not a selective one in the sense that he called this couple, and the nation that would come from them, to exclude the rest of the peoples on this earth. Just the opposite! God's purpose from his first call of Abraham and Sarah was that they might bring his blessing to all the peoples of the earth. He selected them in his sovereign love in order that vast numbers of others would be drawn to that love.

If you are a Christian, this is true for you also; God has called you to himself, indeed, because he loves you despite your sins and failures; but his longing is that through you, many others may also come to know him. At the heart of God's covenant there is always a relationship of love. This was true for Abraham and Sarah. This was true for Moses. This is true for you and me. God commits himself to be in personal fellowship with those whom he calls: "I will . . . be God to you and to your offspring after you."[5] And he calls us to be a fragrance of life to family, friends, neighbors, work colleagues, fellow students, our communities, even the ends of the earth, that many more may enjoy personal fellowship with him.

Every person who knows the Bible, even just barely, is familiar with the story of the deliverance of the people of Israel from Egypt, with the dramatic account of their crossing of the Red Sea, and with the recounting of their journey to Mount Sinai. There at Sinai God promises to reveal himself to *his people*, Israel.

What is essential for the reader of this history to understand is that the law is given to a people who have already been included in the covenant, a people whose very existence is a fulfillment of the promises given by the Lord to Abraham, Isaac, and Jacob.

WHO IS SPEAKING AT SINAI?

The law emphasizes that the God who is speaking at Sinai is the one who is the Creator of heaven and earth. This is brought out many times

---

4 Exodus 19:5.
5 Genesis 17:7.

in the texts surrounding the giving of the law. One simple example to illustrate this point is the commandment about observing the Sabbath:

> Remember the Sabbath day, to keep it holy. Six days you shall labor, and do all your work, but the seventh day is a Sabbath to the Lord your God. On it you shall not do any work, you, or your son, or your daughter, your male servant, or your female servant, or your livestock, or the sojourner who is within your gates. For in six days the Lord made heaven and earth, the sea, and all that is in them, and rested the seventh day. Therefore the Lord blessed the Sabbath day and made it holy.[6]

The text of the law in Exodus 20 is a foundational covenant document, a document that sets out the love of God for his people and the obligations required of those people whom God loves, and whom God has called to love and serve him in return. At the heart of this covenant document is the reminder that the covenant-giving God is the Creator of heaven and earth. This reminder underlines for us how important it is not to separate what we call the covenant of grace from the doctrine of creation.

Why is this so important that I need to draw attention to it here? In the law *the original calling* of our human race, our creational calling, is being revealed more fully. We should notice in this regard that part of the promise that God makes to his people Israel is a land flowing with milk and honey. These words are an intentional echo of the bounty of the garden of Eden before the fall of Adam and Eve. In Eden every tree was pleasant to the sight and good for food, for that place on earth, above all others at any point in history, was indeed a land "flowing with milk and honey."

There are many other echoes of Eden in the accounts of the books of Moses that describe the entry of Israel into the Promised Land. For example, when the Israelite spies enter Canaan to see what the land and its people are like, they return with huge bunches of grapes as a sign to their fellow Israelites of the wonderful fertility of the land the Lord plans to give them. Israel in Canaan following God's law is to be God's new beginning for the human race; they are to be the firstfruits of a new creation. This, of course, is the calling of every Christian today. In

---

[6] Exodus 20:8–11.

Christ we are a new creation, and as his new creation we are designed by the Lord to be the firstfruits of a new world: reminding people of what human life was intended to be in Eden before the fall; and looking forward to what human life shall be like when Christ comes, when the curse is removed, and when earth and heaven are renewed.[7]

What Has the Lawgiver Already Done for His People?

The law is given by the covenant-keeping, faithful God who has *already delivered and redeemed* his people. The first statement of the law is a lovely reminder of this gracious reality: "I am the LORD your God, who brought you out of the land of Egypt, out of the house of slavery."[8] This point needs expanding so that we will grasp its significance. The law is not given to a people who are ignorant of God; it is not given to a people outside the covenant. Nor is the law given in order that Israel might earn a relationship with God; it is not given that Israel might, by obedience, be drawn into covenant fellowship with him. The giving of the law comes not in Exodus 1, when the people of Israel are still in slavery in Egypt. The law is not given that they might obey the commandments and so merit their release from Egyptian bondage. Rather the law is given after the Lord has brought his people out of Egypt. "You yourselves have seen what I did to the Egyptians, and how I bore you on eagles' wings and brought you to myself."[9]

God has already demonstrated his gracious kindness to his people, his power to save them from their enemies, and his mighty works on their behalf. The exodus from Egypt demonstrates the grace of God and his conquering might in behalf of Israel. These people are in no doubt of the Lord's existence or of his amazing grace in saving them. They have already been blessed by him, and they have believed in him before they get to Sinai. After the defeat of Pharaoh and his army in the Red Sea, the text declares: "Thus the LORD saved Israel that day from the hand of the Egyptians, and Israel saw the Egyptians dead on the seashore. Israel saw the great power that the LORD used against

[7] 2 Corinthians 5:17–20; James 1:18.
[8] Exodus 20:2.
[9] Exodus 19:4.

the Egyptians, so the people feared the Lord, and they believed in the Lord."[10] Or listen to the song the Israelites sing as they rest on the shore of the Red Sea and as they realize the extraordinary deliverance that God has wrought for them:

> The Lord is my strength and my song,
>   and he has become my salvation;
> this is my God, and I will praise him,
>   my father's God, and I will exalt him,
> the Lord is a man of war;
>   the Lord is his name.[11]

In addition, before they even left Egypt, they experienced the powerful acts of God in judging Pharaoh and his subjects and sparing Israel repeatedly. These acts of judgment and deliverance culminated in the angel of death striking down the firstborn of every Egyptian household and passing over every house of the people of Israel. In commemoration of this mercy of God, these people receiving the law at Sinai have already been given the ceremony of the Passover. The Passover is theirs so that they can celebrate, year after year for all the generations to come, God's gracious passing over them, his not judging them along with the Egyptians. At the heart of any faithful celebration of the Passover is the recalling of the reason for God's gracious passing over Israel. This reason is that God has already taken this people to be his own treasured possession.

What Is the Motivation for Obeying the Law?

Along with seeing God's gracious acts of salvation as the setting for the giving of the law, we can also see the Lord's intention for the motivation of the hearts of those who receive the law. This issue of motivation for obedience is very significant. Does obedience arise out of attempts to earn God's love? Will Israel merit salvation by hearing and keeping God's commandments? Why should the Israelites keep the law? What is to be the intent of their hearts as they give themselves to obeying God's commandments?

---

[10] Exodus 14:30–31.
[11] Exodus 15:2–3.

This is often where Christians become confused about the law at Sinai, confused about the reasons for the giving of the law and about whether Israel in the Old Testament is a people living in an age of grace. But Moses has no such confusion, and he desires that Israel have no such confusion; and so he repeatedly reminds the people of the Lord's grace and favor to them as the fundamental motivation for the keeping of the law.

> Because he loved your fathers and chose their offspring after them and brought you out of Egypt with his own presence, by his great power, driving out before you nations greater and mightier than you, to bring you in, to give you their land for an inheritance, as it is this day, know therefore today, and lay it to your heart, that the Lord is God in heaven above and on the earth beneath; there is no other. Therefore you shall keep his statutes and his commandments, which I command you today.[12]

This recognition of God's original intention about the motivation for obeying his law will change how we read the New Testament, especially the way we read about the constant conflicts about the law between Jesus and the Pharisees, or between Paul and the Judaizers.

Understanding that the motivation for obedience ought to be gratitude for the grace of God, we will see the Pharisees and teachers of the law in Jesus's day as people who completely misunderstood the law. Without question, some of them saw it as a means of self-justification before God. Think of the Pharisee in Jesus's story:

> He also told this parable to some who trusted in themselves that they were righteous, and treated others with contempt: "Two men went up into the temple to pray, one a Pharisee and the other a tax collector. The Pharisee, standing by himself, prayed thus: 'God, I thank you that I am not like other men, extortioners, unjust, adulterers, or even like this tax collector. I fast twice a week; I give tithes of all that I get.' But the tax collector, standing far off, would not even lift his eyes to heaven, but beat his breast, saying, 'God, be merciful to me, a sinner!' I tell you, this man went down to his house justified, rather than the other."[13]

---

[12] Deuteronomy 4:37–40.
[13] Luke 18:9–14.

It is evident that this Pharisee, and many others like him, had the mistaken belief that righteous acts of keeping the law were the foundation of a relationship with God. Others appear to have believed that their obedience to the law was the means of keeping them in covenant fellowship with God. Clearly, both of these views—obedience initiating fellowship with God and obedience maintaining fellowship with God—are fundamental errors. God initiated fellowship with his people by his gracious acts of deliverance. God maintains fellowship with his people by his continued acts of gracious deliverance and by his ongoing mercy and faithfulness.

Another example of such mistaken views in Judaism at the time of Christ is the question of the young synagogue ruler who came to Jesus and asked, "What *must I do* to inherit eternal life?"[14] This youthful elder of the synagogue clearly believed that there was something he must do in order that he might obtain eternal fellowship with God. This is a profound misunderstanding of the law.

In the same way Paul's apparent critique of the law[15] must be seen as a critique of contemporary Judaism's misuse of the law, not as a critique of Moses and of God's giving of his law (see, for example, Paul's very affirmative words in Romans 7: the law is holy; the commandment is holy and just and good; the law is spiritual).

The purpose of obeying the law is not to achieve salvation, nor to inherit eternal life, but to express one's love and gratitude to the Lord because of the salvation he has already given to his people. This is true at Sinai and for the people of Israel throughout their history. This is true for the Christian church today. And this will be true for all eternity to come. We will walk in the ways of the Lord because we love him who first loved us.

WHAT IS THE CHARACTER OF THE LAWGIVER?

The Lord who gives the commandments is a holy, awesome, and transcendent God. Understanding that the law is a gift of the God who has already been gracious should not lead us to forget that God is to

---

[14] Luke 18:18.
[15] Three passages by Paul that are appealed to as containing a critique of the law are Romans 10:4; Galatians 5:18; and 1 Timothy 1:8–9.

be feared. Indeed, God reveals himself at Sinai in terrifying majesty and holiness. The people are warned to consecrate themselves for the Lord's coming down on Mount Sinai "in the sight of all the people."[16] When he comes, there is a storm theophany that is seen as foundational to our knowledge of God in the rest of Scripture.

> On the morning of the third day there were thunders and lightnings and a thick cloud on the mountain and a very loud trumpet blast, so that all the people in the camp trembled. . . . Mount Sinai was wrapped in smoke because the LORD had descended on it in fire. The smoke of it went up like the smoke from a kiln, and the whole mountain trembled greatly. . . . The sound of the trumpet grew louder and louder.[17]

As we saw in chapter 3, the writer of Hebrews refers back to this account, but not to drive a wedge between the law at Sinai and grace in Christ. Instead, the words given to us by Christ come with an even greater obligation to listen and to obey because he has come from heaven to speak, whereas the law was given on a mountain here on this earth.

> For you have not come to what may be touched, a blazing fire and darkness and gloom and a tempest and the sound of a trumpet and a voice whose words made the hearers beg that no further messages be spoken to them. . . . Indeed, so terrifying was the sight that Moses said, "I tremble with fear." But you have come to Mount Zion and to the city of the living God, the heavenly Jerusalem, and to innumerable angels in festal gathering, and to the assembly of the firstborn who are enrolled in heaven, and to God, the judge of all, and to the spirits of the righteous made perfect, and to Jesus, the mediator of a new covenant, and to the sprinkled blood that speaks a better word than the blood of Abel.
>
> See that you do not refuse him who is speaking. For if they did not escape when they refused him who warned them on earth, much less will we escape if we reject him who warns from heaven. . . . Therefore . . . let us offer to God acceptable worship, with reverence and awe, for our God is a consuming fire.[18]

---

[16] Exodus 19:11.
[17] Exodus 19:16–19; see also 20:18.
[18] Hebrews 12:18–29.

The God we worship is a consuming fire! This is who he was before he created the universe. This is who he was when he made our first parents. This is who he was when he called Abraham and Sarah. This is who he revealed himself to be at Mount Sinai when he gave the law. This is who he revealed himself to be in the person of Jesus Christ, his incarnate Son. And this is who he will be for all eternity to come. Therefore, at every moment in history, his creatures are to worship him with reverence and awe.

The writer of Hebrews finishes his exposition of the wonderful revelation of the grace that comes to us through Jesus's blood with his call to offer acceptable worship that honors the burning brightness of God's purity. Grace and reverent awe because of God's holiness are not set in opposition to each other. Seeing God's fearful majesty, we realize that there must be a corresponding sense of obligation to submit to his commandments. This sense of obligation to obey the Lord is not contradictory to love and gratitude as our fundamental motivation for obeying him.

We should feel obligated to obey God's law because he is holy. Yet our deepest reason for obedience is love for him from hearts that are filled with thankfulness because he has redeemed us. The same thing is true in our marriages and family life. Fear of God and a very strong sense of obligation to be faithful to my wife and children do not contradict love as foundational to my relationship with them.

GIVEN GOD'S HOLY CHARACTER, WHAT KIND OF UNIVERSE IS THIS?

The commandments reveal the character of God as the holy, pure, and righteous one. Therefore, the commandments demonstrate to us the ultimate reality of a moral universe. God's law describes to us who God is—what his very nature is. That is, behind the law of God stands God himself. He is presented as the Holy One, the one who is perfect in righteousness. In his presence the cherubim and seraphim cry continually,

Holy, holy, holy is the LORD of Hosts,
the whole earth is full of his glory![19]

---

[19] Isaiah 6:3.

Moral perfection is God's nature.

Moses affirms, as does the whole of Scripture, that the law is the expression of God's righteous, just, kind, and loving nature. Why do I stress this point? The law is not arbitrary; rather the decrees of the law are righteous and wise, simply because the righteous and wise God has issued them.

> See, I have taught you statutes and rules, as the LORD my God commanded me, that you should do them in the land that you are entering to take possession of it. Keep them and do them, for that will be your wisdom and understanding in the sight of the peoples, who, when they hear all these statutes, will say, "Surely this great nation is a wise and understanding people." For what great nation is there that has a god so near to it as the LORD our God is to us, whenever we call upon him? And what great nation is there, that has statutes and rules so righteous as all this law that I set before you today?[20]

One of the loveliest summaries of God's law appears in Leviticus 19, which begins, "And the LORD spoke to Moses saying, 'Speak to all the congregation of the people of Israel and say to them, You shall be holy, for I the LORD your God am holy.'"[21] Then as we read through the commandments given in this particular list, we find that each one is followed by the words "I am the LORD." This refrain after each commandment teaches us that God's character lies behind every command or decree he makes. This is why the law is beautiful: simply because it reveals the character of God.

WHY ARE THERE LAWS ABOUT SACRIFICES AND CEREMONIES?

Even a rapid reading of the laws within the books of Moses reveals many commandments about sacrifices and other ceremonies. Why is this? Including so many of the requirements of the sacrificial system within the law shows that God is making very careful provision for the constant reality of sin and failure in the lives of all believers. God's covering for sin is, of course, in place long before Sinai. It goes right

---

[20] Deuteronomy 4:5–8.
[21] Leviticus 19:1–2.

back to the early chapters of Genesis. We see God providing sacrifice immediately after the fall into disobedience in the garden of Eden. Abel offers sacrifices to the Lord. Noah's first act on leaving the ark after the flood is to offer sacrifices. We see this repeated in the life of Abraham and the other patriarchs. God gives the Passover with its sacrifice of a lamb before giving the law at Sinai. In the record of the institution of the Passover we see the explicit detail that the purpose of the sacrifice of the lamb is to cover the sins of the people. There are also sacrifices for sin offered at the ceremony of the ratification of the covenant and of the receiving of the law:

> Moses wrote down all the words of the LORD. He rose early in the morning and built an altar at the foot of the mountain, and twelve pillars, according to the twelve tribes of Israel. And he sent young men of the people of Israel, who offered burnt offerings and sacrifices of peace offerings of oxen to the LORD. And Moses took half of the blood and put it in basins, and half of the blood he threw against the altar. Then he took the Book of the Covenant and read it in the hearing of the people. And they said, "All that the LORD has spoken we will do, and we will be obedient." And Moses took the blood and threw it on the people and said, "Behold the blood of the covenant that the LORD has made with you in accordance with all these words."[22]

In addition, of course, the law itself has many sacrifices to deal with sin as one of its central elements. Why are there so many sacrifices? The law instructs its hearers in the righteousness of God, and it therefore necessarily brings conviction of sin. In convicting of sin the law leads God's people to confess their sins and to plead for his forgiveness. Because people need forgiveness, the law provides many sacrifices to deal with this constant revealing of sin and the need for mercy.

The law, in this way, necessarily leads God's people to his grace, mercy, and forgiveness. This grace, mercy, and forgiveness will ultimately be revealed in Christ. He is the reality of whom the sacrifices and the ceremonies are the shadow and promise.[23] The sacrifices and the ceremonies that provide atonement for sin (by prefiguring Christ)

---

[22] Exodus 24:4–8.
[23] Colossians 2:16–17.

precede the giving of the law, they are a fundamental part of the law, and they follow the law.

Given this reality, it is absurd to imagine that God intended anyone to think of the law as a means of earning merit before him, or as a system teaching salvation by works. We should also notice that many of the ceremonies and sacrifices that are part of the law are to take place in the tabernacle. The tabernacle is not only a place for the people to come to worship the Lord, but also a place of worship because the tabernacle is the very sign of God's commitment to dwell in intimate fellowship with his people. The tabernacle is patterned after the true tabernacle in heaven, and it represents on earth God's delight in coming close to his people and walking among them. It is after sacrifices for sin are made that the people may enjoy sweet fellowship with the Lord at his table in the tabernacle. As we noted at the beginning of this chapter, fellowship with God is the heart of all biblical teaching—from the garden of Eden, where God walked with Adam and Eve, to the consummation in Revelation, where God and his people will dwell together forever.

> I will establish my covenant between me and you and your offspring after you throughout their generations for an everlasting covenant, to be God to you and to your offspring after you. . . . I will be their God.[24]

> I will make my dwelling among you, and my soul shall not abhor you. And I will walk among you and will be your God, and you shall be my people. I am the LORD your God, who brought you out of the land of Egypt, that you should not be their slaves. And I have broken the bars of your yoke and made you walk erect.[25]

> And I heard a loud voice from the throne saying, "Behold, the dwelling place of God is with man. He will dwell with them, and they will be his people, and God himself will be with them as their God."[26]

The grace of God's perfect forgiveness through Jesus and the loving fellowship that he brings to us—this is the very heart of the whole biblical revelation, and it is at the heart of the law of God.

[24] Genesis 17:7–8.
[25] Leviticus 26:11–13.
[26] Revelation 21:3.

Questions for Personal Reflection and Group Discussion

1. What do you understand the term *covenant* to mean? What are the essential features of the covenant God made with Abraham and Sarah?

2. What difference does it make to think of the giving of the law at Sinai as a continuation and reaffirmation of the covenant God made with Abraham, Isaac, and Jacob?

3. Is it a new idea to you that God's calling Israel and giving his people a rich and productive land are a renewal of creation? Why do you think this is significant?

4. What difference does this idea of the renewal of creation make in the way we should think about the giving of the law and about its nature and purpose?

5. Do you think there is a problem with seeing obedience to the law as both obligation in the fear of God and a glad expression of love for him?

6. Why is it so important to take note that the law is given in the context of grace and of God's deliverance of his people, rather than as a means of enabling them to become the people of God?

7. Have you ever had the opportunity to join in a Christian celebration of the Passover? How would you express the primary ways in which the Lord's Supper is the fulfillment of the Passover ceremony? As you reflect on this fundamental continuity between the Passover and the Lord's Supper, think about the significance of this continuity in relation to the purposes and context of the giving of the law.

8. Had you noticed before reading this chapter how sacrifices for sin were so carefully included in the law?

9. How would you respond to the following perspective? "The most obvious and striking division of the Word of truth is that between law and grace. . . . Scripture never, in any dispensation, mingles these two principles. Law always has a place and work distinct and wholly diverse from that of grace. . . . Everywhere the Scriptures present law and grace in sharply contrasted spheres."[27]

---

[27] Cyrus I. Scofield, *Rightly Dividing the Word of Truth* (New York: n.p., n.d.), 34, 36.

6

LAW AND THE
IMAGE OF GOD (1)

In chapter 5 we began to think about the giving of the law at Sinai. First, we saw that the context of the giving of the law is the covenant that God already initiated centuries before in the marvelous promises he made to Abraham and Sarah. The law is given to a people who are already included in the covenant, a people whose very existence is a fulfillment of the promises made to Abraham, Isaac, and Jacob, and their descendants after them.

Second, we saw how the law emphasizes that the God who is speaking at Sinai is the one who made heaven and earth, the Creator of all things. So in the law the original calling of our human race, our creational calling, is being revealed more fully.

Third, we saw how the very first statement of the Ten Commandments is that the law is given by this covenant keeping, faithful God who has already delivered and redeemed his people. The law, in other words, is given in the context of grace—not to earn God's favor.

Fourth, we saw that, because the law is given to an already redeemed people, the fundamental motivation for obeying the law is love for God and gratitude for his mercy and grace. The purpose of obeying the law is not to achieve salvation, nor to inherit eternal life, but to offer one's life as a sacrifice of praise.

Fifth, we were reminded that the Lord who gives the commandments is a holy, awesome, and transcendent God who calls his people to worship him with reverence and awe. The fear of God and a strong sense of obligation to obey his commandments do not contradict love as foundational to our relationship with him.

Sixth, we learned that God's character lies behind every commandment or decree he makes. The law, therefore, is beautiful, simply because it reveals the character of God.

Seventh, we observed that in the sacrificial system the law itself makes very careful provision for the constant reality of sin and failure in the lives of all believers. The sacrifices and the ceremonies that provide atonement for sin (by prefiguring Christ) precede the giving of the law, they are a fundamental part of the law, and they follow the law.

In this chapter we turn to another central matter in understanding God's purposes in giving his law to his people. We need to understand that the law is the definition for our human lives. As persons made in the image of God, we were designed to walk in his ways, for this is precisely the life he created us for: to be like him. Being the image of God is the most basic description of what it is to be human. We will go back to Genesis 1:26–28 to look at the account of our creation as we begin our reflections on this issue.

THE IMAGE OF GOD IN GENESIS 1

If we read Genesis 1 purely as a literary document, we see that the high point is verse 27, the account of our creation in God's image. Even as we look at our English Bibles we will see that in most translations verse 27 is set apart from the rest of the text as a brief poem. The purpose of this literary structure in Genesis 1 is to highlight that we are unique in this creation. We are set off from all other creatures, for we are the only beings here on this earth who have been made to bear God's likeness.

The appearance of humans by God's creative act is the crowning moment of the whole story of creation. We might say that the earlier part of the chapter is a preparation for this moment in the account of the origins of everything in our world:

> Then God said, "Let us make man in our image, after our likeness. And let them have dominion over the fish of the sea and over the birds of the heavens and over the livestock and over all the earth and over every creeping thing that creeps on the earth."

So God created man in his own image,
>   in the image of God he created him;
>   male and female he created them.[1]

The text itself also draws attention to our similarity to the rest of God's creatures as well as our uniqueness. We too are living creatures like the birds and sea creatures, the livestock and creeping things.[2] The text presents us as a part of this creation, made from it and cohering with it in all kinds of ways; and yet, we are distinct from all other created things for we are the image of God. Francis Schaeffer used to represent the dual reality of our nature as shown in figure 1.

Figure 1. Humans as finite creation yet personal like God

Infinite	and	Personal God
Finite	and	Personal Humans
Animals	—	Animals
Plants	—	Plants
Physical Structures	—	Physical Structures

In our finiteness we are like every other created thing, rather than like God, for he alone is infinite and eternal in his being, majesty, power, holiness, justice, goodness, and truth. Thus a line in the left-hand column sets God apart from us and other created things. In our being personal, shown in the right-hand column, we are distinct from every other created thing, but like the personal triune God.

What does it mean for us to be God's image? Simply by existing we are God's image. We are made as finite and visible, physical copies of the infinite and invisible God. "Image" and "likeness" are two parallel terms with the same basic meaning. In the ancient world a king or emperor would set up statues of himself in a city. Each statue, an image or likeness of the king, was there to remind the people that he was their ruler. In this way we, as God's image bearers, are visible, physical reminders of the one true King of this world.

[1] Genesis 1:26–27.
[2] See Genesis 1:20, 24; 2:7.

Though the Scriptures do not anywhere give us a simple definition of what it means for us to be God's image, the biblical text draws attention to the following points.

Relationship

We are made for personal relationships as male and female, for our text describes the image this way in Genesis 1:27: "God created man in his own image, in the image of God he created him, male and female he created them." Just as God exists as the three persons of the Trinity—loving, relating, and communicating with each other through all eternity—so we, as those made in his image, are made for love, for relationship, for communication in language (and communication in many other personal ways) with our Creator and with one another. Fundamental to our humanity is that we are made to dwell in families and in community. As the apostle Paul will later write, "I bow my knees to the Father, from whom every family in heaven and on earth is named" (or, "from whom all fatherhood in heaven and earth derives its name").[3]

Dominion

In addition to relationship, it is also clear in the Genesis text that dominion is fundamental to our understanding of the image of God. Notice again the text in 1:26: "Then God said, 'Let us make man in our image, after our likeness. And let them have dominion over the fish of the sea and over the birds of the heavens and over the livestock and over all the earth.'" This purpose of our creation is repeated two verses later, for after God creates male and female in his image, the text says: "And God blessed them. And God said to them, 'Be fruitful and multiply and fill the earth and subdue it, and have dominion over the fish of the sea and over the birds of the heavens and over every living thing that moves on the earth.'"[4]

In these words, God stresses both our fruitfulness in marriage and family and our dominion over this earth and its creatures. Dominion is often referred to as "the cultural mandate." We are made to rule over

---

[3] Ephesians 3:14–15.
[4] Genesis 1:28.

the rest of this creation. We are God's vice-regents. He is the sovereign and infinite ruler over all things, but he has made us to have dominion here on this earth as his stewards.

> The heavens are the LORD's heavens,
>   but the earth he has given to the children of man.[5]

We might express this by saying that the Lord God is the infinite sovereign over all reality and over all history, and that we humans are given a finite sovereignty over this world and over our history, a finite sovereignty under God's infinite sovereignty. To put it another way, as my colleague Michael Williams says: "God is big enough to create significant creatures"; and we may add, God is big enough not to be threatened in his sovereignty by our finite significance as those made to be like him. It does not honor God to deny the significance of humans or to turn us into robots or ciphers.

We may add to these brief reflections on dominion by noting that Genesis 2 draws our attention to the naming of the animals. In the Old Testament text and in its cultural setting, naming implies both understanding the nature of something and having authority over the person or thing that is named. On many occasions in the biblical text we find God naming people. This is an expression of his deep under-standing of who the person will become as he or she serves the Lord in this world.[6] This naming is also an expression of God's authority; the person named is a servant of the Lord, to whom he or she belongs. So dominion speaks of our human understanding of the world in which God has set us, and of our ruling over this world and its creatures. In fact, Francis Bacon taught that it is dominion that led the human race to develop all the arts and sciences.

Other Aspects of God's Image

However, we cannot restrict the meaning of the image of God to these two basic matters of relationship and dominion. God's people have always recognized that there are many consequences of being God's

---

[5] Psalm 115:16.
[6] Think, for example, of Simon who is renamed Peter by the Lord because Peter is going to become a rock, a steadfast and reliable man.

image, many other aspects of our being like God to which the Scriptures draw attention. As believers have read and studied God's Word over the centuries, they have looked for scriptural statements about the nature of God that the Word applies to us, his creatures. This is appropriate, for, in truth, we have been made to be like God and to live like God. So, wherever Scripture draws attention to the similarities between God and us, we may conclude that we are discovering aspects of God's image. Some of the conclusions below are clearly rooted in the statements of Genesis 1 about relationship and dominion; others express additional elements of what it means for us to be like God:

- God is love, and we are made to love him and to love one another.
- God is holy, and we are made to reflect his holiness in all we do.
- God is the Creator and Lord of all things, and we are made as sub-creators to work with this reality that he has made, and to exercise dominion over it to his glory.
- God is the sovereign Lord, and he has given us a finite but significant sovereignty over our lives.
- God is intelligent and rational, thinking only what is right, consistent, and true; and we humans are created to think God's thoughts after him. We are made to be rational, to use our minds to the glory of our Creator. We are to seek to understand our world and our life here in it; and we are to turn our thoughts to reflect on and to treasure all that is right and true.
- God is the Word, the source of all communication and language, and we are all like the Word himself; or we might say that we are "little words"; we are made to communicate with him and with one another, using the marvelous gift of language that he has bestowed on us as persons created to speak as he speaks. There are several significant aspects to God's use of language, and ours:

  - God called all worlds into being by his creative word, and we are to use language in imitation of him by exercising the gifts of creative imagination.
  - God sustains and rules over all things by his powerful and law-giving word, and we are to use the gift of language in understanding and naming the world around us.
  - God reveals himself by his truth-giving word, and we are to reveal ourselves truthfully in all our verbal communication.

- God communicates by his life-giving word, and we are to imitate him by communicating both with our Creator and with one another to build trust and to give life to all of our relationships.

However, there is a very obvious problem as we reflect upon this brief list of ways in which we are God's image bearers. I ask myself: "Am I truly a person who loves like God; who is holy like God; who creates and exercises dominion like God; who is sovereign over my life like God; who thinks with integrity, consistency, and faithfulness like God; who communicates truth like God?" It is very evident, when I ask myself such questions, that I am horribly unlike God! Clearly we are all sinners who have fallen away from this calling to be like God. So how does Scripture speak of the damage to the image caused by sin?

The Image of God, Fallen

The apostle Paul describes our failure to be like God this way: "All have sinned and fall short of the glory of God."[7] This is the human problem: we are no longer conformed to the image and glory of God our Creator. We fail terribly to give a true likeness of God now because of our sin. In effect, we are telling lies about God repeatedly wherever we do not give a true reflection of his character and nature. We should note here that Paul's term "glory" in Romans 3 is very similar to and can be interchanged with "image," which Scripture uses to speak about who we are as human beings. We fail to reflect the image of God. We fall short of the glory of God.

The question then arises, Are we still God's image bearers despite the reality of sin and our failure to measure up to the glory of God? Our answer to this question has to be yes! There must be this affirmative answer, for we find later Scriptures referring back to the creation account when they speak about human life. This is because the creation texts are foundational to our ongoing understanding of our existence and our place in the universe.

In addition to the foundational statement of Genesis 1:26–28, the text in Genesis 9:6 reaffirms that human beings bear God's image well after the fall into rebellion and disobedience. A particularly beautiful

---

[7] Romans 3:23.

reaffirmation of the ongoing dignity of our human nature is Psalm 8 with its teaching that the glory of God transcends the majesty of the heavens, but rests on us as human beings. Particularly fascinating is that this psalm comes within a series of psalms reflecting on the problem of human wickedness. Then we find Psalm 8 with its question for God:

> When I look at your heavens, the work of your fingers,
>   the moon and the stars, which you have set in place,
> what is man that you are mindful of him,
>   and the son of man that you care for him?[8]

God's answer to this question is not to focus on the dreary record of our sins recorded and lamented in the surrounding psalms, but to remind us of our original and continuing glory.[9]

> You have made him a little lower than the heavenly beings
>   and crowned him with glory and honor.
> You have given him dominion over the works of your hands;
>   you have put all things under his feet.[10]

In another passage which affirms that we continue to be God's image, the apostle James is writing about the tongue and says: "With it we bless our Lord and Father, and with it we curse people who are made in the likeness of God. From the same mouth come blessing and cursing. My brothers, these things ought not to be so."[11] So despite the terrible reality of the fall, Scripture insists that human beings are still the image and glory of God. Calvin in one place calls us ruined statues in which we can still glimpse the remnants of our former glory. He affirms that, despite the terrible decline, the "misshapen ruins"[12] that

---

[8] Psalm 8:3–4.
[9] Remember the psalms are a book, just like any other book of Scripture. In fact there are five books of psalms, reflecting the five books of the law written by Moses. This reminds us that the psalms are also law, just like the books of the law. God's people could refer to the Old Testament Scriptures under the threefold division of Law, Prophets, and Writings, or under the twofold division of Law and Prophets, or simply as the Law. That is why we find Jesus quoting a psalm as law. See, for example, John 10:34, where Jesus refers to Psalm 82 as law. Or see Jesus's summary of the whole Old Testament as the Law and the Prophets in Matthew 22:34–40.
[10] Psalm 8:5–6.
[11] James 3:9–10.
[12] John Calvin, *Institutes of the Christian Religion*, ed. John T. McNeill, trans. Ford Lewis Battles (Philadelphia: Westminster, 1960), 2.2.12.

the fall has brought upon our race, the image of God is not completely obliterated, for there are "remaining traces of the image of God."[13] Francis Schaeffer would say simply that we are "glorious ruins." J. R. R. Tolkien used the expression "rags of lordship." He wrote to his friend C. S. Lewis:

> . . . Though now long estranged,
> man is not wholly lost or wholly changed.
> Dis-graced he may be, yet is not dethroned,
> and keeps the rags of lordship once he owned.[14]

In *Prince Caspian*, one of Lewis's *Chronicles of Narnia*, we find a wonderful expression of this human glory and tragedy. Caspian says:

> "I was wishing that I came of a more honourable lineage."
> "You come of the Lord Adam and the Lady Eve," said Aslan. "And that is both honour enough to erect the head of the poorest beggar, and shame enough to bow the shoulders of the greatest emperor on earth. Be content."[15]

William Shakespeare also captured this noble reality, our God-likeness, and the shame of our rebellion and sin, in some of the most powerful words ever written about what it means to be human:

> What a piece of work is a man, how noble in reason, how infinite in faculties, in form and moving how express and admirable, in action how like an angel, in apprehension how like a god! the beauty of the world, the paragon of animals—and yet, to me, what is this quintessence of dust?[16]

Later in the play, Hamlet addresses the problem of his own sinfulness, and the sinfulness of all other people in this world, and he does so with a painfully honest account of his own heart:

---

[13] Ibid., 2.2.17.
[14] J. R. R. Tolkien, *Mythopoeia*. This is the poem that Tolkien wrote for Lewis shortly after the long conversation that occurred between the two of them and another friend, Hugo Dyson, late one night in September 1931. It was just a few days after this conversation that Lewis came to faith in Christ. See my book *Echoes of Eden* (Wheaton, IL: Crossway, 2013), for an account of this discussion and how God used it in Lewis's life.
[15] C. S. Lewis, *Prince Caspian* (New York: Macmillan, 1951), 211–12.
[16] William Shakespeare, *Hamlet*, act 2, scene 2.

Why wouldst thou be a breeder of sinners? I am myself indifferent honest, but yet I could accuse me of such things that it were better my mother had not borne me: I am very proud, revengeful, ambitious, with more offenses at my beck than I have thoughts to put them in, imagination to give them shape, or time to act them in. What should such fellows as I do crawling between earth and heaven? We are arrant knaves all; believe none of us.[17]

RESTORATION TO THE IMAGE OF GOD

If we turn from a biblical exposition of our sinful condition to understand the nature of our salvation through Christ, we discover that the key to understanding sanctification and the Christian life is restoration to the image, or glory, of God. Three particular texts set out this calling for us and will inform our reflection:

But that is not the way you learned Christ!—assuming that you have heard about him and were taught in him, as the truth is in Jesus, to put off your old self, which belongs to your former manner of life and is corrupt through deceitful desires, and to be renewed in the spirit of your minds, and to put on the new self, created after the likeness of God in true righteousness and holiness.[18]

Do not lie to one another, seeing that you have put off the old self with its practices and have put on the new self which is being renewed in knowledge after the image of its creator. Here there is not Greek and Jew, circumcised or uncircumcised, barbarian, Scythian, slave, free; but Christ is all, and in all.[19]

We all, with unveiled face, beholding the glory of the Lord, are being transformed into the same image from one degree of glory to another. For this comes from the Lord who is the Spirit.[20]

Each of these three texts leads us to meditate on Christ as the one who has given us life, Christ as the one who indwells us and enables us by his Spirit, and Christ as the one who is our model because his life perfectly reflected the image of God. Christ is the example to us

---

[17] Ibid., act 3, scene 1.
[18] Ephesians 4:20–24.
[19] Colossians 3:9–11.
[20] 2 Corinthians 3:18.

of a human who thought, spoke, and acted as humans were created to think, speak, and act. Christ demonstrated who we should be and what we are to become. He shows us the nature of true humanity.

Christ shows us a truly human life, a life after the image of God; and Jesus does this by living in full obedience to God's law. This is our calling too: to submit to God's law gladly because the law is good for us. The law is not a hindrance or barrier for our lives; rather, God's law defines how human life was intended to be lived. As we saw in our last chapter, what we might call the holiness code in Leviticus 19 teaches us that we are created to live in imitation of God: "And the LORD spoke to Moses, saying, 'Speak to all the congregation of the people of Israel and say to them, You shall be holy, for I the LORD your God am holy.'"[21] After each of the commandments that follow this initial statement in Leviticus 19 there is the added affirmation, "I am the LORD." God is saying in essence, "This is my character—to be just, to be merciful, to be kind, to be faithful, to be generous. You are to be like me." We are to be faithful in relationships, kind to the needy, just in the application of law, merciful to the broken, because this is who God is.

If we think back to our first chapter, we should recall that Psalm 25:4–14 teaches us to walk in God's ways, in the way of the covenant-giving and covenant-keeping God. The Lord is "good and upright . . . , therefore he instructs sinners in the way."[22] The law expresses the way in which God walks, and we need instruction in that way so that we might truly reflect God's likeness and be the kind of people God originally designed us to be.

Because the law is a definition of true humanness, the biblical texts remind us that God's law is good and is for our own good.

> And now, Israel, what does the LORD your God require of you, but to fear the LORD your God, to walk in his ways, to love him, to serve the LORD your God with all your heart and with all your soul, and to keep the commandments and statutes of the LORD, which I am commanding you today for your good?[23]

---

[21] Leviticus 19:1–2.

[22] Psalm 25:8.

[23] Deuteronomy 10:12–13. See also Deuteronomy 4:1–8, where God stresses to the people that the laws he gives them will cause all the nations around them to recognize what a wise and understanding people they are because of the righteousness and obvious goodness of the commandments.

Walking in the ways of the law will bring blessing, life, and freedom to us, for we will be living as God created us to live. We will be more and more restored to the image of God in genuine righteousness and holiness.

Questions for Personal Reflection and Group Discussion

1. Did you find the diagram from Francis Schaeffer helpful as it sets out the difference and likeness between humans and the rest of creation?

2. What do you think is the most significant aspect of what it means for us to be God's image bearers?

3. Psalm 8 teaches that each person displays God's glory far more fully than the most beautiful night sky or fall day that you have ever seen. Does this thought excite you, or do you find this a challenging and problematic idea?

4. We all fall short of the glory of God. What areas of your life trouble you most as you consider that you do not faithfully show forth the image of God in your daily life?

5. Christ, we are taught, is the perfect representation of the image of God. As you think about his life, what characteristics do you most admire? Or to put the question another way, in what parts of your life are you most eager to become like Christ and so reflect faithfully the image of God?

6. Was it a new idea to you that the law expresses our original human calling, that God's commandments show us how to reflect God's image? What do you think is particularly significant about this; and in what ways do you think this is very different from the way much of our surrounding culture thinks about how we should live?

7

Law and the Image of God (2)

In the previous chapter we continued our study of the giving of the law at Sinai, and we focused on the way the law expresses what it means for us to live as God's image bearers. We begin this chapter by returning to the final section of chapter 6 in order to expand those reflections.

We saw that our calling is to submit to God's law gladly because the law defines for us what it means to be God's image and to live in imitation of our Creator. This means that we should never regard the law as a hindrance to our happiness and fulfillment; nor should we think of the law as a barrier in the way of the good life. Rather, God's law defines for all of us how human life was intended to be lived. We saw also how the holiness code of Leviticus 19 teaches us that we are created to live in imitation of God: "You shall be holy, for I the Lord your God am holy."[1] And each subsequent commandment in Leviticus 19 is followed by the emphatic statement "I am the Lord." It's as if God is saying, "This is my character: I am just; I am merciful; I am kind; I am faithful; I am generous. You are to be like me."

So we are to be faithful in relationships, gracious to our enemies, kind to the needy, just in the application of law, merciful to the broken, generous to those who work for us—because this is who God is. We are never to curse the deaf, never to put stumbling blocks in the way of the blind, nor to defer to the powerful, to slander, or to bear grudges—because the Lord never behaves in such ways.

---

[1] Leviticus 19:1–2.

In our previous chapter we were also reminded of how Psalm 25 teaches that we are to walk in the way of the covenant-giving and covenant-keeping God. He is "good and upright, therefore he instructs sinners in the way."[2] Because we are so easily led astray from moral wisdom—by our own sinful natures, by the culture in which we live, and by the Devil, who seeks to distract us from God's calling and bring about our ruin—the Lord has been kind enough to set out for us in his commandments the way of life he designed for us from creation. Turning again to Psalm 25, where we began this book, we should be able to see how much sense this psalm makes in light of the way the law depicts our conformity to the image and likeness of God.

> Make me to know your ways, O LORD;
>> teach me your paths.
> Lead me in your truth and teach me,
>> for you are the God of my salvation;
>> for you I wait all the day long.
>
> Remember your mercy, O LORD, and your steadfast love,
>> for they have been from of old.
> Remember not the sins of my youth or my transgressions;
>> according to your steadfast love remember me,
>> for the sake of your goodness, O LORD!
>
> Good and upright is the LORD;
>> therefore he instructs sinners in the way.
> He leads the humble in what is right,
>> and teaches the humble his way.
> All the paths of the LORD are steadfast love and faithfulness,
>> for those who keep his covenant and his testimonies.
>
> For your name's sake, O LORD,
>> pardon my guilt, for it is great.[3]

David clearly does not think of the law as a means of justification for those who are confident that they are serving God and meriting his favor. Instead, David sees the law as instruction in the ways of the Lord

---

[2] Psalm 25:8.
[3] Psalm 25:4–11.

for the humble sinner. His desire to have the Lord teach him about the Lord's character and way of living so that he might imitate that way of life comes within a context of confession of sin and an acute understanding of his need for forgiveness.

We need to put away from our thoughts any notion that the law was given as a means to earn fellowship with God. This was never the purpose of the law. The law was given to those aware of their constant need for mercy and pardon. It was given to those who lived in the Lord's grace and steadfast love and who were dependent on his faithfulness to his promises. In such a setting the appropriate response to the Lord is the words of this psalm:

> Make known to me your ways, O Lord;
>   teach me your paths.

The law expresses the way in which God walks, and we need instruction in that way so that we might truly reflect God's likeness and be the kind of people God originally designed us to be. Because law is a definition of true humanness, there are many biblical texts that remind us that God's law is good and is intended for our good, for the good life. Walking in the ways of the law will bring blessing, life, and freedom to us, for we will be living as God created us to live. We will be more and more restored to the image of God. Think of how Psalm 1 expresses this:

> Blessed is the man
>   who walks not in the counsel of the wicked,
> nor stands in the way of sinners,
>   nor sits in the seat of scoffers;
> but his delight is in the law of the Lord,
>   and on his law he meditates day and night.
>
> He is like a tree
>   planted by streams of water
> that yields its fruit in its season,
>   and its leaf does not wither.
> In all that he does he prospers.
> The wicked are not so,
>   but are like chaff that the wind drives away.[4]

---

[4] Psalm 1:1–4.

Human flourishing in all of life is the consequence of meditating on God's laws and living by them. This is the teaching of the New Testament just as much as the Old. The apostle James makes exactly the same point in the first chapter of his epistle. "But the one who looks into the perfect law, the law of liberty, and perseveres, being no hearer who forgets but a doer who acts, he will be blessed in his doing."[5]

THE LAW, THE TRUE SELF, AND SELFLESSNESS

As I have stated earlier, such a view of the good life is dramatically different from the way contemporary Western cultures teach us to think. We are told that blessing will come as we follow our own inner longings and as we think about our personal needs and desires. "Be true to yourself." "You need to think about what will make you happy." "The important question is, how will this make you feel?" "Will this bring the fulfillment of your desires and your longings?"

These are the constant cries of most of our television, movies, music, and literature. These are the directions that many parents give to their children, including many Christian parents. Such voices in our moment of history are widespread and constant. They call out a siren cry that is very appealing. It is appealing because the heart of original sin pursues its own way rather than the Lord's way, putting self at the center of reality rather than acknowledging our Creator's central place. In addition, because we are born in sin and have a sinful nature from the womb, we all have many desires and longings that are so powerful that they seem to define who we are, though they are vastly different from the desires, longings, and fulfillment for which the Lord has designed us.

One of the most challenging aspects of our cultural setting confronts us right at this point. We are urged on every side, even in many of our churches, to consider our inner feelings the expressions of the true self: such wishes define our nature, the essence of who we are, and therefore we ought to follow these inner voices. What this view forgets is that we are all fallen creatures and, consequently, many of these inner voices are not worthy of God, not worthy of humanity, and not worthy of ourselves. If we listen to them, we will bring sorrow

---

[5] James 1:25.

upon sorrow into our lives and the lives of our spouses, our children, our wider families, our colleagues, our friends, and our fellow citizens.

In addition, our cultures insist that we have a right to personal happiness. Indeed, a fundamental part of our American understanding of freedom is that we have the right to follow that inner call. Resisting that self-centered call is the most challenging part of living in our world. This is the primary reason why poll after poll tells us that while anywhere from 30 percent to 45 percent of Americans claim to be born again, only 8 to 10 percent say that their faith directs their lives and that they seek to live in obedience to the Lord.

The law teaches me something very different from this devotion to fulfilling my own desires and passions. At the heart of the law is our calling to show grace, love, and mercy to others as God has shown them to us, his people. This is brought out in many of the laws, including the ceremonial laws.

For example, the Sabbath is to be an occasion for mercy because God was merciful to Israel. The festivals that mark Israel's year are to include the alien, the widow, the orphan, and the poor because God was merciful to Israel when they were aliens and poor. Israel is to include such people in the celebration of the festivals because God included Israel by delivering his people into intimate fellowship with himself.

The laws about debts, sabbatical years, Jubilee years—all these laws are about graciousness and generosity and not holding people's failures against them. Instead, these laws are about giving people a new beginning, just as God constantly does for his people.

There are many laws about rulers imitating God by being advocates for the poor, the needy, the widow, the orphan, and the alien. Indeed, the Scriptures declare that this is one of the primary responsibilities of all authorities at any level in a nation.[6]

There are laws about agriculture and business that demand mercy and generosity to those in need. These laws mirror the goodness and

---

[6] See, for example, Proverbs 31:8–9. This passage sets out the obligations of a king, for those in authority have a particular responsibility to imitate the graciousness of God and his intervention on behalf of those who have no voice of their own. See also Psalm 82:1–4, where rulers are called "gods" because of their obligation to be like God; and where they are rebuked for their failure to stand up for the weak and poor against the powerful.

kindness of God to Israel. There is what Gordon Wenham calls a gap between law and ethics; or to put it another way, God's design is that we always ask, what is the law about, what is its ethical intent? The Old Testament itself constantly reminds God's people to do this, insisting that the law is about justice, mercy, and faithfulness, or about doing justice, loving mercy, and walking humbly with God, or about loving God and loving our neighbors. It is not simply about obeying the letter of a particular law. Rather, we are to go deeper in every aspect of obedience to the law and ask the fundamental question, in what way is this law calling us to be like God?

For example, the law of Moses required that widows, orphans, the poor, and the aliens be allowed to gather what they could find after the harvesters had gone through the fields, and after they had made their first cutting and gathering of the grain. Farmers were forbidden to reap their fields a second time to harvest what the first cutting missed, and the harvesters were forbidden to harvest the corners of their fields. Also, they were to make sure that the poor had plenty to eat at the time of harvest. There was no way to obey this demand without including the needy in one's family celebration of the festivals. These laws are beautiful in their requirement of generosity to those in need, and it will aid our understanding to quote several of them in full:

> When you reap the harvest of your land, you shall not reap your field right up to its edge, neither shall you gather the gleanings after your harvest. And you shall not strip your vineyard bare, neither shall you gather the fallen grapes of your vineyard. You shall leave them for the poor and for the sojourner: I am the LORD.[7]

> When you reap your harvest in your field and forget a sheaf in the field, you shall not go back to get it. It shall be for the sojourner, the fatherless, and the widow, that the LORD your God may bless you in all the work of your hands. When you beat your olive trees, you shall not go over them again. It shall be for the sojourner, the fatherless, and the widow. When you gather the grapes of your vineyard, you shall not strip it afterward. It shall be for the sojourner, the fatherless, and

---

[7] Leviticus 19:9–10.

the widow. You shall remember that you were a slave in the land of Egypt; therefore I command you to do this.[8]

At the end of every three years you shall bring out all the tithe of your produce in the same year and lay it up within your towns. And the Levite, because he has no portion or inheritance with you, and the sojourner, the fatherless, and the widow, who are within your towns, shall come and eat and be filled, that the LORD your God may bless you in all the work of your hands that you do.[9]

Harvesting by hand leaves a lot of grain behind, and so from a purely economic viewpoint the command not to go through the fields a second time was very costly. However, rather than thinking of their own economic advantage, the farmers were required to leave the excess for the poor, the fatherless, the widow, and the alien in the land. Widows, the fatherless, and aliens made up the great majority of the poor in Israel, as they do in every society throughout history.

We should notice that there are no statements in these laws about whether the poor are the "deserving poor" (as some speak about such matters of charity). Whether a person was poor because of tragedy or because of sin and laziness is not an issue for consideration in these commandments. A lazy or otherwise sinful man has a needy wife and children, quite apart from his own needs.

Rather than considering what is deserved or the character of the person in need, the fundamental issue in these laws is to remember the undeserved kindness of God to us and, therefore, to be generous to anyone in need. At the heart of these laws is the call to imitate the character of God and to remember his mercy in redeeming his people. Israel was never to forget its history. Twenty generations after the exodus the people were still to base their actions on the reminder that they had been slaves in Egypt, and that the Lord had shown mercy to them.

Just so for the Christian today, I am not to consider what people merit, but rather how God has shown to me his extraordinary grace, his unmerited favor, in giving up his Son for my salvation. The cross of Christ takes account of my sins, my demerits—not my goodness!

---

[8] Deuteronomy 24:19–22.
[9] Deuteronomy 14:28–29.

The Godly Example of Boaz

One example of obedience to these commandments is the beautiful fulfillment of these requirements in the life of Boaz when he encounters Ruth and Naomi in their need.

The events of the lives of Ruth and Boaz take place at the end of the twelfth century BC. What do we know of this period of history? If we turn to the very last verse of the book of Judges we read the words, "Everyone did as he saw fit."[10] The period of the Judges was a terrible time, a time of perpetual upheaval for the people in the land of Palestine. There was almost constant warfare, there was occupation by the surrounding nations, and the people of Israel were ruled harshly.

The years leading up to the time of Ruth are a history of the people turning away from God, a narrative of unbelief and idolatry among God's people, and a sorry record of disobedience and rebellion against the Lord and his commandments. When we read the book of Judges, we see an overwhelming picture of human sin, unbelief, and unfaithfulness to God. It was a time of abandoning the worship of God and of ignoring his law. And because of this, it was a time of continual political, social, and economic crisis. This is the big picture against which the book of Ruth is set.

The book gives us another picture, a miniature held up against the backdrop of faithlessness; but this other picture is a portrait of faithfulness. In it we read about the faithfulness of two women and of one man: Naomi, Ruth, and Boaz. These three people honored and loved God, were faithful to him, and obeyed his Word despite the pattern of life around them. Theirs is a story of three people who were faithful when the surrounding culture was characterized by faithlessness to God and by faithlessness between people. We might describe our time in a similar way. Today people live autonomously, that is, as a law unto themselves. Everyone is doing what is right in his or her own eyes.

This is the big picture, both in the time of Ruth and Boaz and now, three thousand years later. In such a time as this, what miniatures are there that contrast to this backdrop? What stories in our nations, in our cities, in our churches, on our campuses, in our families parallel

---

[10]Judges 21:25, niv.

the story of Ruth, Naomi, and Boaz? What stories are there of people who are committed to serving God: stories of people being faithful, stories of people loving God and walking in his ways, stories of people living for others and living for God—and all this happening in a time where everyone around us is doing what they see fit?

As we read the story that brings Ruth and Boaz together, it is evident that behind the scenes God's hand is guiding the lives of Ruth, Naomi, and Boaz because the Lord loves to care for those who make him their refuge. Naomi and Ruth, in the providence of God, a particular providence of which they are as yet unaware, arrive back in Bethlehem during the time of the barley harvest. Barley fields ripen first in the cycle of yearly harvests. The wheat harvest comes several weeks later. What does this have to do with Ruth and Naomi and the providence of God?

To understand how beautiful this story of God's care is, we need to consider Ruth and Naomi's situation. As widows coming back to Bethlehem they have no resources, no means of making a living. They are going to be completely dependent on the readiness of their neighbors to obey God's laws about the treatment of widows. There are many compassionate laws of God, laws about kindness to widows, orphans, and aliens, which Moses gave to the people of Israel. However, in most of the nation's history these laws have been ignored. And for Ruth and Naomi, their well-being depends upon how the people of Bethlehem feel about obeying these laws.

The two women have returned in desperate circumstances. In that society, as in most societies throughout history, widows have no means of making a livelihood. To put bread on the table, both for herself and for her mother-in-law, Ruth goes gleaning behind the harvesters in a field where she hopes that the owners will treat her favorably. She is in an agrarian society in which every family has land and every family farms. Each family was granted an allotment of land by the Lord when Israel first entered the land of Canaan.

As we have seen, the people are commanded to allow gleaning, and the law reminds them that they are to be generous in remembrance of God's generosity to them. These same motivations to be generous to those in need are just as applicable to the Christian today. We are called to imitate God's generous character and to remember his gracious salvation. The principles of these gleaning laws still apply to every believer throughout this present age.

Of course for the poor to be able to glean, the owner of the field had to be willing to keep the demands of the law, and the owner might not be willing, even though these laws are not options but requirements, obligations. Just as we are commanded not to commit adultery, not to murder, not to steal, so too we are commanded to obey the gleaning laws. We can be sure that the majority of the landowners did not obey these laws, even when they were faced with people who met the requirements of the law.

Ruth meets three of the four categories of need: she is poor, she is an alien, and she is a widow. She probably also meets the fourth category of being an orphan, as her father-in-law is dead, and she has left her own parents and people, thus having neither a husband nor a father to provide for her once she chose to go with Naomi.

When Ruth goes into the field to glean, it is apparent that she has no idea whose field she is in. But in God's providence, and because of his unseen gracious care for her, "she happened" (2:3) to choose the field of Boaz. Even though Boaz is not present, it is obvious that he has given instructions to his foreman to allow gleaning, for when Ruth makes her polite request (2:7), the foreman gladly agrees. Notice the greeting between Boaz and his harvesters, "The LORD be with you!" and their reply, "The LORD bless you" (2:4). It is evident that this entire household is one of faith. The foreman is aware, of course, that it is the newly arrived Moabitess who is gleaning. Ruth no doubt has a foreign accent, and, in addition, the whole community knows of the extraordinary choice she has made in leaving her land, her gods, her people, and her family to return to Bethlehem with her mother-in-law (1:19). We also see that the foreman is aware of Ruth's hard work (2:7).

What is Boaz's response when he discovers that this alien widow is gleaning in his field? He urges Ruth to stay in his fields, knowing that some of his neighbors would not be so ready to let her glean in their fields, and also being acutely aware that she might even be in danger of rape elsewhere (2:8–9). Naomi also is concerned about Ruth's vulnerability to sexual assault (2:22). Remember that this is a time of great wickedness in the nation of Israel. (Think, for example, of the raping to death of the Levite's concubine recorded in Judges 19.) There are likely many men working in those fields who would gladly take advantage of a woman in need and without a man's protection, as is true of Ruth. Boaz, in effect, chooses immediately to become Ruth's protector and guardian.

Several times on the news over the past few years I have heard about the widespread abuse of women and their daughters in aid situations around the world. Men from the aid organizations, as well as locals employed by them, regularly and systematically demand sexual favors of women and their daughters in return for grain and other food. Women in such settings of poverty have to accede to such demands for sex—unless they are prepared to starve to death—if they are committed to feeding their children. Of course, there are many occasions when a woman is not given the choice to accede to such demands, but is forced into sexual subjugation.[11]

However, in Ruth's case, God in his merciful providence is watching over her and protects her by bringing her to the field of this good man, Boaz. We see Boaz going far beyond the letter of the law in his care for this widow and alien (2:9, 14–16). This is, of course, what God desires of us all—that we follow the spirit of the law rather than merely the letter. We are neither to ignore such laws nor to keep them strictly to the letter while doing the minimum of what God commands for those in need. The laws simply spell out the basics. God's laws are the floor of what we should do.[12] They are not the reality of the spacious room of obedience to the Lord. And so we are to ask ourselves: What is the intent of the law? What is the principle that God desires us to observe?

God's people in the time of Ruth and Boaz and today are commanded to be generous to those less fortunate. We are not simply to tolerate any person in need who happens to have the courage to take advantage of provisions such as the gleaning laws. This generosity, this obedience to the spirit and intent of the law, is what we see in the life

---

[11] In addition, many women in need are forced into slavery prostitution with false promises of employment, marriage, green cards, etc. See the outstanding Jack Reacher novel by Lee Child, *Worth Dying For*, which addresses this issue.

[12] I am indebted to Gordon Wenham for this beautiful insight into the nature of God's law.

of Boaz. He urges Ruth to stay in his fields, to return each day, and to keep gleaning there for her own safety. He orders his men not to take advantage of her or abuse her in any way. He invites her to drink with the men and to eat lunch with them. He ensures that she is given so much extra food at lunchtime (not what she has gleaned, but from the bounty he provides for himself and his laborers) that she is able to take some home to share with Naomi for dinner that night. He commands his men to let sheaves fall so that she can pick them up, and thus glean plenty of grain. Boaz, as a man of true faith, is deeply moved by the account he has heard of the faith and courageous decision of Ruth (2:11–12). Boaz acts like God in his graciousness and kindness to the less fortunate. This is, of course, exactly what the law requires!

At the end of the first day, because of the instructions Boaz has given his men, Ruth returns to Naomi with far more grain than a gleaner would normally gather and thresh, and also with the excess of the roasted barley from her lunch. Naomi is deeply moved by these evidences of God's care for Ruth, for she realizes that God has providentially directed Ruth to the field of a kind and generous man (2:19–22). As she listens to Ruth's account of her day, Naomi also realizes that Boaz is a close relative.

But this is just the first day! Ruth's gleaning in Boaz's fields continues for a period of up to seven weeks, from the beginning of the barley harvest to the end of the wheat harvest. All through this time Boaz makes sure that Ruth and Naomi will have enough to live on, perhaps even enough extra to sell and to store up for the months ahead when the harvest is over. In fact, by the end of the harvest, Ruth almost certainly has gleaned sufficient grain that she and Naomi will have plenty to eat through the coming hard times of winter. Boaz is indeed a man committed to observing the full intent of the law, thus imitating the character of God. And this is our calling today: our lives are to be miniatures of faithfulness to God's law, miniatures set against the backdrop of our culture's pursuit of personal fulfillment and pleasure.

I want to add here one more beautiful detail from the book of Ruth. Later in the story we hear Boaz referring to Ruth's coming to glean in his fields as a kindness to him (3:10). What could he possibly mean by such an expression? Boaz is saying that he regards the presence of Ruth in his fields as a blessing to him. He sees her need and her gleaning as a privilege not for Ruth, but for him. Boaz is a man who constantly asks, "Where do I see opportunities to express the grace, mercy, and love that God has shown to me?"

Boaz is a near descendant of the prostitute Rahab, whom the Lord had redeemed. He comes from a family that has in its own history a deep appreciation for the unmerited favor of God, a profound knowledge that God delights to rescue people from their misery and sin, and a true understanding that the heart of fellowship with God is his refusal to remember our unbelief, our failings, and our disobedience. Boaz is filled with the love of God toward him, and so that love flows out of his heart toward those in need of his mercy and graciousness. Protecting Ruth, being generous to Ruth, seeing that Ruth and Naomi are well provided for—this is not a burden to him, but a joy, a privilege.

Is this how we think when we meet people in need of our protection, our generosity, our provision? Do we see the tasks set before us as unpleasant burdens, as unfortunate obligations, as annoying interruptions in our busy and self-centered lives? Or will we join Boaz in seeing opportunities to meet needs as a kindness to us?

Questions for Personal Reflection and Group Discussion

1. Do you find yourself enticed by our culture's call to seek your own fulfillment and happiness rather than to find fulfillment and happiness in following the desires of the Lord and his pattern of life for you? I am convinced that, if we are honest, we will all have to answer this question with a yes. It would be helpful to consider where we feel this enticement most pressing in upon us, where we find it most difficult to resist. This, if we are prepared to have the Lord wound us, will be a painful undertaking.

2. Are you convinced that the law was given to an already redeemed people, to a people who are repentant sinners in need of God's mercy, like David in Psalm 25, rather than as a means of earning God's favor and love?

3. As you look at your own life and the life of your family or close friends, what do you see to be the areas in which you most need the Lord's instruction so that you might walk in his ways?

4. What is your reaction to the statistics that between 30 and 45 percent of Americans claim to be born again, but that only 8 to 10 percent say that they

believe Scripture to be true and to have authority over their personal lives and that they seek to obey Christ's commands as the only appropriate response to his love and forgiveness?

5. Have you thought of mercy, kindness, and generosity to others as being central to the Old Testament law? Had you noticed how the laws about generosity and mercy are constantly related back to the mercy of God? What difference should this make for you as you think about ways in which you might bring your life more fully under God's law and in line with his mercy to you?

6. Boaz is a man who lives out the spirit of the law and not simply the letter. What do you find to be most beautiful about this story of his kindness to Ruth? Do you know of similar examples today of this same kind of obedience to the spirit of the law by Christian believers, obedience that creates a miniature to set against the patterns of the culture in which we live?

7. Is it a new idea for you to think about opportunities for obedience and generosity as a kindness to us, rather than simply as challenging obligations? Where do you need to see that obedience to God is a kindness to you?

8

The Spirit of the Law

We have been reflecting on the relationship between the commandments of the law and the image of God. We looked at Psalm 25 and David's desire to have God teach him how he might walk in the same paths of righteousness, faithfulness, and love that characterize the way of the Lord. We saw that David clearly does not think of the law as a means of justification; rather it is gracious instruction for the humble sinner. His passionate hope is that he might learn to imitate the Lord's way of life. This expression of longing to be like the Lord comes in the context of confession of sin and an acute understanding of his need for forgiveness.

Because there is such widespread misunderstanding on this point, I will reiterate here what I stated earlier: the law was never given as a way to earn fellowship with God. It was given to those aware of their constant need for mercy and pardon. It was given to those who lived in the Lord's grace, to those whose trust is his steadfast love, to those who walk in the light of his faithfulness to his covenant promises. When you and I know that we are loved and forgiven by the Lord, the appropriate response to him is to say with the psalmist,

> Make known to me your ways, O Lord;
>   teach me your paths.[1]

We also saw that human flourishing in all of life, what I am calling the good life, is the consequence of meditating on God's laws and

---
[1] Psalm 25:4.

living by them. To live in obedience to the law of God brings beauty into our lives, rather than ugliness. We thought about the manner in which our culture teaches us to live for ourselves and how it promises us that such self-centered living will bring us freedom and happiness. We contrasted this with the way the law teaches us to live for others in imitation of God, for at the heart of the law is our calling to show grace, love, and mercy to others, as God has shown them to us, his beloved people.

We also saw that the Old Testament laws about agricultural and business practice demand mercy and generosity toward those in need, for these laws mirror the goodness and kindness of God to Israel. I pointed out that the laws about gleaning and being generous to the widow, the orphan, the alien, and the poor do not demand that we first ask whether these people are "deserving poor."

AFFIRMING BOTH RESPONSIBILITY AND MERCY

Some readers will have problems with that last statement and respond, "But what about the need for responsibility and hard work?" It is true, of course, that the Bible teaches people to work hard and to support themselves and their families. God's Word encourages responsibility, it speaks passionately against laziness, and it rejects a culture of dependence. The following story may help to show I strongly believe in the need for people to give themselves to hard work and supporting themselves.

A young man who had lived as a thief came to stay with us. He responded to the gospel and, one day, professed faith in Christ in our kitchen, praying with me a prayer of commitment to the Lord. I then opened the Bible to Ephesians and read Paul's words: "Let the thief no longer steal, but rather let him labor, doing honest work with his own hands, so that he may have something to share with anyone in need."[2]

Challenging the young man on this issue, I told him that, as a new believer in Jesus, he now had a calling to stop stealing, to work hard, to become independent, and to become generous. He responded, "But, Jerram; that is too hard! Living as a thief is so much easier than finding

---

[2] Ephesians 4:28.

a job and working at it every day." I replied that, despite the challenge this would be to him, this was the Lord's requirement.

He went away, found a job that he worked at for a time, then returned to his life as a thief. His church disciplined him, as the New Testament demands, and again, for a time, he found work. The stealing way of life was so familiar to him, however, that eventually he went back to it. We had warned him that if he did, the Lord himself would intervene and severely discipline him. This happened. He was caught by the police, tried, found guilty, and imprisoned. There in prison he finally learned a trade and, upon release, gave himself to work in a new way. I still pray for him whenever I think about him. The Lord does indeed insist that his people be hardworking, faithful, and generous.

Nonetheless, the point still stands: when we see someone in need of food and clothing, our first question is not to be whether this person is poor because he is lazy or because of misfortune. God does not look at our merit or our deserving when he is generous to us. The point of the grace of God is that we merit justice and judgment; we do not deserve the love and mercy of Christ. In just the same way, we are to be gracious, generous, and kind, whether people are deserving and responsible or not. As we seek to obey any of God's commandments, the Lord's design is that we always ask: What is this law about? What is its ethical intent? What are the spiritual and moral principles at the heart of this particular law? How does this law teach me to be like my loving and gracious Savior?

We spent the major part of our last chapter looking at the example of Boaz. Obedience to the spirit and intent of the law is precisely what we see in the life of Boaz. He urges Ruth to stay and glean from his fields for her own safety. He orders his men not to take advantage of her. He invites her to have lunch with them and ensures that she has extra food to take home to Naomi. He commands his men to let sheaves fall so that she can pick them up. In short, Boaz acts like God in his graciousness and kindness to the less fortunate, just as the law requires. I finished our reflections on Boaz with a challenge. This is our calling today: our lives are to be miniatures of faithfulness to God's law, miniatures set against the backdrop of our culture's pursuit of personal fulfillment and pleasure.

The Spirit of the Law as "Extraordinary" Generosity

One modern-day example of someone applying the spirit of the law involves the agricultural laws from the book of Leviticus:

> And the Lord spoke to Moses, saying, "Speak to the people of Israel and say to them, When you come into the land that I give you and reap its harvest, you shall bring the sheaf of the firstfruits of your harvest to the priest, and he shall wave the sheaf before the Lord, so that you may be accepted. On the day after the Sabbath the priest shall wave it. And on the day when you wave the sheaf, you shall offer a male lamb a year old without blemish as a burnt offering to the Lord. And the grain offering with it shall be two tenths of an ephah of fine flour mixed with oil, a food offering to the Lord with a pleasing aroma, and the drink offering with it shall be of wine, a fourth of a hin. And you shall eat neither bread nor grain parched or fresh until this same day, until you have brought the offering of your God: it is a statute forever throughout your generations in all your dwellings."[3]

I offer the story below as an encouragement to live by the spirit of the law in glad obedience and in earthy, concrete ways. The example is that of my father-in-law, along with his dear wife.

I was a student at Covenant Theological Seminary in the late 1960s. Each summer during those student years my wife, Vicki, and I would drive out to Central California, and I would work for several months on the family farm. My own father died in 1972, so he was still alive at this time, but from our wedding in 1967, I always called Vicki's father Dad. Dad had a small farm of forty to sixty acres in the San Joaquin Valley, thirty miles south of Fresno, and he grew tree fruit such as peaches, nectarines, plums, and persimmons, as well as some grapes and kiwis. In the summer of 1969 we were staying with Mom and Dad, enjoying their wonderful hospitality, as we did so many times, and I was helping pick and pack watermelons.

One day, when I was walking back through the fields to the house for lunch, I came across Dad kneeling in his orchard before one of his

---

[3] Leviticus 23:9–14; see also 23:15–21 for the Feast of Weeks, a further feast of firstfruits. In other passages we see this requirement of offering firstfruits to the Lord applied to grapes, olives, tree fruit, etc.

young peach trees. When a peach tree is three or four years old, it will bear its firstfruits. The young tree will have four or five large and beautiful peaches, and these will be some of the finest fruit the tree will ever bear. Dad was kneeling there holding up a peach in each hand and saying: "Lord, these peaches are yours. These trees are yours and all the fruit they will ever bear. This orchard is yours. My farm is yours. I am yours. Thank you for your love to me in Jesus. Help me to serve you in all I do."

I waited quietly till he had finished his prayer and got up from his knees. He was a bit embarrassed to find me watching and listening to what was intended to be a private moment between him and the Lord. I asked him about what he had just done, and he explained that he had this service of firstfruits every time any of his trees started bearing their peaches, nectarines, plums, or persimmons, or his vines their grapes or kiwis. "I read that the Lord taught Moses to command the people to bring the best of their firstfruits to the house of the Lord and offer them to him," he said, "so I decided that I would have this little service with my firstfruits."

Dad loved to read the Scriptures, and as he studied the laws in the books of Moses, he decided for himself that he wanted to put into practice some of the various offerings and services in the Old Testament law that were required of the people of Israel. He knew that believers today are not obligated to obey all the Mosaic law according to the letter, but he understood that the spiritual principles and intent of these laws still apply to believers in Christ for, as he said, "Paul teaches us that everything in Scripture from former times was written down for our instruction."[4]

So Dad's plan was that he would regularly have this service of firstfruits just between himself and the Lord. He never told anyone about this ceremony; it was a private matter between him and the Lord. Dad had never been taught in his church the true meaning of the various offerings and services in the Old Testament law that were required of the people of Israel; and certainly his pastor had never suggested that Dad put them into practice. But reading the Bible himself, Dad understood the intent of these laws, and so he had decided that he would do this on his own. His pastor was not the kind of man with whom

---

[4] See Romans 15:4.

he could have spoken about such a matter. I remember having lunch with the pastor one day (that same summer) and the pastor telling me that he preached short sermons without much content because his congregation was made up of ignorant farmers. I am sure Dad knew the Scriptures far better than that pastor. And the results of Dad's little ceremony were remarkable.

First, it shaped his attitude toward his employees and toward anyone with whom he did business. He did not ask about his "bottom line" when thinking about paying the men who worked on his farm. For the Christian in business, or in any line of work, the bottom line is seeking the kingdom of God and his righteousness. So it was for Dad. Many of the laborers on the farms in California's Central Valley were at that time, just like today, immigrants from Mexico, some legal, some illegal. Many of the farmers (including some of those who claimed to be Christian) paid them a minimum wage and treated them quite poorly. But Dad knew that this was deeply disobedient to the Lord and to his commandments, for the law requires that we treat aliens in the same just, fair, and generous way as we treat the native-born. Rather than asking what he could afford to pay the men who worked for him, Dad asked what would be pleasing to the Lord, what was just, merciful, and fair. He knew that one day he would have to give an account to the Lord, the same Lord who had not counted the cost of redeeming us, but who was rich and yet made himself poor for our sakes.

Within the last two or three years of Dad's life a man came by the house to thank him, someone who had worked for Dad many years before. "Every summer I would come up from Mexico and I would make a beeline for your farm," the man said. "You treated us so much better than the other farmers. You did not pay the minimum wage or the 'going rate.' You paid us far more. You often ate lunch with us. You brought us treats at break time. On very hot days you would come by with ice cream or ice-cold drinks. You asked about our families. Working for you changed my whole life and the way I have raised my own sons. I have tried to raise them to be like you. I am sorry I did not come back to thank you before." By this stage of his life Dad had dementia, and so he did not fully understand what the man was saying, but everyone else present did.

Dad died in October 2007 at the age of ninety. At his memorial service I had the privilege of preaching, and I told this story of his ceremony of firstfruits. It was new to almost everyone there. We also heard testimony that he paid people more than they were worth, and some would tell him so when he handed them their checks. Even when others, including relatives, took advantage of his integrity and generosity, Dad never held it against them. He continued to treat them as well as he treated everyone else, with the same kindness and mercy he always showed people. When a neighbor moved his boundary line to try to steal some of Dad's land, Dad refrained from rebuking him, though it certainly distressed him. I am sure almost everyone who knew him, who worked with him, or who did any business with him in any setting could tell numerous stories about this aspect of his commitment to treat people with justice and mercy.

Second, when he gave, he gave generously without thinking about how much precisely he could afford. Rather he would ask, "What does the Lord want me to give?" He would pray that the Lord would lead him in his giving, and that the Spirit would put on his heart people who were in need and the ministries to which he should give. He understood in a very deep way that the laws about tithing were not fulfilled by giving an exact 10 percent of his income, but that these tithing laws were a floor, a kind of basic minimum, and so he always gave much more. Though not a wealthy man, many years he gave away more than half his income. He gave to his church, to ministries, to orphans, and to many individuals. He did not keep records of all his giving, because often he would just give cash spontaneously, though with more regular gifts, he received tax deductible receipts.

He was once audited by the Internal Revenue Service because they could not believe that he was giving away so much of his income. After the audit the IRS wrote him a letter, which he kept and showed to me. I have never seen another like it. "Mr. Buxman," it said, "your bookkeeping is impeccable and your accounts clear; and your generosity is extraordinary!" They informed him, however, that he could not give so much and claim it all as tax deductible. He was giving over the limit! Of course, that did not cause him to give less. It had not occurred to him that there was a limit to what one could give. He carried on giving just as generously, but was careful only to enter onto his tax return the portion of his giving that was within the IRS rules.

Dad was indeed extraordinarily generous. He would invite the local rescue mission to come and glean from his orchards, for he had read about gleaning in the law of Moses and in the book of Ruth, and he loved the story of Ruth and Boaz. Almost every week he would take boxes of fruit and vegetables to a distribution center to give free produce to elderly people on fixed incomes, and to others who were poor for whatever reason.

The third consequence was Dad and Mom's hospitality, their readiness to be generous with their home, their possessions, their food, and their time. I will give just two examples. In 1971, after I graduated from Covenant, Vicki and I went back to England to work at the English L'Abri and to serve in a Presbyterian church we helped to plant in our community there. One of the people who came to the English L'Abri that year was a young man from Southern California, I will call him Tom, who had become a Christian simply by reading the New Testament. His parents had divorced and no one had paid much attention to him, so Tom had often skipped school. He had never been to church and knew nothing about Christianity, but one day he found a family Bible at home that looked as if it had never been opened, so he started reading the New Testament. By the time he had read halfway through the book of Acts he decided that it was true and thought, "I believe this; so now that I believe in Jesus, I should do something useful with my life instead of just living to please myself." So Tom joined the Peace Corps and went to work for several years in French-speaking West Africa.

There he met other Christians and started studying the Bible with a team leader who had worked at L'Abri in Switzerland. When Tom's term in Africa finished, the ex-L'Abri worker sent him to the English L'Abri to get a solid foundation for his faith before he returned to California. It was there at the English L'Abri that Vicki and I met him, and we became good friends. When he left after a year with us, he asked whether we had any suggestions of where he might go, and of Christians with whom he could make contact. Without thinking out the consequences, we encouraged him to visit Vicki's parents. We

wrote to them and mentioned that we were sending this young man
to them, and they said that would be fine.

So that is what Tom did—he turned up at Mom and Dad's home,
and they had him stay with them for quite some time. Dad gave him
a job on the farm and so he got his start. He still lives in that area. I
often see him when I go out to Central California. He is still working
in farming and is married with grown children of his own. He still
refers to Vicki's parents, both now with the Lord, as Mom and Dad.
At the memorial service for Dad, Tom spoke about their love for him
and their extraordinary hospitality: "I was a stranger and you took me
in. I was hungry and you fed me." He could hardly get his words out
through his weeping. Many years after we sent him to Mom and Dad
we thought, "That was such a presumption on our part to assume that
they would take him in." But their willingness simply shows what
kind of people they were.

Let me share one other story about their hospitality. One summer
evening we were driving up into the Sierra foothills to have dinner
with Vicki's younger brother and his wife. On the little winding back
road climbing up into the mountains we saw a man in his fifties walking and lugging a large and heavy-looking suitcase. We stopped to give
him a ride, and the man, Kurt, turned out to be a German high school
teacher of geology. All his life he had longed to come to California
to look at rock formations in beautiful places like King's Canyon and
Yosemite Valley. On this occasion Kurt was on his way up to see the
giant redwood trees at General Grant and to explore King's Canyon
and Cedar Grove. His suitcase was indeed heavy because, along with
his clothes, he had collected many rock samples as he traveled around
California. We were chatting in the car and then invited him to dinner
at my brother-in-law's. Later that evening, Mom and Dad invited him
to return with us to stay the night.

Dad's parents were Germans, part of a German community that
had lived in Russia for many generations. The community comprised
mostly Mennonites and some Lutherans who had been invited to Russia by Catherine the Great in the 1760s. They had settled in the area
near the Volga River and continued to speak German. Dad's parents
immigrated to the United States around 1900 and spoke only German

all their lives. So Dad was delighted to have this teacher to converse with in German. Kurt ended up staying with Mom and Dad for several days, and they became excellent friends. For the next few years each summer some of Kurt's German high school students would turn up at Mom and Dad's, usually unannounced, and would of course be invited to stay for dinner and the night, and often for a couple of days. Mom and Dad saw God's laws about hospitality as simply a normal part of the Christian life. They did not think of themselves as doing anything extraordinary, but as simply being committed to obey the spirit of the law, and thus to practice the kind of hospitality that the Lord had shown them and that the Lord would show them for all eternity to come.

The fourth consequence of Dad's dedication of himself and his possessions to the Lord was its impact on his three sons and daughter. Today two of their sons are farmers and the third is a doctor. All of them are men whom people love to work for and with because of their integrity, fairness, and kindness. The fourth child is, of course, my wife. Vicki is like the noble wife of Proverbs 31. Each one of them is generous and hospitable, just like Dad and Mom.

I have told parts of this story in many sermons and lectures in various places in the world. For example, I used Dad's service of firstfruits as an illustration when I was lecturing in Hungary at the European Leadership Forum, a meeting with large numbers of young Christian leaders from perhaps forty European nations. Many people were profoundly moved by Dad's story. Toward the end of the week someone said to me, "Who would have thought, at the beginning of this week, that the most significant person during this conference would be a ninety-year-old farmer who left school at the age of twelve?"

When I returned to their home, I told this story to Mom and Dad at dinner one day, and even despite his dementia he was embarrassed and he blushed as I recounted what had been said. I finished by telling him that at the end of the lecture I said to the people gathered there at that conference in Hungary, "Soon he is going to be with the King whom he served all his life." Then I started singing, "Soon and very soon we are going to see the king." Dad joined right in singing it with us. Mom said, "He hasn't sung that song for more than thirty years!"

Even with dementia, though he had forgotten many things he had once known, he never forgot scriptural passages or songs that he had learned; nor did he forget any member of the family.

Now his mind and memory are fully restored, and he is singing in the presence of the King. Even more beautiful, the King is singing over him, and he and the King are filled with delight in each other. I am confident that the Savior welcomed him with the words, "Well done, good and faithful servant. . . . Enter into the joy of your master."[5]

Questions for Personal Reflection and Group Discussion

1. Are you troubled by the statement that we are not to think about whether the poor are deserving poor when we are generous to the needy, but that we are to remember God's undeserved kindness to us?

2. It is important to think about the spiritual principles invoked by Old Testament laws about agriculture, business, and the ceremonies (including combinations of ceremony and agricultural, such as the service of firstfruits). The law of Moses is like a treasure chest full of delights, surprises, and challenges for the one who begins to study it. Are there aspects of the law that you would particularly like to reflect upon and apply in your own life?

3. Do you know of striking examples of believers among your family members or friends who have taken a part of God's law, just as my father-in-law did, and sought to live in obedience to the principles made known in the law?

4. The story of Dad's firstfruits ceremony recounted in this chapter is very moving, just as is the story of Ruth and Boaz. Why is such a story inspiring? (We will return to this issue of the power of stories later in this book, because story is a very significant part of communicating God's commandments.)

5. How might you adapt Dad's service of firstfruits to your own life, either in your home or in your workplace? What elements would you need to include in such a ceremony?

6. Are there other parts of the law that you might like to use to create a ceremony for your own life, your family, your home, or your workplace? Consider spending some time to develop such a service for your personal worship of the Lord.

---

[5] Matthew 25:21, 23.

9

Jesus Expounds the Law

In our last chapter we considered a contemporary example of obedience to the spirit of the law. We thought about my father-in-law reading the law of Moses and seeing how the Israelites were commanded to offer their firstfruits to the Lord. Dad designed his own service of firstfruits for offering his peaches, plums, nectarines, grapes, kiwis, and persimmons to the Lord whenever his trees and vines started bearing their fruit. He understood at a deep level the principles that lie behind these Old Testament ceremonies and laws. He realized that there are a series of fundamental issues involved in all these commandments.

First, Dad believed that everything we have comes to us as a gift of grace from our kind heavenly Father. He saw his life, his health, his marriage, his family, his orchards, his farm, his money, and his home as belonging to God rather than to him.

Second, he knew that without God's mercy in Christ, he would have been lost forever, trapped in his sins and unbelief. He understood that the one who bows to the Lord has two reasons to see himself as owing everything to God: (1) we are creatures utterly dependent on our Creator, and (2) we are sinners who could not live a moment before God without his constant forgiveness.

Third, Dad saw himself as a temporary overseer of all that the Lord had entrusted to him, a steward who would one day give an account for all that the Lord had given him. Would he be a faithful servant, managing what truly belonged to the Lord, or would he believe the lie that it was all his to spend on himself, his family, his own needs, and his pleasures?

Fourth, Dad realized that many of the commandments and ceremonies had at their heart, and as their motivating power, the love and graciousness of God to his people. The Lord had been so kind and generous to him; how could he harden his heart against others in need of his kindness and generosity?

Fifth, he believed that it is our human calling to seek to be a little bit like God, to display to others in some small way the loveliness of God's character. Dad knew that people around a believer draw conclusions about the Lord from what they see in the lives of his people.

It was these deep understandings of the law—understandings he was never taught in his church, but that came to him through the Spirit as he read the Word for himself and reflected on it—that lay behind his merciful and gracious treatment of his employees, his extraordinary generosity with his money, his and Mom's commitment to hospitality, and his seeking to live as such a wonderful example before his three sons and daughter.

Some reading this may well have felt both inspired and discouraged by it. That is a wonderful and an appropriate response, because such a response raises some very significant questions about the nature of God's law and how we are to teach it, both to our own hearts and to others'.

THE TEACHER, THE LAW, AND THE GOOD SAMARITAN

How should we teach the law in a way that exposes its inner principles and therefore challenges the heart at a deep level? The best place to turn is to the example of Jesus's expounding the law, so in this chapter we will look at a familiar passage, an account in the Gospels of Jesus's confrontations with "a lawyer" (ESV), "an expert in the law" (NIV), or as we might describe him today, "a Bible teacher"; for this is what the man was, a leading Bible scholar of his generation. Luke's story of this meeting contains Jesus's exposition of the second great commandment: what it means to love my neighbor. In addition, in the course of his conversation with this Bible teacher, Jesus tells one of his best-known parables, in fact one of the best-known stories in the world, the parable of the good Samaritan. Luke 10:25–29 presents the beginning of the encounter between Jesus and the scholar:

And behold, a lawyer stood up to put him to the test, saying, "Teacher, what shall I do to inherit eternal life?" He said to him, "What is written in the Law? How do you read it?" And he answered, "You shall love the Lord your God with all your heart and with all your soul and with all your strength and with all your mind, and your neighbor as yourself." And he said to him, "You have answered correctly; do this, and you will live."

But he, desiring to justify himself, said to Jesus, "And who is my neighbor?"

The Bible Teacher's Question

The expert in the law, or as I will call him, the scholar or Bible teacher, has spent his life studying and teaching the Scriptures and is clearly confident of his knowledge. This man approaches Jesus as a fellow Bible teacher and presents him with a question: "Teacher, what must I do to inherit eternal life?" We might respond, "What a great question to be asked!" Wouldn't we be pleased if someone, anyone, were to come to one of us with such a question? This is the kind of question for which an evangelist longs and prays. Imagine being a Sunday school teacher or a speaker at a conference and being asked such a question. Think of a neighbor or someone at work asking such a question. How would we have answered? I think almost all of us would jump into an account of how to be saved and then urge this inquirer to follow us in a prayer of commitment.

But if we hold our eagerness for a moment and read the record of Jesus's response, it becomes evident that he does not seem to have answered this man's great question. Jesus does not tell this fellow scholar how he might inherit eternal life. This failure of Jesus to answer the question leaves us with many of our own questions. How would we reply if someone were to come to us and ask this kind of question? Why does Jesus not answer it? What can we learn from Jesus's reply? What is going on here? Is there more in this encounter than immediately meets the eye?

Luke helps our understanding by letting us know that the scholar's question is not sincere; rather, he is testing Jesus. He is not coming to learn from Jesus. He is saying in effect: "Let's try to find out if you know the Scriptures. Are you fit to teach the Word? Are you properly trained, like me?" He believed that he had gone to the best Bible school or seminary of the day, and he knew that Jesus had never been a student there or at any other school with which he was familiar.

Jesus's Question in Reply

Jesus sees deep into this Bible scholar's heart. Observing his insincerity, Jesus responds not with a direct answer, but with a question of his own: "What is written in the Law? How do you read it?" At that time "the Law" could refer to the Ten Commandments, to all the laws of Moses, to the five books of the Pentateuch, or to the whole Old Testament, the Word of God. Here Jesus is essentially asking, "What do you think God's Word teaches about the way to inherit eternal life?" The scholar could have replied, "I asked first!" Or he could have felt ashamed of his heart's attitude to Jesus and said, "Teacher, forgive me for my attempt at proving your inferiority as a student of Scripture, but I would indeed like to know what you think." However, he cannot resist showing off his knowledge, and so he gives his answer, demonstrating that he is not at all interested in learning from Jesus.

The Bible Teacher's Answer

The scholar gives a wonderful answer. He displays a deep knowledge of Scripture. He summarizes the whole law of God in his reply: "You shall love the Lord your God with all your heart and with all your soul and with all your strength and with all your mind, and your neighbor as yourself."[1] In fact, this man's summary of the law of God is the same as that which Jesus himself gives on another occasion.[2] Theoretically, this is an accurate answer to the question. If any of us were to keep these commandments of loving God with our whole being and of loving our neighbor as ourselves, we would indeed inherit eternal life.

However, as we have seen in earlier chapters, God never intended to give his law as a prescription for attaining eternal life, for when he handed the law to his people, the Lord understood that they were all sinners who needed his forgiveness. The law is a gift of God's grace to the people he already loves, the people he has already delivered from

[1] Luke 10:27.
[2] Mark 12:28–34.

bondage to be his own. As a gift of grace, the law gives a description of how God has designed human life to be lived, but certainly not a prescription for attaining life with God. In all the long history of our race, there is only one human being who has ever kept these two great commandments fully and truly, and that, of course, is Jesus himself.

Jesus's Reply

How will Jesus respond to this beautiful and accurate summary of the law? He could give a brief exposition of his Father's purpose in giving the law (much as in the paragraph above). However, Jesus understands this man's heart. He knows that if he were to enter into an exposition of the purpose of the law, the Bible teacher would be delighted and would pursue a long debate about the law, thereby showing off even more of his knowledge. It is clear that his desire is still to flaunt his learning and, if possible, to prove Jesus's inadequacy, either in biblical knowledge or in debate. Because Jesus sees the motives of the man's heart, he does not go that route. Instead Jesus commends the teacher for his answer: "You have answered correctly." However, Jesus adds a stinger to his words of commendation: "Do this, and you will live."

Avoiding the Challenge

Jesus's answer to the Bible teacher implies that if he were to obey the two great commandments perfectly, then he would in truth inherit eternal life. So, what should be the Bible teacher's response at this point? Something like this: "I know that the Word of God teaches these two great commandments as summarizing the whole duty of every man and woman. And I believe that at least to some small degree I have tried to keep these laws, but I find myself incapable of obeying them fully. I look into my heart and I see that very often it is cold to God; and to be honest with you, I am afraid that I do not love my neighbor as I love myself. I have never perfectly kept these laws, and neither has anyone else I have ever met. Jesus, please tell me what to do."

If the scholar were prepared to answer in this way, we may be sure that Jesus very gladly would have answered his initial question about how to inherit eternal life. But instead of being open and honest and acknowledging his sin and need, the Bible teacher tries to justify himself. Perhaps he also hopes to gain some time, as Jesus's words are not at all what he is expecting. Jesus's reply unsettles him and rocks him back a little. The teacher hopes to get back to safer ground and to a further demonstration of his knowledge, so he raises the question, "And who is my neighbor?" We should imagine that his hope is to try to engage Jesus in a comfortable and technical discussion as to how exactly "my neighbor" is to be defined.

Jesus Tells the Story of the Good Samaritan

Again, Jesus refuses to play the intellectual games the Bible teacher desires. Instead of giving a direct answer about the meaning of "my neighbor," Jesus tells a story. The story does of course answer the teacher's question, and many other questions as well. Jesus's story is the one we know as the parable of the good Samaritan.

> A man was going down from Jerusalem to Jericho, and he fell among robbers, who stripped him and beat him and departed, leaving him half dead. Now by chance a priest was going down that road, and when he saw him he passed by on the other side. So likewise a Levite, when he came to the place and saw him, passed by on the other side. But a Samaritan, as he journeyed, came to where he was, and when he saw him, he had compassion. He went to him and bound up his wounds, pouring on oil and wine. Then he set him on his own animal and brought him to an inn and took care of him. And the next day he took out two denarii and gave them to the innkeeper, saying, "Take care of him, and whatever more you spend, I will repay you when I come back."[3]

UNDERSTANDING PARABLES

How are we to read this parable? We can begin to answer this question by looking at what Jesus himself has to say about his use of parables in general.[4] Jesus declares that the parables reveal the good news of the kingdom to those with open ears and hearts, to those who are eager to hear his message; but, Jesus also teaches that the parables are bad news, revealing only judgment for those whose ears and hearts are

---

[3] Luke 10:30–35.
[4] Jesus speaks about his use of parables in Luke 8:8–10; Mark 4:9–13; and more fully in Matthew 13:9–17, 34–35.

closed to his message of salvation. Parables have two opposite effects, depending on the hearer. To some they are a rich treasury of truth; to others they are an offense.

How is it possible that a story can work in such contrary ways? At one level most of the parables seem to us to be simple stories, often drawn from everyday life. This is part of the reason why they are a word of judgment for those who are proud of their wisdom and knowledge. The Pharisees and teachers of the law desire to parade their learning before Jesus and to engage with him at the level of sophisticated theological and ethical discussion. Jesus usually resists their attempts to engage him at this level, as he sees that this would simply cater to their arrogance, their idolatrous love of learning, and their desire for endless disputation without ever coming to a heartfelt commitment to practice the truth. So Jesus tells stories to theological heavyweights to throw them off balance, and as a way of refusing to play their game. Their tendency is to dismiss his teaching as naïve stories for the "commonfolk" and for "ignorant sinners." In their minds Jesus the storyteller is merely a crowd pleaser, an entertainer rather than a serious teacher.

However, Jesus's stories are rarely as simple or straightforward as they seem. In fact, they do communicate profound theological and moral truths, and often they do answer the testing questions that the Pharisees and the teachers of the law bring to Jesus. This is true of this parable of the good Samaritan. But when Jesus does answer their questions, his answer is not straightforward. It is hidden within the parable, packaged in a manner that is much more challenging personally than a straightforward reply would be.

Parables can be very simple, or they may work on as many as four levels. First, parables are frequently stories, wonderful stories, that capture the imagination and memory of the reader or hearer. Second, parables may teach moral behavior; they may reveal something about character, what it is to be a truly good person, or how people ought or ought not to behave. In other words, parables sometimes expound the law of God. Third, parables may teach concerning the nature of the kingdom of God: what kind of a kingdom does the Lord want to establish in our world? Fourth, parables may communicate something about the Lord himself.

The parable of the good Samaritan works on all these levels. First, it is a marvelous story, an unforgettable story, appealing to our imaginations and holding its place in our memories. Second, it certainly teaches us how we are to live, showing us what it means to keep God's commandment to love our neighbors. Third, this story reveals the nature of the kingdom of God and the transformation of life in this world, the turning upside down of a society's ways of relating to other people. And, fourth, this parable teaches us about Jesus. But before we develop some of these four points, we need to ask, What is this particular story teaching the Bible scholar? And as Jesus teaches this man, what is he also teaching us?

The Parable's Lessons for the Bible Teacher

A Theological Put-Down

Jesus's story is first of all a theological put-down. Jesus refuses to engage in the kind of theological game the teacher desires, a game in which each player in turn shows off his knowledge and verbal acuity and dexterity, and then the cleverest is declared the winner of the debate. Instead of a debate, the Bible teacher hears what he likely considers a story for children or for uneducated people.

What Is True Love for My Neighbor?

The story, however, offers a very challenging lesson in keeping the second great commandment. The parable teaches that true love for one's neighbor requires the sacrifice of time, money, energy, convenience, and even safety—in other words, the sacrifice of oneself—for another. This is the kind of love that the Samaritan shows for the man who has fallen among thieves. He endangers himself by stopping to care for the robbed and wounded man. He puts the man on his animal, and so he himself has to walk. He uses the supplies he has with him to care for the man. He spends a considerable amount of time and money to ensure that the man recovers.

This is true love for one's neighbor: spending on others the time, energy, money, service, and sacrifice that one would spend on oneself. Jesus is challenging the Bible teacher, "Think before you declare God's commandments so lightly! It is easy enough to say that God's law requires us to love our neighbor as we love ourselves. However, it is another matter altogether to put this into practice."

Who Is My Neighbor?

Jesus's reply to the teacher's question is challenging, moreover, in how it defines "neighbor." My neighbor, the one whom God demands that I love, is not just my spouse, my children, my family, and my close friends; that is, people I already love. My neighbor is anyone in need of my help, a stranger, or even an enemy.

The Old Testament law itself is clear about this.[5] Jesus adds an extra challenge for the teacher. He says, in effect, "For you, a Jew, 'your neighbor' includes a needy Samaritan, just as in my story, a needy Jew is the neighbor of the kind Samaritan." Like this Bible teacher, we all tend to want to restrict the scope of God's commandments to make them more manageable. Jesus exposes this as self-justifying hypocrisy. I am sure that everyone reading this has individuals and groups of people whom he or she wishes to set outside the boundaries of the command "Love your neighbor as yourself."

Knowing and Doing

The good Samaritan parable is pushing the Bible teacher, and us, to think about the relationship between knowing the truth and doing the truth. People who think they have a deep knowledge of God's Word may not necessarily be obeying that Word. Even those called by God to be scholars and teachers of the law may not be practicing what they preach. The priest and Levite, examples of those whom God appointed to model and teach his law to the people, are not obedient to the law in Jesus's story. They are the ones who pass by on the other side of the road. In this parable, expert knowledge and professional calling do not lead to living the law of love. Again, this is an indirect challenge to the Bible teacher. He has come to Jesus to test him and to prove how knowledgeable he himself is. By giving the examples of the priest and Levite as failures of obedience in his story, Jesus is reminding this

---

[5] See, for example, Exodus 23:4–5; Deuteronomy 22:1–4. The Deuteronomy text requires us to help our brother who is in need. The Exodus law makes precisely the same demand of us when we meet an enemy in need.

scholar that teachers will be judged with greater strictness.[6] In effect, Jesus says to him, "Stop parading your knowledge of Scripture until you have started practicing what you know."

Revealing the Prejudices of the Heart

The story is intended to make the Bible teacher, and us, examine the prejudices that dwell within our hearts. The Samaritans were regarded as unclean, immoral, and heretical by the religious leaders of Jesus's day. But Jesus's parable suggests that a despised Samaritan is here fulfilling God's law, while the honored leaders of God's people are not. Jesus uses the most difficult example possible to make his story scandalous to the scholar. The one obedient to God's law is the one least expected! To get some idea of the power and offense of this example, we need to ask ourselves, whom would I least like to find as the hero of this story? (A gay-rights activist? a left-wing politician? a right-wing politician? a wealthy businessman? a liberal lawyer? a feminist scholar? a Muslim imam? You fill in the blank.)

A Final Question and One Last Challenge

Jesus finishes the story with another question: "Which of these three was a neighbor to the man who fell into the hands of thieves?" The teacher cannot bring himself to say, "The Samaritan," and so he replies, "The one who had mercy on him." The encounter between the two comes to an end, probably very much to the scholar's relief, with Jesus's parting words: "Go, and do likewise." Jesus challenges him to bring his practice of truth up to the level of his knowledge. That, of course, is the challenge for us all.

Questions for Personal Reflection and Group Discussion

1. Is the parable of the good Samaritan your favorite parable? If not, which one is your favorite? What do you enjoy about the parable of the good Samaritan?

2. What do you think would have been the most difficult part of the encounter with Jesus for the Bible scholar? If you were in his place, what would you have found to be difficult?

---

[6] James 3:1.

3. Jesus tells a story that describes kindness that is truly lovely. Yet this story is also very challenging to us, just as it was for the lawyer. Why is it both inspiring and challenging—perhaps even discouraging?

4. Jesus expounds what it means for you and me to love our neighbors. Certainly, our most immediate neighbors whom we are called to love are those nearest to us: wife, husband, children, parents, and dear friends—the people that each of us cares for most. Do you believe that love means sacrificing energy, time, money, convenience, and security for others to the same degree that you expend on yourself? Do you show even those you love this degree of love?

5. Jesus also teaches us that loving our neighbor means loving people who are in need, even those we may never have met before. It is very easy to restrict the love commandment to what is easier for us. Where have you been tempted to restrict the command to love your neighbor; or to put it another way, whom have you wanted to exclude from its scope?

6. Who are the people excluded from "neighbors to be loved" in our society right now, or in the Christian circles in which you move?

7. Jesus's parables are subversive. Where is the parable of the good Samaritan working away subversively in your heart and mind?

10

Jesus Fulfills the Law

In the previous three chapters we have explored the loveliness of true obedience to the law. We looked at the example of Boaz, who committed himself to live by the spirit of the law as he managed his fields and as he meditated on the true faithfulness, mercy, and costly obedience that God requires of those who know God's love. We considered a contemporary illustration in the story of Vicki's father and his offering his firstfruits to the Lord and how that dedication of his heart and his orchards to his Savior resulted in a life of kindness, generosity, and hospitality. Then, in chapter 9 we studied the beautiful example of love shown by the Good Samaritan in the story that Jesus told the expert in the law.

The Power of Stories

There are, of course, many other biblical stories we could examine that would reveal to us one or another aspect of what it means to live in accord with the true meaning of the law. Most readers will be familiar with the following story from the Gospels:

> Now when Jesus was at Bethany in the house of Simon the leper, a woman came up to him with an alabaster flask of very expensive ointment, and she poured it on his head as he reclined at table. And when the disciples saw it, they were indignant, saying, "Why this waste? For this could have been sold for a large sum and given to the poor." But Jesus, aware of this, said to them, "Why do you trouble the woman? For she has done a beautiful thing to me. For you always have the poor with you, but you will not always have me. In pouring this ointment

on my body, she has done it to prepare me for burial. Truly, I say to you, wherever this gospel is proclaimed in the whole world, what she has done will also be told in memory of her."[1]

Jesus tells those who observed the woman pouring the ointment over him that her story would be told throughout the world. Stories of true obedience to the commandments do indeed get repeated over and over again. The reason for this constant retelling is that such stories are so memorable in their expression of deep understanding of what God deserves from us and what he asks of us in his law. This story of the woman pouring the ointment on Jesus's head reveals what it means for us to love the Lord truly. The ointment might well have been an heirloom, something passed down in her family, generation after generation. It must have been one of this woman's most valuable possessions.

In that culture such heirlooms were a form of personal savings or investment (one that would not decrease in value—unlike our stocks and shares). This jar of ointment would have cost a year's salary. Imagine giving such an extravagant gift to the Lord—one that is poured out and then can never be used again; a year's labor for any of us, expended in a moment in a gesture of gratitude and love. But this is the kind of love the Lord does indeed demand of us; and he most certainly is worthy of it.

This woman's story teaches us what obedience to the first great commandment truly requires, just as the parable of the good Samaritan reveals to us the meaning of the second great commandment. All such stories are inspiring to us, whether actual accounts of obedience to the law, such as the stories of Boaz, Dad, and the woman who anointed Jesus, or parables that Jesus made up in order to reveal moral beauty, such as the stories of the good Samaritan, the prodigal son, the good shepherd. I am sure that every reader has his or her favorites. Think about the stories that you particularly treasure: both actual histories and fictional ones.

Almost all of us have films we watch repeatedly, perhaps every Christmas, because we find them to be joyful and inspirational: *A Christmas Carol*; *It's a Wonderful Life*; *The Lion, the Witch and the Wardrobe*;

---

[1] Matthew 26:6–13.

The Lord of the Rings; *The Secret Garden*; *Persuasion*. In addition, many of us have stories that we remember from childhood, stories that we read or that were read to us. Many of these we return to again and again, rereading them either to ourselves or to our families; and each time they offer us the same joy and inspiration. In the Barrs family we are constantly adding new stories to our repertoire. My most recent one is *Hannah Coulter*, a novel by Wendell Berry. It is not simply the imaginative appeal of such movies and books that captivates us; it is even more their moral insight. Perhaps the appeal of good stories is their perfect union of imaginative and moral power that delights and inspires.

A Christmas Story: The Law Fulfilled

The stories of Jesus reveal the beauty of the law and its deep demands on our lives. Indeed, Jesus makes it explicit that he did not come to set the law aside. In the Sermon on the Mount he makes this very point with great authority and passion: "Do not think that I have come to abolish the Law or the Prophets: I have not come to abolish them but to fulfill them. For truly, I say to you, until heaven and earth pass away, not an iota, not a dot, will pass from the Law until all is accomplished."[2]

This word of Jesus, that he came to fulfill the law, brings us to the most wonderful story of all, the story of Christmas. When we celebrate the birth of Jesus we are retelling the only human story of perfect obedience to the law. Think of the way Paul expresses this: "When the fullness of time had come, God sent forth his Son, born of woman, born under the law, to redeem those who were under the law, so that we might receive adoption as sons."[3] Why did Christ come into this world? Why was the eternal second person of the Trinity conceived in the womb of Mary, and why was he born as a human baby in a stable in Bethlehem just over two thousand years ago? To understand the answer to this question we need to return to the account of the creation of our first parents.

Eve and Adam were made to be like God, to reflect perfectly his kind, merciful, loving, just, faithful, and holy character. Yet they rebelled against God's creational purpose for their lives and turned to

---

[2] Matthew 5:17–18.
[3] Galatians 4:4–5.

a life of self-centered disobedience. Instead of following the creation mandate of the first great commandment, to love their Creator, they refused to love God with heart and soul and mind and strength. They turned away from this great love for God to an inordinate love of themselves. This wrought havoc in every aspect of their lives.

What are the consequences of this disobedience? We can summarize all the consequences of Adam and Eve's sin and refer to all of it as the judgment of God. This is easily said, but what does this judgment mean? How does God's judgment work itself out? We can try to capture it by speaking of the sevenfold effects of sin, or the seven-pointed curse.[4]

The Seven-Pointed Curse: A Story of Alienation

The first curse of sin is that *God is alienated from Adam and Eve, and from all of us.* As the righteous, perfect, holy judge of all reality, whose standard is moral perfection, he can have no dealings with sin or sinners. His face is turned away from us, as Isaiah expresses it in one passage,[5] so that he cannot hear us, for he can have fellowship only with what is good and perfect. This is true now and it is true for all eternity. That is the first and central impact of disobedience: God's wrath and anger is directed against Adam and Eve, against sin, against sinners.

We may not want to think in such a way, but this is clearly what Scripture teaches us in many places. Paul says that we are all "by nature children of wrath, like the rest of mankind."[6] This is the reality and the first consequence of turning from God's commandments. Some readers will object: "God hates sin, but loves sinners!" While this sounds like a more pleasant sentiment, we should remember that it is sinners who will face God's judgment, and not simply sin disembodied from the person who committed those sins. It is not a handful of particularly obnoxious sins but rather actual men and women who will "appear before the judgment seat of Christ, that each one may receive what is due him for the things done while in the body, whether good or bad."[7]

---

[4] This expression "the seven-pointed curse" is my adaptation of a phrase by Francis Schaeffer, who spoke of a four-pointed curse. See Schaeffer, *Genesis in Space and Time.*
[5] Isaiah 59:2.
[6] Ephesians 2:3; or see Romans 1:18–32; 3:19–20.
[7] 2 Corinthians 5:10, NIV.

The second curse of their disobedience is that *Adam and Eve are alienated from God, and so are we all.* In Genesis 3, we read of Adam and Eve trying to hide from God because they no longer love him, because they have disobeyed him, because they have ceased to trust him, because they now doubt him, because they no longer seek the enjoyment of his company, and because they are now afraid of him. So they turn away from him. They become, and we all become, enemies of God, hoping and trying to hide from him our sin and our rebellion. We find ourselves longing to honor ourselves rather than honor our Creator, for the very heart or essence of sin is pride.

At the center of the Genesis account of the fall is the problem of arrogance with which we all wrestle: we seek to put ourselves in the place of God. We all find this tension in our hearts every day of our lives. This is still true of us Christians who have bowed before God and who have prayed repeatedly that he would humble us before the infinite power and glory of his divine majesty. We are constantly eager to put our hope and confidence in ourselves rather than in God.

The third curse of sin is that *Adam and Eve are alienated from themselves*; and so are we all, each one from himself or herself. What is meant by this self-alienation? As we look within ourselves, we are aware of an internal disorder. We experience shame and even self-loathing because of who we are. We have all woken up in the middle of the night and reflected on things we have done, said, or thought, and even though there is no one else to see us (apart from the Lord), we have been overwhelmed utterly with a sense of shame. We find ourselves blushing and sweating in the dark.

Eve and Adam experience this sense of shame before God, before each other, and even in their own hearts. Like them, we experience disgust with ourselves. Paul said of himself many years after he had become a believer and an apostle of Christ, "Wretched man that I am! Who will deliver me from this body of death?"[8]

Such self-loathing sometimes expressed itself in extreme ways. It is present in teenage girls (and occasionally boys) wrestling with problems like anorexia or bulimia, or various forms of self-mutilation. But even short of such extremes of self-hatred, wherever we are honest

---

[8] Romans 7:24.

about ourselves, we find that we all struggle with a sense of dissatisfaction in our life, in our character, our choices, and our behavior. I find a profound lack of happiness when I face the question, who am I, deep within myself? There is no longer any perfect happiness for us in knowing ourselves and in having to live with ourselves, either because we do indeed know ourselves too well, or because we are trying desperately to avoid knowing ourselves.

The fourth curse of sin is that *Adam and Eve are alienated from each other*. In this aspect of the curse we observe the beginning of alienation or the breakdown of relationships across all human contacts. Each one of us wrestles with this alienation from every other person we meet, and even from those we love the most dearly or to whom we are bound the most closely. In the very next chapter of Genesis we find Cain killing his brother, Abel, because he is jealous and angry. In the account of the curse on Adam and Eve we see described for us how this disintegration affects even those relationships most treasured by us, such as the bond of marriage, this most precious relationship of all, where two become one. God spells out for Adam and for Eve the particular effects of sin in the relationships between a man and a woman.

The impact of the curse on Adam is to "rule over" his wife, to turn his headship into domination. It is the temptation of every man to treat his wife, the one whom he should regard as his equal and partner, instead as "his woman," to use her like a servant, to regard her as an object for doing his bidding or for meeting his needs for sex, companionship, food, laundry, a comfortable home, or a trophy of pride before other men.

All of us have observed or practiced or suffered from this pattern of behavior. The desire to dominate is something against which all men have to wrestle. It is particularly acute in the relationship between a man and a woman, which is why Paul has to challenge husbands to "love your wives, and do not be harsh with them."[9] We also observe this desire to rule in all other relationships between men and those to whom they relate: between fathers and children, in sibling rivalry, in the workplace, at play, in the church. In fact, we have to state it as a

---

[9] Colossians 3:19.

general principle that wherever there are men, there will be this urge to be first and to dominate.

Of course it is possible to work against this and to put such sin to death and so experience a deep level of delight in one another, rather than indulge in constant competition and the need to be superior. But such joy in male relationships is not found without a profound commitment to work against these innate pressures, whether in the workplace, in school, or in the family. This is why the apostle Paul reminds fathers, "Do not provoke your children, lest they become discouraged."[10] Men have to resist this desire to rule over their children if they long to have a close and permanent relationship of love and friendship with them.

The impact of the curse on Eve in her relationship with Adam is expressed this way: "Your desire will be to your husband, and he shall rule over you." A woman's temptation is to long for a good relationship with a man so deeply that she may endure almost anything in order to gain it, even if it is to her own hurt. This inordinate desire seems to be what Genesis is describing. An extreme example of this is wife abuse, in which a wife will simply give in to her husband; will submit repeatedly, no matter how unreasonable and even absurd his demands; and will subject herself to verbal and even physical abuse. She endures all this in the desperate and thoroughly unlikely hope that forbearance and even greater submission will produce a fruitful change in the relationship. The movie *Sleeping with the Enemy* is a graphic picture of this destructive pattern.

Even in what should be the most fulfilling human relationship, sin brings alienation, tension, and trouble into every close encounter between men and women. And, of course, this alienation and breakdown apparent in marriage is present in every other human relationship. The rest of Scripture spells out for us innumerable examples of the way this disease of our sin corrupts every relationship we touch.

The fifth curse of sin is that *Adam and Eve are alienated from creation*, the creation they were made to rule. As with the other curses, this affects every one of us. Genesis spells out this loss of dominion by focusing on the difficulty of producing food from the ground. I earlier

---

[10] Colossians 3:21; see also Ephesians 6:4.

introduced my father-in-law, the farmer. He grew peaches, plums, nectarines, persimmons, grapes, kiwis, and other tree fruits all his life, and
like every other farmer in the world, he could testify as to the reality
of this curse. Farming is hard work, literally backbreaking work. The
farmer is constantly facing new difficulties, constantly having to try
to figure out how to get the ground, his crops, his machines, and his
body to accomplish what needs to be done, so that the ground might
bring forth a harvest, the bills might be paid, and food might be set
on the family table.

Whether in the area of farming or gardening, where we literally
produce food from the ground, or in any other area of work, we all
experience loss of dominion as we labor in the world in which God has
set us. Work in this fallen world is a joy, as we use body, mind, heart,
and imagination to do fulfilling tasks in seeking to exercise dominion;
but work also always has an element of trouble, sorrow, and pain in it.
We all experience a sense of frustration at not being able to accomplish
what we want to. Things seem to work against us. There is "a spanner
in the works" in every task we try to accomplish. All human beings are
faced every day with the impossibility of creating a utopia, for we are
confronted daily with our failure to exercise dominion, and also with
our abuse of dominion. Even driving through the traffic on our way
to work or school or play, we experience loss of dominion.

And, of course, we all abuse our dominion over creation, sometimes in very obvious personal ways, like littering the countryside or
neglecting a once well-tended garden or farm and letting it go to ruin.
Or we abuse dominion in more subtle ways, like overgrazing a pasture
so that the cattle on it not only eat the leaves of nourishing and beautiful plants such as wild clovers, but in their hunger also tear up all
good plants by their roots, leaving only noxious weeds like ragweed or
thistles. Or we may have what seems like an innocent idea and end up
unwittingly creating enormous environmental problems.

As a well-known example, at the end of the nineteenth century a
lover of Shakespeare's plays decided that it would be a wonderful plan
to bring several pairs of every kind of bird mentioned in Shakespeare's
plays into the United States. He carried out this plan, and today we
live with the consequences of untold millions of starlings and house

sparrows that cause great damage to crops and overwhelm native species of birds.

Or we may over-catch some kinds of fish and drive them to the edge of extinction, or pollute streams, ponds, rivers, lakes, and oceans so that vast areas of water become virtual deserts. Or we may tear down forests with no thought for the erosion of land and destruction of species in our drive for meeting obvious needs. We may even change the climate of our nation or the whole world by our lack of thought for the future of this earth and our failure to care for the generations yet unborn. We become a curse to the very earth that God gave us to tend as his tenants and stewards.

The sixth curse of sin is that *Adam and Eve are alienated from their own bodies.* Again, this alienation affects us all. There is a kind of disintegration between body and spirit. At the end, we experience this most terribly in death, when body and spirit are torn apart. God did not create us for this tearing apart; rather the Lord created us for a permanent union between body and spirit. However, the consequence of sin is physical death, as well as spiritual death.

We experience this disintegration all through our lives as we suffer sickness, pain, and aging. When I turned forty, someone said to me, "If you wake up on your fortieth birthday with no aches, you're in heaven already." We all are familiar with physical decline as we and our loved ones age. Sometimes this becomes particularly acute as when a person is diagnosed with Lou Gehrig's disease. A relative of mine died a few years ago of this terrible sickness after her body had become less and less responsive to her wishes as the years passed and the disease progressed. She became unable to speak, unable to swallow, unable to walk, unable to order her muscles to do the simplest task. We all are familiar with such tragedies, because this bodily brokenness, this physical mortality, is a universal human experience.

Eve, in particular, feels the effects of this in that most marvelous process, the bearing of children. Genesis 3 expresses this very clearly as one of the consequences of sin: the increased pain and trouble of childbearing. Giving birth to a child is still a wonderful gift from God, yet all women know what a struggle, a labor, childbirth literally is.

The seventh and final curse of sin is that *Adam and Eve have to live in an environment that itself is under judgment and experiences alienation.* The earth is cursed because it is their home, the place of their dominion. This earth is the setting in which we have to face the reality of our sin and its bitter fruits every day of our lives. God has not allowed us to live in a perfect world where we can hide ourselves from the reality of human sin or sin's consequences.

This earth is still very lovely—it still declares the glory of God— but it is "subjected to futility," as Paul expresses it in Romans 8. The earth resists our attempts at dominion. Nature itself is "red in tooth and claw," and, according to Paul, longs to be set free from its bondage to decay.[11] There is nothing that can be made completely whole here in our present lives, not even this beautiful earth on which we live. God has judged the earth as part of his judgment on our race. The Lord declares that the "earth he has given to the children of men."[12] Because it is our home, our world is subjected to the curse that we deserve. The earth has been given to us as our dwelling place and as the sphere of our rule; and so it has been subjected to vanity along with us.

These are the seven consequences of sin, and as a result of Eve and Adam's disobedience, we see breakdown and alienation coming into every aspect of our human existence. There is nothing that is untainted by our failure to obey the commandments of God, and in particular by our failure to worship God alone. Each one of us experiences all seven of these curses of sin every day of our lives. This is the reality we all inhabit in our present human existence in this world.

Another Story: One Perfect Life in Our Place

We all know the daily struggle of living in disobedience to the law. We do not love God with heart and soul and mind and strength, and we do not love our neighbors as ourselves. We experience the reality of that seven-pointed curse both because we are descendants of Adam and Eve and because we ourselves are sinners every day.

Each one of us was born under the law, obligated as humans to live in obedience to these commandments of God. Yet we do not obey

---

[11] Romans 8:20–23.
[12] Psalm 115:16.

them, and this is why stories of moral beauty both inspire and discourage us. We see the loveliness of the law and the loveliness of obedience. But, at the same time, we are also convicted of our own lack of loveliness.

However, there is one story that does not ever discourage us. That is the story of the incarnation. Jesus was also born under the law, obligated, by his being one of us, to live in obedience to these commandments of God. He has done so perfectly. From infancy until his death he loved God with his whole being. Every moment of his life he loved every neighbor as he loved himself. Each story we read in the Gospels tells of a life lived entirely without sin. Jesus declares about himself, "My food is to do the will of him who sent me and to accomplish his work."[13] He says of his daily life, "I do as the Father commanded me, so that the world may know that I love the Father."[14] "He who sent me is with me. He has not left me alone, for I always do the things that are pleasing to him."[15] "I have not spoken on my own authority, but the Father who sent me has given me a commandment—what to say and what to speak [or "what to say and how to say it"—NIV]. And I know that his commandment is eternal life. What I say, therefore, I say as the Father has told me."[16]

Try to imagine a life in which every thought, every word, every motive, every act, every facial expression and the emotion behind it is perfectly in obedience to the Father's command. Our lives are so very different from this. But this is the life that Jesus lived, the life he lived in our place. This is the life with which we are credited by our heavenly Father when we put our hope in Jesus. This is the life that does not discourage us or threaten us in any way, for his life has been accounted to us.

When I read the story of the life and words of Christ, I am reading my own story. It is the story of my life as the Father sees me, the story of my life as I am accepted in and clothed by the life of the beloved Son. This is what we celebrate at Christmas, and every other day of our

---

[13] John 4:34.
[14] John 14:31.
[15] John 8:29.
[16] John 12:49–50.

lives: Christ born under the law to redeem those under the law, so that we might be adopted as God's beloved children and heirs.

Questions for Personal Reflection and Group Discussion

1. What favorite stories of yours reveal the beauty of righteousness? Which stories of moral goodness do you delight in returning to again and again? (Think about stories in print or in film.)

2. What movies might you watch again this coming Christmas? What qualities of these films lead you to want to see them repeatedly?

3. What favorite books, either children's stories (as they are called) or adult stories, do you read many times? Again, what is it about them that brings you back to them so many times?

4. Try to put into your own words, relating to your own life, why stories of moral beauty, courage, and heroism can sometimes be discouraging.

5. Have you noticed before this how the story of Jesus, the most beautiful story of righteousness, is never discouraging to us? This will be true for us only if we understand appropriately why he came to live a perfect life. If we see Jesus simply as a moral example and not as the one who came to bear our sin and judgment, then even his story will become discouraging to us.

6. Have you thought of the story of Jesus's moral perfection as your story?

11

JESUS OVERCOMES THE
CURSE OF THE LAW

In our tenth chapter we thought about how each of us has favorite stories of human virtue, tales that we return to many times to relive our smiles and tears of joy. In the questions at the end of the chapter, I asked you to think about the films you watch repeatedly and the books you read over and again: stories that make your hearts glad with their accounts of faithfulness, integrity, generosity, kindness, love, and a life renewed by the goodness of God.

Toward the latter part of our last chapter I pointed out how, though we are all inspired by stories of the beauty of obedience to God's law, yet we are sometimes discouraged by these very same stories. The reason for this discouragement is that we all know in the depths of our hearts the daily reality of our disobedience to the law. We do not love God with heart and soul and mind and strength; and we do not love our neighbors as ourselves. In consequence, we experience every day what I called the seven-pointed curse.

Though we were all born under the law, obligated to obey all the commandments of God as summarized by the two great commandments, yet we do not live in full and cheerful obedience. We all experience the daily reality of the coldness, reluctance, and obduracy of our hearts, and sometimes our outright refusal to walk in the ways we know to be right or even our intentional and eager pursuit of ways we know to be wrong. Because of this, stories of moral beauty both inspire and discourage us.

THE ENCOURAGING WORD

Yet, we saw that there is one story that never discourages us—the story of Jesus. Like us, Jesus was born under the law, obligated by his humanity to live in obedience to all the commandments of God. And Jesus did this perfectly. Not even his enemies could find real fault with him. Every moment of every day of his life he loved God the Father with heart and soul and mind and strength. Every moment of every day he loved every human being around him as he loved himself. We saw how Jesus repeatedly claimed moral perfection about his daily life. He could make this claim with no fear of contradiction from Mary or Joseph, or from his brothers and sisters, or from his friends and neighbors, or from his disciples or even from his enemies. Of course, the Gospels tell us that some of those enemies tried to charge him with faults and crimes; but none of their charges held up to examination.

I asked us to try to imagine a life in which every thought, word, motive, act, facial expression, and emotion is perfectly in obedience to the Father's command. Our lives are far from this. But this is the life that Jesus lived from the moment of his birth when he took his first cry to bring air into his lungs until the moment that he drew his last breath when he died on the cross and commended his spirit to the Father.

Christians all over the world celebrate the coming of Christ at Christmas. But we also celebrate his coming every day of our lives, for we understand that his birth, life, and death here in our world are the most significant birth, life, and death in history.

THE "MOTHER PROMISE"

The Lord God first announces this coming of Christ into our world to Eve in the garden of Eden after she and Adam fall into sin.[1] God gives Eve the good news of the coming of a deliverer. This is the first promise of ultimate redemption that we find in the Scriptures. One of my colleagues, Michael Williams, calls this promise "the mother promise" for it is the promise to the first mother, or ancestor, of the Redeemer, and this promise is also the mother, or source, of all the other promises that will come. God declares that he will send One into the world who

---

[1] Genesis 3:15.

will overcome Satan and sin. This One to come will do this for Eve, for Adam, and for all of us who believe in him. However, this overcoming of Satan will be at great cost to the deliverer when he comes. The One descended from Eve will crush the Serpent's head, but he himself will be bruised, or crushed, in the process.

Why do Christians see this brief prophecy in Genesis 3 as such a wonderful promise? God is committing himself, through the coming Seed of Eve, to overcome the seven-pointed curse that is his judgment on our race for its rebellion and disobedience. God promises to heal the seven states of alienation described in our last chapter. This original promise, this mother of all promises, is repeated as the generations come, and with each repetition the outlines and details of this initial picture of redemption—this "protoevangelium," the first proclamation of the gospel—are filled in.

As the prophecies of the Messiah unfold, so we see in greater detail a portrait of his life and work. This unfolding portrait reveals that the Messiah's goal in coming into this world is the full restoration of all that was lost, the complete healing of every alienation that has come into our lives as a result of human sin, both of that original sin of Adam and Eve, and of our ongoing sin. In figure 2 I have given a list of texts to read during Advent, the days leading up to our celebration of Christ's birth each year. Each reading has been assigned a title that attempts to capture the central facet of the promise in the text.

Figure 2. Advent readings

Day	Text	Title
December 1	Genesis 3:1–20	Seed of Eve
December 2	Genesis 22:1–18	Only Beloved Son and Sacrifice
December 3	Genesis 48:15–16; 49:8–10	Lion of Judah
December 4	Numbers 23:18–24; 24:3–9, 15–19	Star of Jacob
December 5	Deuteronomy 18:14–22	Prophet like Moses
December 6	2 Samuel 7:1–17	Son of David

DAY	TEXT	TITLE
December 7	Psalm 2	Messiah: Son of God and King
December 8	Job 19:23–27; Psalm 16	Holy One and Resurrected Redeemer
December 9	Psalm 22	The One Forsaken by God
December 10	Psalm 72	Royal Son and Deliverer of the Afflicted
December 11	Psalm 110	Priest and Lord at God's Right Hand
December 12	Isaiah 7:14; 9:1–7	Immanuel, Mighty God, and Prince of Peace
December 13	Isaiah 11:1–10	Branch from Jesse's Roots
December 14	Isaiah 42:1–10	Covenant and Light of the Nations
December 15	Isaiah 49:1–7; 50:4–11	Servant of Kings, Sustainer of the Weary
December 16	Isaiah 52:13–53:12	Suffering Servant and Lamb of God
December 17	Jeremiah 23:1–6; 33:14–18	Righteous Branch
December 18	Ezekiel 34:1–31	The Good Shepherd
December 19	Daniel 7:9–14; Micah 5:2–5a	The Son of Man and Ruler from Bethlehem
December 20	Zechariah 9:9–10; 12:10–13:1	King on a Donkey and Pierced Firstborn
December 21	Malachi 3:1–4; 4:1–6	Covenant Messenger and Righteous Sun
December 22	Luke 1:5–38	Son of the Most High
December 23	Luke 1:39–80	The Tender Mercy of God
December 24	Matthew 1:18–25; John 1:1–14	Savior from Sin and Word Made Flesh
December 25	Matthew 2:1–12; Luke 2:1–20	The Birth of Jesus

FAR AS THE CURSE IS FOUND

Because we are rebels against God as those who disobey his law, we all live under the curse of the law expressed in the sevenfold alienations we studied in our last chapter. How does Christ overcome this sevenfold curse of the law?

First, *Jesus faced the wrath of his Father, the just anger of God, against our sin.* Jesus appeased this wrath and propitiated the universal Judge by bearing all of our sin, disobedience, and punishment himself. He was condemned for our failures to obey the law though he himself lived in perfect obedience to its every command. He was able to accomplish this amazing work because—though he is the eternal Son, the Word, the agent of creation and revelation, the second person of the triune God—he was also born of a woman, born under the law, that is, he was born as one of us, one truly human, and also one born as an Israelite.

Jesus was born as one committed to keeping God's law. This is true both because of his membership in the human race, a race that is called, by virtue of our being human, to live in obedience to our Creator; and also because of his birth as an Israelite, this people who bound themselves with solemn oaths to honor God's every word.[2] The people of Israel were a nation chosen by God and a nation that, therefore, had committed itself to keep covenant with God and to obey his commandments.

Jesus was the one who fulfilled the calling of Israel. He was the true Israel by his life of perfect fulfillment of all the requirements of the law. He was the representative of Israel and the human race. As one in whom the whole fullness of deity dwelt, and who also fully shared our human life, he lived a life of complete and glad obedience to all of God's commandments in your place and in my place. This descendant of Eve was crushed. He was put to death and bore God's just penalty for our disobedience and rebellion. In his perfect life and sacrificial death, he reconciled our heavenly Father to us and overcame that first and most terrible alienation between our Creator and us his creatures. My guilt and your guilt were assigned to him, so that he would bear their punishment; and his perfect obedience was assigned to you and

---

[2] See Deuteronomy 27 and 28 for the blessings and curses that Israel took upon itself in binding the nation and its generations to come to live in obedience to the Lord and his law.

to me so that when the Father looks at my life or your life, he sees us as those who live each day in glad righteousness. The Father sees our lives as the very life of Jesus recorded for us in the Gospels.

The life Jesus lived, he lived in our place. This is the life with which we are credited by our heavenly Father when we put our hope in Jesus. This is the life that does not discourage us or threaten us in any way, for his life has been accounted to us. As I wrote at the end of chapter 10, when I read the story of the life and words of Christ, I am reading my own story, the story of my life as the Father sees me, the story of my life as I am accepted in and clothed by the life of the beloved Son. This is what we celebrate at Christmas and every moment: Jesus Christ born under the law to redeem those under the law, so that we might be adopted as God's beloved children and heirs. Jesus kept the law for me and for you.

Second, *Jesus brought new life to each one of us so that we are no longer alienated from God.* He pours his love into our hearts so that we may freely and gladly love God. He frees each of us from our sins by his sacrificial death, so that not only the condemnation due to sin, but also the guilty conscience we all rightly have before God will be cleansed and given liberty.

This freedom of the conscience and the renewal of our inner being enable us to want to know and to love God. We can cry to him, "Daddy," "Father," "I love you." With confidence we can call God our Father because the Seed of Eve, a member of our own race, leads us into the presence of his Father and assures us that we are loved—loved even as he, the beloved Son, is loved. We can now have complete and unlimited access to the throne of God. This free entry into heaven's counsels is available when we come in the name of our representative, Jesus, for he is the one who shared our humanity, the one who shared our struggles, and also the one who resisted temptation and sin, even though it cost him his life. Though I have a guilty conscience because of my ongoing disobedience to the law, yet I can come to God as my beloved Father with a clear conscience because I am clothed in Jesus's full obedience to the law.

Third, *Jesus, in bearing our sin, in setting us free from sin's condemnation, and in renewing us, enables you and me to love ourselves.* I no longer need to feel worthless because I so often give in to my tempter, or to other weaknesses and passions, or to the pressures of those around me. I no longer need to feel overwhelmed with guilt and shame, for even if my heart condemns me, Jesus's love is greater than my heart.

I look inside myself and find that whenever I try to do right, there is a principle, a deep-seated law of my soul, that wants to do wrong and to resist what is good and true and beautiful. However, I can know now that this insistent sinner is part of the "old me," not the "new me" that belongs to God and longs to love God and walk in his ways. Of course, this "new me" is never perfectly realized in this life. However, there is within each one of us who belongs to Christ the glimmerings of a newness that he has created within by the power of his Spirit, a new me who loves the law of God and who sees the law as holy, good, and perfect.

So I am able to conclude with Paul, it is no longer I, no longer my true self, but rather it is the "old me," the sin that dwells within me, that has this ongoing commitment to evil.[3] The true me with a new name, the new me that Jesus is creating, will one day be the only me, and on that day I will obtain the glorious liberty of being a child of God, a sister or brother of Christ who will only desire what is good, whose longing will be to obey the law wholeheartedly and fully. But already, because I know my true identity, because I know who I am becoming, I can begin to love and to accept myself.

Fourth, *Jesus has died to reconcile us to each other and to restore all broken relationships in all of our lives.* My elder brother Jesus has died to reconcile me to other people, to overcome every barrier that exists between me and anyone else. He calls me to love my spouse as he has loved me; and he empowers me so that I am enabled to do this. He calls me to love my children (or my parents) and, in this love, to imitate my heavenly Father, the Father from whom every family in heaven and on earth derives its name.[4] He calls me to friendships that mirror the perfect love that Jesus showed to John, his beloved disciple, the disciple who dwelt in his heart just as Jesus lived in his Father's heart.[5] He calls me

---

[3] Romans 7:7–25.
[4] Ephesians 3:14–15.
[5] John 1:18; 13:23. Jesus, the beloved Son, dwelt in the bosom of the Father; John, the beloved disciple, dwelt in the bosom of Jesus.

to live in delighted obedience to the second great commandment and to love every neighbor as I love myself.

In every relationship I have he calls me to be a servant as he has served me, whether at home, at work, or in the wider society. He calls me to be reconciled across all barriers of gender, race, social status, or whatever other barrier there might be, for he is my peace who has made the two one and destroyed the barriers, the walls of hostility, between hostile individuals or hostile social groups, by his death on the cross.[6] This is one of the glorious mysteries of the good news that our representative died to bring us: the mystery of formerly hostile groups of people becoming united and loving each other.[7]

The greatest mystery of all is that we who were God's enemies now have the privilege of knowing the One who became man and who became sin for us so that we might be at peace with God. But this greatest mystery carries within it the additional mystery that through his love we might be able to love one another across every social barrier erected by sinful humanity. He longs to make the angels marvel by showing them that wherever his love enters human hearts, what new delight in one another and what self-giving there can be between those who were formerly alienated from each other.[8] As someone who belongs to Jesus I know that I am to be like my heavenly Father, and that, therefore, I am to love my enemies and do good to them, for they are also my neighbors, to whom I am obligated by the law of love.

Fifth, *Jesus restores our dominion over creation.* He first enables us to have dominion over ourselves and our sinful passions, and then calls us and enables us to begin to restore dominion over every aspect of our lives, for even the smallest part of our lives is his. As the Dutch Reformer Abraham Kuyper put it: "Oh, no single piece of our mental world is to be hermetically sealed off from the rest, and there is not a square inch in the whole domain of our human existence over which Christ, who is Sovereign over *all*, does not cry: 'Mine!'"[9]

---

[6] Ephesians 2:11–22.
[7] A mystery in Scripture is something that we could not know without God revealing it to us, something we could not experience without God's work, the resolution of problems that we could never resolve apart from God's marvelous intervention.
[8] Ephesians 3:1–10. In this passage Paul writes about the mystery of reconciliation between Gentiles and God, and between Jew and Gentile, along with the way the angels marvel at this wonderful reality.
[9] Abraham Kuyper, the inaugural address of the opening of the Free University of Amsterdam, October 20, 1880, quoted in *Abraham Kuyper: A Centennial Reader*, ed. James D. Bratt (Grand Rapids: Eerdmans, 1998), 488.

We begin to see this renewal of our dominion when we acknowledge Jesus Christ as Lord, as the one who has the right to rule us in all of life, and when, submitting to his authority and his law, we begin to seek to serve him in all we do. He longs for us to be his salt and light to bring new life to this world, to restrain its evil, to push back the darkness and to overcome the consequences of the fall. He wants our lives to be the firstfruits of the new creation, outposts of his kingdom, "pilot plants," as Francis Schaeffer used to say, of the new day that will come to the whole world when Christ descends from heaven to claim the kingdoms of this world as his own. He desires that we display to the world the beauty of glad obedience to the law.

Jesus also longs for us to begin to rule this earth wisely. He desires that we cease polluting it, that we stop bringing our fellow creatures to the brink of extinction, that we refrain from damaging the extraordinary resources with which he has filled this earth. Instead he asks of us that we see ourselves as his tenants, that we recognize that the earth belongs to the Lord, and not to us. He calls us to learn to be stewards who pass on our particular corner of the earth, and indeed the whole earth, to future generations in better shape than we ourselves inherited it.

Sixth, *Jesus promises us that the separation of body and spirit, the coming of death into human experience, will not be permanent.* Even now we begin to see the first glimpses of the healing of the separation between the body and the spirit that the curse has brought into our lives. Our mortality is most certainly ever with us, the corruptible nature of our flesh, for in this life the outer nature is wasting away. Yet one day we will be made completely new, and our bodies will be raised immortal and incorruptible.

However, even now, our bodies are the Lord's, and the Lord is for the body,[10] and so we take pleasure in the gifts of food and drink, sexuality and marriage, creation around us and the physical well-being of ourselves and of others. Think again of Eric Liddell saying, "God . . . made me fast. When I run I feel his pleasure."[11] In the years of Jesus's ministry on this earth, we see some promising signs of the kingdom

---

[10] 1 Corinthians 6:13.
[11] From the film *Chariots of Fire*, 1981.

to come and of the ultimate restoration of the body as he heals every kind of sickness and disease, as he casts out demons that bring suffering to those they possess, and as he even raises the dead. We too are to work at setting back the boundaries of the fall by honoring the healing arts and by welcoming into our homes those whose lives are troubled. Hospitals and hospitality, where we see comfort, care, and healing for the whole person, body and spirit, have been two of the marks of the church of Jesus Christ from the earliest centuries.

Jesus invites us to sit and eat at his table now, in this present age, as he calls us to intimate fellowship with him and as we partake of the bread and wine that represent to us his body and blood offered up for us, that proclaim his death and victory to us, and that nourish us spiritually with his life. He also invites us to sit at his table and to be served by him at the consummation of his kingdom at the wedding feast he is preparing for us all.[12]

He calls us, in turn, to welcome friends, neighbors, and strangers to our tables so that they may share in our enjoyment of his good gifts to us. This is the central meaning of all our exercise of hospitality: that is, celebrating the hospitality of Christ so liberally shown to us, and inviting others in need to enjoy with us the firstfruits of that hospitality that we will enjoy forever.

In addition to delight in the renewal of the gifts of the physical creation, we may even see from time to time—like "arrows of glory from heaven" (Michael Green's phrase)—the miraculous healing of someone suffering with severe illness. There are, of course, many examples of such healings in the ministry of Jesus, and there are a considerable number in the accounts of the ministry of the apostles. We also find a few cases of such miraculous healing at other moments of history scattered throughout the Old Testament record. Such signs of the coming kingdom can be found in clusters during times of climactic events in the unfolding of God's reign of redemption.

In the New Testament the apostle James commands us to pray for those who are sick, to anoint them with oil, and to lay hands on them.[13] Believers have been assured all through the twenty centuries of the

[12] See Luke 12:37; Revelation 21:9.
[13] James 5:13–16.

history of the church that God does, from time to time, intervene to bring healing to his people. However, in even the most dramatic cases, we know that the healed person will eventually die, like everyone else, and wait in paradise for the final resurrection of the body. This was true for Lazarus, who was commanded by Jesus to come out of his grave and was raised up from the state of death. But Lazarus had to die again. Only at the return of Christ will the tearing apart of body and soul be completely overcome.

Seventh, *Jesus promises us that the judgment on this earth will one day be removed*. At the present time, we await with eager anticipation the lifting of the curse from creation. We may know with confidence that there will one day be a renewed earth with no more thorns and thistles to infest the ground, no more violence of any kind. There will be a peaceable kingdom, in which even the wolf will lie down with the lamb, and the little child will be able to play with snakes.[14] A time is coming when there will be nothing to bring harm or hurt in this world. When Jesus comes, he will bring to an end, once and for all, the cursed way in which we have abused our dominion of this earth. One day there will be, as Jesus declares, the regeneration of all things, for the earth itself will be made new.[15] Every one of the seven points of the curse will be finally and fully overcome.

Already, even now while we live in this "valley of tears," we know that God loves us with a perfect love through his Son, our Mediator and advocate. The first of our alienations is fully resolved: God's love for us is complete. He could not love us any more fully than he already does. In giving Christ for us he has given us the greatest gift imaginable. That "inestimable gift" will one day bring about Christ's return in glory and the full establishment of his kingdom.

We know that we have to wait until that "last day" of this age for the resurrection of our bodies, the renewal of the earth, and the utter removal of the seventh point of the curse. But what of the other five alienations? What can we expect now, in this life?

Francis Schaeffer used to say that there should be substantial healing in the life of the Christian—not complete, not perfect, but sub-

---

[14] Isaiah 11:1–9.
[15] 2 Peter 3:13; Revelation 21:1–5.

stantial. In each of the other five areas of the curse we should begin to see the firstfruits of the victory of Christ: a growing confidence in our being loved by God and a growth in loving him; a growing acceptance of ourselves and a delight in the renewing work of his Spirit within us; a readiness to love one another more fully as the days go by and to extend that love to more and more people and so to break down one barrier after another; an increasing commitment to offer our lives in every area to the lordship of Christ; a greater delight in the creation and a growing commitment to steward it well; a steady confidence that though our bodies will decay, yet he will not leave us unclothed, but will swallow up our mortality with life; and with this a growing delight in the good gifts of God that we are to share with others in anticipation of the glory that will one day be ours.

We are to see God's law as setting out for us both directions and boundaries in these five areas of our lives. Even a little advance in these five areas will indeed bring substantial healing in this life. This all-pervasive salvation is what that first promise of Christ's coming opens up to us, a window into the inheritance and the joy prepared for us by our heavenly Father and won for us by Jesus, the second Adam. In this life, as we commit ourselves to put our hope in Jesus and to obey his commandments because we love him, the Lord promises us:

> The path of the righteous is like the light of the dawn,
>   which shines brighter and brighter until full day.[16]

Questions for Personal Reflection and Group Discussion

1. Have you been accustomed to thinking about the work of Christ in such a comprehensive manner, as affecting every aspect of the brokenness of our life in this world? If this chapter has given you a new and deeper understanding of why Jesus came, what facets of his work are particularly interesting to you?

2. Do you struggle with the teaching that as the central meaning of his death, Christ had to propitiate the wrath of God against us and against our sin? Why do many people, including Christians, find this such a difficult idea?

3. As you reflect on Christ's life of obedience imputed to you, which parts of his obedience in your place are most precious to you? To put this question

---

[16] Proverbs 4:18.

another way, as you read the Gospels, what aspects of Jesus's perfect obedience do you delight in most?

4. Thinking about Christ's renewing us in love for God, the second aspect of his overcoming the curse, where do you find this most encouraging and most challenging?

5. Do you find it always easy to love yourself, the third part of the curse that is overcome by Christ? If you find a proper self-love difficult, why is that?

6. Looking at your own life, where do you begin to see a fuller reality of greater dominion over part of your life (the fifth area of Christ's overcoming the curse)? To put this question another way: where do you begin to see victory over areas of personal sin?

7. Where do you long for "substantial healing" to be a greater reality in your life?

8. Are there ways in which you are attempting to exercise stewardship over this earth more wisely?

9. What excites you most about the prospect of every aspect of the curse being overcome when Jesus returns in glory to reign on this earth?

12

How Substantial Is the Healing We Can Expect?

In our eleventh chapter we reflected on the way Jesus took upon himself the curse of the law as he died on the cross, bearing our failures, our shame, our guilt, and our punishment. We saw how Jesus overcame by his death all seven of the areas of the curse. We rejoiced in the well-nigh incredible truth that the first aspect of the curse, God's alienation from us, is already completely set aside by the work of Jesus.[1] The Father now loves us fully: from his perspective there is no barrier of sin at all between him and us. He sees us as perfect through the death of Jesus in our place and through our being clothed with the perfect life of Jesus. As he looks upon each of our lives, he sees, day by day, the full obedience to the law that characterized every moment of Jesus's life.

As we reflected on the seventh point of the curse, the frustration to which the creation has been subjected, I argued that we will not see this aspect of the curse set aside until Jesus comes. Only then will the earth be set free from its bondage to decay and the whole creation renewed. We have to wait for the fulfillment of the promise of the new heaven and the new earth. When the New Jerusalem comes down from heaven to this earth, then finally the curse on creation will be

---

[1]This truth is "incredible" in the sense that it seems to us too good to be true, and therefore we almost disbelieve for joy.

removed, and the kingdoms of this world will become the kingdom of the Lord and of his Christ, and he will reign here forever.

I used Francis Schaeffer's expression "substantial healing" to suggest that in the other five areas of the curse we begin to see some overcoming of the consequences of the fall as we look to Jesus in trust and hope, and as we commit ourselves to walking in the ways of God's law. These other five areas, the second through sixth points of the curse, were (2) the barrier between us and God; (3) the alienation between us and ourselves; (4) our broken relationships, the alienation between people; (5) the loss of dominion over our lives and over creation; and (6) the separation of body and spirit expressed most violently in death.

QUESTIONS ABOUT HEALING

I am sure that many of you reading chapter 11 had questions about this issue of substantial healing. For example: How much healing can we expect? If we see very little healing or perhaps even no healing in one of these areas, should we doubt our salvation? Does this absence of healing indicate that we are not true believers and are in danger of being cast out of God's presence and love? As a pastor and teacher, I have been asked such questions repeatedly throughout my years of ministry. I know that many believers struggle with such questions, and I sympathize deeply with those who ask them. What can we say regarding such questions to encourage our hearts?

The Bible takes very seriously the brokenness of our present experience. In fact, it is appropriate to say that only biblical Christianity has any kind of adequate account of the reality of suffering in human life. Only Christianity declares that sin, death, and all the tragedies of our life since the fall are abnormal. Every other religious and secular worldview has to regard sin, death, and tragedy as normal parts of human life on this earth. Other religious and secular worldviews declare that just as day and night, light and darkness are a normal and necessary part of ordinary life, so also good and evil, kindness and cruelty, justice and injustice, joy and sorrow, celebration and grief, blessing and tragedy, life and death are all normal and necessary parts of human existence. Scripture denies this with great passion and insists that all the sadness of life is a result of our rebellion against God and that all sadness and tragedy are therefore abnormal. This is why we rejoice in the advent of Jesus, both his first and second comings, because through him all these problems will be overcome, and even death will be swallowed up in victory.

The Scripture does teach that there is the possibility of the first-fruits of renewal (Schaeffer's "substantial healing") in our present life. These firstfruits, or foretastes of the coming kingdom, are possible because of what Jesus has already done in his life, death, and resurrection. However, God's Word is also very clear that there are many sorrows for which the tears will not be wiped away in this life. Think of Hebrews 11: some by faith saw all kinds of extraordinary blessings, answers to prayer, dramatic victories, and even resurrection from the dead; others by faith experienced grief, tragedy, sorrows of every kind, and death in all sorts of miserable ways. Yet all are commended for their faith. Edith Schaeffer, in her wonderful book *Affliction*, uses the image of God's portrait gallery to capture this diversity of experience of the people of God in this world. Biblical passages like Hebrews 11 warn us that it is of the utmost importance that we do not judge either one another or ourselves by the extent of healing or renewal that we or our fellow believers experience.

AWAITING HEALING IN FIVE AREAS

We can look at this variation of experience in each of the five areas of the curse mentioned above. But first we need to understand very clearly that in the second through sixth points of the curse, just as in the seventh, we will not see the kingdom of God in its fullness until we see Christ face to face, that is, until our bodies are raised up and the earth is made new.

For example, consider the overcoming of the second point of the curse, the removal of the barrier between us and the Lord. We are told in Scripture that God's perfect love casts out our fear and that we can be confident of our salvation, we can be sure of the love of God for us in Jesus. Yet, there is nobody who has complete assurance of faith in the present life, not one Christian who is at every moment utterly confident of the love of God and absolutely sure always of his or her ultimate salvation. Given the reality of ongoing sin in our lives, given the ever-present nature of our psychological frailty, given the veil that exists between us and the Lord until death tears that veil down, no one experiences total and constant assurance. The Lord's love for us is most certainly perfect, but our trust in that love is never perfect.

So all Christians have imperfect faith. In addition, there is a great variation in the levels of confidence in the Lord and in our sense of assurance. This variation is caused by many factors. Take, for example, the matter of sound instruction. Calvin, in his biblical wisdom and in the beauty of his language, taught that Christ is the "mirror of salvation." His point was that it is only by looking at Christ, at Christ's love, at Christ's perfect life, and at Christ's death and resurrection that we can gain any assurance at all. If we turn to our own hearts and our own inner experience, then we will always be doubtful of whether we are loved by God and whether we can see the marks of a genuinely saved person inside us.

Many denominations, including those in the Reformed tradition, have denied Calvin's perspective and instead taken the view that only internal experience can grant the believer assurance. There are Scottish Presbyterian churches, Dutch Reformed churches, and Reformed Baptist churches that teach this with deep conviction. The consequence of this unhappy teaching is utterly predictable. No matter how strong a person's inner emotional stability is in other areas of life, there is almost no one in many of these churches who has any assurance at all that they will be saved. Hardly anyone in many such churches takes the Lord's Supper. Indeed, to be admitted to the Lord's Table, members have to prove to their elders, to their consistory, or to their deacons' board that they have the internal marks of an elect and regenerate person: that they have had particular experiences that they can recount in terms of the day, hour, and minute, and the details of the visitation, in which the Holy Spirit witnessed to their spirit that they were children of God, loved by him, elected by him, justified by him, and in the process of being sanctified by him.

I have personally known people of great godliness who never in their lives took the Lord's Supper and who doubted their salvation right up until they died. I have heard of funerals in churches where the pastors refused to give any comfort to the grieving families, even when the deceased were Christians who led lives of outstanding moral beauty. At one funeral the pastor declared to the family and friends of such a man that we can never know if a professing Christian is truly saved. I know of churches that will not even put a sign outside showing that a church meets in the building on Sundays, lest an unelect person wander into the service. This is all a tragedy, and it illustrates in a very profound way Jesus's words about the truth setting us free—and, we may add, the lack of truth binding us in chains.

There are also, of course, many churches that focus solely on the free-will side of the sovereignty/responsibility spectrum, and that, therefore, see assurance entirely in terms of gazing into one's own heart and seeing one's own spiritual experiences as the measure of one's personal security. Some such churches demand particular experiences of the Spirit, like speaking in tongues or some other "second blessing," as an indication that the person is truly saved. All such problematic teaching produces lack of assurance in the hearts and minds of believers.

In addition to the problem of wrong teaching, there is also our personal brokenness. All of us have areas of frailty because we are fallen persons. Some of this comes to us simply by virtue of our descent, initially from Adam and Eve; some of this comes from the particular heredity that each of us has, the family into which we were born. Because we are children of Adam and Eve, all of us are born with bodies that are imperfect, mortal, and corruptible; many of us are born with hereditary diseases, and all of us are born with physical weaknesses and limitations that vary from family to family.

In the same way all of us are born with psychological and emotional damage because of our descent from Adam and Eve. It is impossible to be psychologically and emotionally whole when one is born in sin. Indeed we may say that it would be wrong for any of us to feel emotionally whole, simply because we are not whole in any way. We are all born with particular areas of hereditary psychological weakness that vary from family to family; and some of us are born with very severe emotional damage. In addition, not one of us is raised in an ideal home, because even the best of parents are sinners who sometimes fail to love their children perfectly and to affirm them appropriately.

I remember one of my own sons saying to me, when he was about fourteen, "Dad, what do you have against me?" His words almost broke my heart. I thought, "How did I ever manage to communicate such an awful notion to him?" I said to him, "My dear son, I have nothing against you. Please forgive me for communicating such an abominable idea to you."

Even when we do a reasonably good job at this task of loving and affirming our children, even then, others can come in and wreak terrible damage in a child's life. When one of our sons was seven, he suddenly became very down on himself. He seemed very sad, almost depressed, much of the time. He started spanking himself. Finally we managed to get out of him what was going on at school, and at such a young age he found it difficult to explain the problem. His second-grade teacher had taken an intense dislike to him and had said many completely inappropriate things to him, both privately and in front of the whole class. Even after I had gone to talk to the teacher to put a stop to such outrageous practice in her classroom, and even with my wife and I giving him lots of extra assurance of our love and of his worth, the teacher's few weeks of damage undermined his self-confidence for many, many years.

Some of us are born with very severe emotional frailties; others of us have backgrounds from homes that would tear to pieces the strongest psychological constitution; others of us have had experiences of such tragedy and such pain that self-confidence and assurance are impossible in this life. Some examples will help us to think about this.

William Cowper was a famous poet and hymn writer (incidentally, one of the favorite authors of Jane Austen). Almost all Christians in the English-speaking world will have sung hymns he wrote: *There Is a Fountain Filled with Blood*; *God Moves in a Mysterious Way*; *The Spirit Breathes upon the Word*; *Jesus, Where-e'er Your People Meet*; *O for a Closer Walk with God*; *Sometimes a Light Surprises the Christian While He Sings*. Some of these hymns are filled with expressions of confidence in the love of God and in the atoning work of Christ. Yet if you have read anything at all about Cowper's personal life, you will know that he suffered from dreadful depression. Cowper's depression plunged him into a state of terror that he was irretrievably lost. He was desperately sure that he was heading to hell. You may also know that John Newton, the ex-slave trader, pastor, and hymn writer, cared for Cowper for many years in his home. From time to time Cowper's illness was so severe that he would be taken into the main hospital in London for people suffering from serious psychological troubles. This was Bethlehem Hospital, a place of such misery and chaos that its abbreviated name "Bedlam" has become a word signifying a state of total breakdown of order and sanity. Despite all Cowper's anxiety and fear, who would doubt that he is with the Lord with all his troubles removed and his spirit made whole and perfect?

A friend I have known for many decades, a young woman who became a Christian one day in our home, has perhaps the worst case of schizophrenia that I have ever encountered. She spent years in a psychiatric hospital before she came to stay with us, and there is little doubt that she will be on very heavy doses of antidepressant medications her whole life to try to control her moods and her behavior. On the one hand, she has one of the most brilliant and rapidly working minds of anyone I have ever met; on the other hand, she is like a completely unstable two-year-old emotionally. She will never hold down a job. She got married but is incapable of sustaining the constant commitment and faithful other-centeredness that is essential to marriage. She has children but cannot care for them. Her mind and her emotions are like a woodland in storm, constantly being tossed this way and that and thrashing about without apparent purpose or meaning. I believe that she is a miracle; without her having become a Christian, she would be hospitalized all her life, and her days would be utterly chaotic with internal anguish and confusion. Yet, for even the semblance of normality, she will have to wait until she is with the Lord.

I think, too, of a dear friend who was a brother in the Lord and in ministry. He was diagnosed with early-onset Alzheimer's and, as is usual in such cases, the disease progressed very rapidly. Until then he had been fit and healthy, leading an active life physically and in every other way. But within two or three years of the onset of his illness he did not know his children, relatives, or friends. He would quickly get distressed when people he had once loved came to visit. He could cope only briefly with extra people in his home and with the added input of sights, sounds, and emotional pressures. Soon he reached the point where he would wake at all hours; he would want to get up and go out in the middle of the night. He had lost all sense of direction and location and would no longer listen to reason. Then he became physically aggressive and ceased to recognize anyone at all. If you have seen the movie *Iris*, you will understand a little of what both he and his family endured.

Consider, also, the biblical example of Tamar, the daughter of David, who was violently raped by her half-brother Amnon. Her life was left desolate. I will never forget the first time I gave a public lecture about her life and about the terrible rape that destroyed any possibility of a normal existence for her. After the lecture two women in their late seventies and early eighties were able to speak about their experience of having been raped as teenagers. They were bringing this into the open for the first time in their lives, and so for the first time were able to gain a tiny bit of healing. But for such sorrows there is no wiping away of the tears until we meet Jesus in the kingdom to come. That is why Revelation says:

> Then I saw a new heaven and a new earth, for the first heaven and the first earth had passed away, and the sea was no more. And I saw the holy city, new Jerusalem, coming down out of heaven from God, prepared as a bride adorned for her husband. And I heard a loud voice from the throne saying, "Behold, the dwelling place of God is with man. He will dwell with them, and they will be his people, and God himself will be with them as their God. He will wipe away every tear from their eyes, and death shall be no more, neither shall there be mourning, nor crying nor pain anymore, for the former things have passed away."
>
> And he who was seated on the throne said, "Behold, I am making all things new." Also he said, "Write this down, for these words are trustworthy and true."[2]

Whether it is our psychological and emotional healing or our physical healing we all know that any firstfruits are only an infinitesimally small part of the glory that shall be ours in the life to come. We

---

[2] Revelation 21:1–5.

all know that for many believing family members or acquaintances, there is no healing in the physical area in this life, but only the longing for the new body.

A member of the church where I was a pastor died as a result of brittle bone disease. When this hereditary disease progresses, one cannot stand without one's legs and feet shattering, and coughing will break one's ribs. This member of our church died of pneumonia in terrible agony. During the last couple of weeks of his life I went to visit him in the hospital several times so that we could plan his funeral service. He was desperate to be free of his wretched body and to be with the Lord, and he looked forward with passionate longing to the day when he would be raised up with a new, restored body, one with strong bones and complete health.

He wanted a funeral service that would be a celebration of going to be with the Lord, of the life to come, and of the resurrection. His funeral, in accord with his wishes, was more like a wedding ceremony. The church was filled with white flowers. The hymns he chose were the most joyful hymns he could discover. It was an amazing occasion of gladness in the wonder of Christ's promises of victory. But it was also a time of deep sorrow for his wife and children, who were now bereft of husband and father.

We all know people like this who have died, or who are dying of appalling diseases or of terrible injuries sustained through accidents. And we all have been in funeral services that have this excruciating mixture of joy and sorrow, of hope and pain, of promise of life and present reality of death.

What is true for some in the physical aspect of life is true for many others in the psychological and emotional aspects of life. And it is true for all of us with the fifth area of the curse, the restoration of dominion. We all struggle with having natures that are prone to sin. Paul expresses this battle in summary form: "For the desires of the flesh are against the Spirit, and the desires of the Spirit are against the flesh, for these are opposed to each other, to keep you from doing the things you want to do."[3] In Romans 7, Paul expands on this brief account of our losing battles against sin, and he sets out in painful

---

[3] Galatians 5:17.

detail the constant reality of our failure to do what we long to do. The inability to live righteously, the incapacity to obey the commandments that we love and that we long to obey—this is a daily reality for each one of us. The longer we are believers, the more acutely we feel this conflict, and the more sorrow our failures give us.

Consider the fourth area of the curse, the breakdown of relationships between us and others. We may see progress in this area, but we are all acutely aware of the ongoing problems we all experience. Our society is divided on Sunday mornings along racial lines. Discrimination around the globe is a constant part of human life in every nation. The healing that we see in this area of life is a wretchedly tiny answer to the vastness of the problem.

If we look at the abuse of dominion, we have to acknowledge that our generation has done the greatest damage to the earth of any generation in history. We may try to resist such knowledge, but it is indeed the truth.

WE SHALL SEE HIM

There are indeed many discouragements that confront us personally, nationally, and across the globe. However, we need to place our hopes where the Lord directs us. All of us are called to walk by faith rather than by sight, for as John says: "Beloved, we are God's children now, and what we will be has not yet appeared; but we know that when he appears we will be like him, because we shall see him as he is."[4] The apostle Paul addresses directly the problem of overexpectation of deliverance from troubles when he writes to the false teachers in Corinth who taught that there can be complete healing now:

> Already you have all you want! Already you have become rich! Without us you have become kings! And would that you did reign, so that we might share the rule with you! For I think that God has exhibited us apostles as last of all, like men sentenced to death, because we have become a spectacle to the world, to angels, and to men. We are fools for Christ's sake, but you are wise in Christ. We are weak, but you are strong. You are held in honor, but we in disrepute. To the present hour we hunger and thirst, we are poorly dressed and buffeted and homeless,

---

[4] 1 John 3:2.

and we labor, working with our own hands. When reviled, we bless; when persecuted, we endure; when slandered, we entreat. We have become, and are still, like the scum of the world, the refuse of all things.[5]

So, do not be discouraged when areas in your life are yet without healing. This is the common lot of all Christians in the present age. The sober truth is this: "Through many tribulations we must enter the kingdom of God."[6]

Our confidence is not to be in the beginnings of healing that we see here and there in our lives; nor in the advances we make in obedience to God's wonderful laws; nor in our loving the Lord more deeply day by day. Nor should our confidence be in answers to prayer for physical healing; nor in the realization of a society in which all barriers are torn down and in which we see God's kingdom coming; nor in advances we make in caring for this earth. Our hope is to be in Christ and in his ultimate victory. Paul writes these sober words:

> If in Christ we have hope in this life only, we are of all people most to be pitied.
>
> But in fact Christ has been raised from the dead, the firstfruits of those who have fallen asleep. For as by a man came death, by a man has come also the resurrection of the dead. For as in Adam all die, so also in Christ shall all be made alive. But each in his own order: Christ the firstfruits, then at his coming those who belong to Christ. Then comes the end, when he delivers the kingdom to God the Father after destroying every rule and every authority and power. For he must reign until he has put all his enemies under his feet. The last enemy to be destroyed is death.[7]

Questions for Personal Reflection and Group Discussion

1. Make a list of books or movies that reveal substantial healing. Is this the same list that you made earlier when you wrote down the books and movies that you read or watch repeatedly?

2. Have you come across the kind of teaching that demands intense inner experience as the test of salvation? Such teaching exists in many different kinds

---

[5] 1 Corinthians 4:8–13.
[6] Acts 14:22. This is the message that Paul felt constrained to teach the recent converts when he returned to the churches he had newly planted.
[7] 1 Corinthians 15:19–26.

of church settings, ranging from those that are ultra-Reformed to those that stress only human freedom.

3. In what areas in your life do you long for healing and yet very often feel that there is no progress at all? All of us have such areas in our lives, though they are not easy for us to talk about. (This is obviously a very personal question and needs to be handled very carefully and gently if you are in a group setting.)

4. What are sources of encouragement in your life? These could be areas of advance in your own inner life or could be things you find encouraging as you seek to persevere in faith and in serving the Lord: Scripture, the sacraments, other believers, music, the beauty of the commandments. Many things could be mentioned here, for God has an infinite variety of means to serve us; and the ways he helps us differ for each person because he knows us intimately and sees our different areas of frailty and our particular needs.

5. As you look forward to the new heaven and the new earth, what are you most eager to do that you do not have time or the ability or opportunity to do in the present life? This could include victory over sin or sorrow; or it could be aspects of life you long to enjoy but, for whatever reason, cannot do now.

13

How Have Different Traditions Understood the Law?

In chapter 12 we asked how substantial is the healing that we can expect as those who have come to faith in Jesus. Scripture leads us to the hope that we will all see growth and healing in some aspects of our lives, and that we will experience some setting back of the consequences of the curse of the law. We must also acknowledge that there are wounds in many areas of life that receive either no healing or only slight healing in this present age. Just as some believers have to live their whole lives with inherited diseases that waste their body, so other believers may have to endure sicknesses that waste the mind and destroy the personality, as we saw in several examples.

Our hope is in the Lord, the one who fulfills the law and lifts the effects of the curse we suffer now. He will complete the work he has begun, overcoming the curse that manifests itself in our struggle to gain a sense of God's love and presence, in the breakdown of our inner well-being, in the dissolution of even our most precious human relationships, in the loss of proper dominion over our lives and over our world, and in our limited physical renewal.

In this chapter we turn from our discussion of the curse of the law to consider some of the different ways Christians have thought about the law. This is important for several reasons. First, all of us will have heard teaching that makes us wonder just how we ought to think about the law. Second, a number of very common teachings seriously undermine confidence in the law, some even insisting that the law no longer has a place in the Christian life. As I write this chapter my wife has just heard from a relative who is listening to a series of sermons in which the teacher declared that Christians are completely freed from the law. Third, reflecting on these differing views of the law should help us to think more clearly about what God's Word has to say about the blessings of the law.

INADEQUATE VIEWS OF THE LAW

To my sorrow and to the detriment of God's people, there has been within the church for many centuries an inadequate understanding of God's law. In Lutheranism the primary place of the law is to bring conviction of sin; and some in the Reformed churches are deeply influenced by this view and seem to forget that the primary use of the law is to instruct us in the character of God and in his design for our lives as his creatures and beloved children. Though John Wesley himself had a high view of the necessity of teaching obedience to the law, in parts of the holiness tradition within the wider Wesleyan movement, including the tradition in which the Pentecostal churches arose, emphasis on active obedience to the law is only slight, and this neglect has become deeply influential right across the evangelical movement.

As an example, think of the influence of Watchman Nee, who stood in this holiness tradition, with his passionate rejection of any emphasis on active obedience or on any effort of one's will to do God's law.[1] For Nee this is the mistake of carnal Christians, those he saw described by Paul in Romans 7. Nee insisted that we are delivered utterly from the law. And this teaching is present, though less strongly, in many other popular writers on the Christian life.

We will look at some of the more common problematic views in a bit more detail.

---

[1] See, for example, Watchman Nee, *The Spiritual Man* (New York: Christian Fellowship, 1968).

Lutheran Views of the Law

The Formula of Concord, the creedal statement of Lutheranism, distinguished three uses, or purposes, in the law according to Article 6:

> The Law was given to men for three reasons: . . . that thereby outward discipline might be maintained against wild, disobedient men [and that wild and intractable men might be restrained, as though by certain bars]; . . . that men thereby may be led to the knowledge of their sins; . . . that after they are regenerate . . . they might . . . have a fixed rule according to which they are to regulate and direct their whole life.

While each of these statements is accurate, we should notice how the focus is on the restraining aspect of the law for unbelievers and on the convicting purpose of the law for believers. There is a formal acknowledgment that the law has the third purpose of regulating and directing the life of the regenerate; but in practice many Lutheran churches place little emphasis on this. Friends of mine who have grown up in Lutheran homes and churches acknowledge this readily. Martin Luther himself was suspicious of the very positive emphasis on the law found in the letter of James. The apostle James, in his first chapter, writes the following wonderful words:

> But be doers of the word, and not hearers only, deceiving yourselves. For if anyone is a hearer of the word and not a doer, he is like a man who looks intently at his natural face in a mirror. For he looks at himself and goes away and at once forgets what he looks like. But the one who looks into the perfect law, the law of liberty, and perseveres, being no hearer who forgets but a doer who acts, he will be blessed in his doing.[2]

Luther called James an "Epistle of straw" because of James's passionate teaching on the necessity of submission to the law as a positive good in the life of the believer and as an essential fruit of saving faith. The woodcut *Law and Grace* (fig. 3), by a close friend of Luther's, Lucas Cranach the Elder, captures the problem with its depiction of law and grace.

---

[2] James 1:22–25.

Figure 3. *Law and Grace*, by Lucas Cranach the Elder

In the first panel, a minister is proclaiming the law, represented by the tablets of the Ten Commandments, and a man is running from the proclamation of the law. In the background we see the fall of Adam and Eve into disobedience, and also the holy God on his throne of judgment. The Devil and a skeleton holding the spear (and representing death) are chasing the one who hears the law into the mouth of hell. The message is very clear: the law leads only to conviction and to judgment.

In the second panel, the man is happily hearing the preaching of the gospel. The preacher is pointing to Christ on the cross, and the dove, representing the Holy Spirit, is directing his blessing and the blood from Christ's side onto the man. The skeleton of death and the Devil are lying on the ground, defeated by Christ. In the background we see Old Testament saints outside the tabernacle looking at the serpent on the bronze pole, an Old Testament picture of the coming work of Christ. Again, the message is clear: grace comes from Jesus Christ.

This second panel is, of course, a fine representation of the grace of Christ and of the power of the cross. However, there is a problem with this wonderful woodcut: the law is seen only in a negative way as an enemy that convicts people of sin and leads them to judgment. We will return to this problem later. For the present I will simply point out that even this work of conviction of sin by the law is the work of a friend, for it is conviction of sin that leads me to the knowledge of my need of a Savior.

Dispensational Approaches to the Law

In dispensational circles law is necessarily played down because of a strong discontinuity between the old and new covenants in dispensational teaching. Traditionally, dispensationalists have seen the law of Moses as having been given to Israel as the means by which the people were to establish and maintain a relationship with God. It is only with the death and resurrection of Christ that salvation by grace through faith in Christ is revealed. Dispensationalists also see God dealing with the church and the people of Israel in two radically different ways, for Israel and the church are understood to be two separate peoples of God. Many Christians in the United States have been exposed to dispensationalist teaching through the very popular writings on the end times by people like Hal Lindsay, author of *The Late Great Planet Earth*, or the Left Behind series, produced by Tim LaHaye and Jerry Jenkins. Christians often do not realize that the prophetic views of such men are bound up with other teachings about Scripture, about the law, and about Israel—teachings that contain serious errors.

By far the most extreme example of dispensationalist teaching I have ever heard was the opinion that Jesus was hard, cold, and unmerciful in comparison with Paul, for Jesus's teaching still comes as part of the old covenant of salvation through obedience to the demands of the law. Extreme views such as this have been moderated as traditionally dispensational seminaries and Bible colleges have moved toward a view of greater unity between the Testaments. Today, many such educational institutions are teaching a view very similar to a Reformed understanding of the law.

However, despite these changes, many churches and many believers remain steeped in the older views. So, what is the fundamental characteristic of traditional dispensationalism in its views of the law? In the words of John Nelson Darby (1800–1882): "Even this (law qualified with mercy), so far from being the gospel, is what the apostle calls the ministration of death and condemnation. Then, in contrast with this, he speaks of the gospel—of Christ's work—as the ministration of the Spirit, and of righteousness." Darby adds, "There is no mercy, or salvation, or redemption in the law; it is a ministration of death and condemnation."[3]

Darby was the founder of the Brethren churches and one of the creators of the central ideas in dispensationalist teaching. In context, he is commenting on Moses's being merciful to the people of Israel and Moses's speaking of God's forgiving Israel, though he distinguishes this forgiveness from the forgivness the Christian receives. "There is no mercy, or salvation, or redemption in the law."

Most Christians today who have been influenced by Darby's views have learned them through the notes in a Scofield Bible, with its fundamentally negative view of the law. Cyrus I. Scofield (1843–1921) was greatly shaped in his thinking by the teaching of Darby and became, via the many Bibles bearing his name, the most influential exponent internationally of dispensationalist teaching. He wrote:

> The most obvious and striking division of the Word of truth is that between law and grace. . . . Scripture never, in any dispensation, mingles these two principles. Law always has a place and work distinct and wholly diverse from that of grace.
>
> Everywhere the Scriptures present law and grace in sharply contrasted spheres.[4]

In the Scofield Reference Bible the biblical text and the commentary appear on the same page. This arrangement, especially with dispensational headings over particular passages of Scripture, led many Christians to associate these notes with God's Word. The following are comments on John 1:17:

> Grace is "the kindness and love of God our Saviour toward man . . . not by works of righteousness which we have done"; Titus 3:4,5. It is, therefore, constantly set in contrast to law, under which God demands righteousness from man, as, under grace, he gives righteous-

---

[3] John Nelson Darby, "The Law and the Gospel of the Glory of Christ," in *The Collected Writings of John Nelson Darby*, accessed May 22, 2013, http://bibletruthpublishers.com/the-law-and-the-gospel-of-the-glory-of-christ/john-nelson-darby-jnd/collected-writings-of-j-n-darby-miscellaneous-3/la63243.
[4] Cyrus I. Scofield, *Rightly Dividing the Word of Truth* (New York: n.p., n.d.), 34, 36.

ness to man; Romans 3:21,22; 8:4; Philemon 1:3,9. Law is connected with Moses and works; grace with Christ and faith; John 1:17; Romans 10:4–10. Law blesses the good; grace saves the bad; Exodus 19:5; Ephesians 2:1–9. Law demands that blessings be earned; grace is a free gift; Deuteronomy 28:1–6; Ephesians 2:8; Romans 4:4,5.[5]

A crystal clear opposition between law and grace is apparent in the notes. We might summarize the impact of this teaching with the commonly heard expressions: "Christians today are not under law, but under grace." "Christians are freed from the law and its demands." "The law was for the people of Israel; faith in Jesus is for Christians."

In addition to the widespread influence of dispensational teaching, much fundamentalism and many believers within the evangelical movement are dominated by a negative reaction to the secular culture and a corresponding attraction to the security that legalism offers. Any teaching that is legalistic will add cement to the basically negative disposition many believers have toward all law. We will look at this problem in detail in a later chapter.

Problems regarding the Law in Reformed Churches

In Reformed traditions we should expect to find a central emphasis on the grace of God, as this is the heart of all historically Reformed church confessions. However, in the actual teaching and practice of numbers of Reformed churches, grace has sometimes been replaced by moralism. What do I mean by moralism? The word is difficult to define, but perhaps the following questions will help: Do the sermons beat up the congregation? Is the clear intent and consequence of the teaching that believers are made to feel worthless so that, motivated by guilt, they will go out and live better lives? Do we find an emphasis on living the Christian life entirely through human effort? Do members of the church define the Christian life as primarily a list of things they have to do? The fruit of such teaching is that, while congregations would insist that justification is by faith in Jesus, they believe that sanctification is by what believers do.

Back in the early 1950s Francis Schaeffer gave a series of sermons

---

[5] Notes on John 1:17 in *The Scofield Reference Bible*, ed. C. I. Scofield (New York: Oxford University Press, 1917).

in many Presbyterian churches in the United States the content of which was to become his book *True Spirituality*. The heart of this teaching was that the beginning, middle, and end of the Christian life is faith in the work of Christ. One of the common responses to those sermons on sanctification through faith was: "This is an entirely new teaching, which we have never heard before. There must be some ulterior motive for such different ideas. Schaeffer has developed these views as a power play!"

In fact, of course, there was nothing new about Schaeffer's teaching. It is clearly taught on every page of the Scriptures. It is also present very powerfully in the teaching of John Calvin and of most of the greatest Reformed theologians and teachers of the past five hundred years. However, in the 1950s, this biblical emphasis on living the Christian life out of faith in Christ's finished work and in dependence on the Holy Spirit was sadly missing in many circles.

Even today there are still Reformed churches that have teaching characterized by moralism and legalism. By *legalism* I mean simply adding human rules to the law of God and teaching these human rules as the way of Christian obedience. We will address this problem later, but it should be sufficient to acknowledge here that legalism is very widespread in evangelical churches of almost every denomination and kind. Both moralism and legalism undermine the sufficiency of Christ's work and the power of the Holy Spirit for the life of faith.

Thankfully, there has been a healthy reaction to this loss of the biblical teaching on the power of God for living the Christian life. This reaction has led to a beautiful emphasis on grace in the Christian life, a rediscovery of the active obedience of Christ, and of sanctification by faith. This renewed discovery of grace has been wonderfully salutary in the lives of many Christians. Yet some, in their wholly understandable reaction to moralism and legalism, and in their zeal for grace, have unwittingly neglected the law, as if law and grace were always in tension with each other; or they have rejected any emphasis on holiness lived in the fear of God, as if such an approach were always in opposition to dependence on the grace of Christ.

To help us come to a better understanding of the law we turn to Calvin.

JOHN CALVIN ON THE LAW

In several passages we find Calvin emphasizing the law in a much more positive way:

> That the whole matter may be made clearer, let us take a succinct view of the office and use of the Moral Law. Now this office and use seems to me to consist of three parts. First, [the law] by exhibiting the righteousness of God,—in other words, the righteousness which alone is acceptable to God,—it admonishes every one of his own unrighteousness, certiorates, convicts, and finally condemns him. . . .
>
> The second office of the Law is by means of its fearful denunciations and the consequent dread of punishment, to curb those who, unless forced, have no regard for rectitude and justice. . . .
>
> The third use of the Law . . . has respect to believers in whose hearts the Spirit of God already flourishes and reigns. . . . For it is the best instrument for enabling them daily to learn with greater truth and certainty what that will of the Lord is which they aspire to follow, and to confirm them in this knowledge.[6]

In his first point Calvin emphasizes that the law teaches us about God. When we begin with the law as revealing the character of God, this helps us to see the law as good, holy, wise, and perfect. We should also observe how Calvin points to the way the law sets out how we as humans are to live before God. Calvin recognizes, of course, that the effect of this is that we are convicted of sin. But we should notice that the law convicts us because it is a presentation of perfect righteousness, not because it is our enemy. Indeed this work of conviction is the work of a friend for the law leads us to Christ who is, in his life, our righteousness and, in his death, our justification.

Consider also the positive nature of Calvin's third use of the law, which he called "the principal use, and more closely connected with its proper end."[7] Calvin makes it clear that this third use is for believers, those who have already put their hope in Christ, those in whom the Spirit dwells and over whom the Spirit reigns. For Calvin the law

[6] John Calvin, *Institutes of the Christian Religion*, trans. Henry Beveridge, 2.7.6, 2.7.10, 2.7.12, accessed at http://www.ccel.org/ccel/calvin/institutes.i.html. Certiorari is a writ from a higher to a lower court requesting a transcript of a case for review.
[7] Ibid., 2.7.12.

is the Christian's guide in holy living, a treasure chest for us to consult so that we learn what kind of life the Lord desires for us to be living.

Grace and Law

One issue that often troubles our understanding is the relationship between law and grace. I will try to summarize some essential points for us to grasp:

1. The law is given to us by the God of all grace.
2. The law reveals God's character of grace, mercy, love, and justice.
3. The law is good, holy, wise, perfect, and spiritual because it reveals God's character.
4. The law defines how we are to live as humans made in God's likeness.
5. Therefore the law convicts us of sin, for it exposes our failures.
6. The law convicts us because it is a presentation of perfect righteousness, not because it is our enemy; indeed this work of conviction is the work of a friend.
7. The law leads us to Christ, who, in his life of perfect obedience to the law, is our righteousness, and who, in dying to bear our failure to obey the law, is our justification.
8. We are led by the law to Christ for forgiveness.
9. Once we are forgiven, Christ returns us to the law, which defines for us his desire for our life.
10. Christ's longing is that we be transformed into his likeness, which is set out in his law.

All faithful teaching of God's law will produce humility in our hearts because our sin is exposed and we are driven to our knees to seek the mercy and forgiveness of Christ. If moral teaching in our churches produces pride or despondency, then we can conclude that the law is not being properly taught.

My next conclusion may surprise some readers. We may be sure that where the law is not deeply taught and loved, there will be little appreciation for Christ and for his work; and there will be little transformation of life and little genuine discipleship. It is only as we see the righteousness that characterizes God and that he desires in us, only as we understand the full requirements of the law, that we will be deeply convicted of sin and see our need of Christ's love. The truth is that we need to delight in the law in our inmost being and to teach this delight to others. Only this love for the law will bring utter dependence on Christ and on his grace for both our justification and our sanctification. There are no shortcuts, no quick routes to sanctification.

This summary of a proper evaluation of the law brings us back to the teaching of Psalm 19 on the beauty of the law. Seeing what David says about the law may now make more sense to us than when I first reflected on this psalm.

> The law of the Lord is perfect,
>   reviving the soul.
> The statutes of the Lord are trustworthy,
>   making wise the simple.
> The precepts of the Lord are right,
>   giving joy to the heart.
> The commands of the Lord are radiant,
>   giving light to the eyes.
> The fear of the Lord is pure,
>   enduring forever.
> The ordinances of the Lord are sure
>   and altogether righteous.
> They are more precious than gold,
>   than much pure gold;
> they are sweeter than honey,
>   than honey from the comb.
> By them is your servant warned;
>   in keeping them is great reward.[8]

In chapter 4 we looked at six affirmations about the law set forth in verses 7–9 of this psalm. We may review them briefly here to see God's gracious provision for his people in his law.

Six Affirmations about the Law
1. David tells us that "the law of the Lord is perfect." Without blemish, it gives new life to the soul, "reviving" it over and over again.

---
[8] Psalm 19:7–11, niv.

This word "reviving" is the same word used in Psalm 23 for restoring the soul!

2. "The statutes of the LORD [or "the testimony of the LORD"—ESV] are trustworthy" or sure, faithful and beyond any doubt. God himself has told us what true virtue is, both in his *acts* of justice, mercy, and faithfulness revealed in history and in his *words* of wisdom about genuine righteousness. Therefore, his words enable us to become wise.

3. "The precepts of the LORD are right," morally beautiful and upright. They reflect God's own goodness; and so they bring joy to the heart of the one who gives his or her life to observing them.

4. "The commands of the LORD are radiant," like sunlight on our path. If we follow God's laws, we will always have light to direct our lives.

5. "The fear of the LORD is pure." God's way is pure and wholesome, worthy of reverence. And it will endure forever. True righteousness is always in style and does not change from culture to culture, from one moment to another, or from one situation to another.

6. "The ordinances of the LORD are sure"; they are right and good. When you see them observed in business or in the political sphere, you can rejoice, for they are "altogether righteous."

In verses 10–11 David teaches us to treasure the laws of God more highly than our possessions, our pension fund, or our savings. Our food and drink should be to delight in doing the will of our heavenly Father, as Jesus did. And our wealth should be to commit ourselves to walk in the ways of the Lord.

David adds in verse 11 that God's laws warn us, showing us so clearly where we are sinful. At the same time, David urges us to enjoy the rewards that God delights in giving us, his children, whenever we make any step forward in keeping the commandments. The psalm continues with David turning to examine his own heart and life:

Who can discern his errors?
  Forgive my hidden faults.
Keep your servant also from willful sins;
  may they not rule over me.

Then will I be blameless,
    innocent of great transgression.

May the words of my mouth and the meditation of my heart
    be pleasing in your sight,
    O LORD, my Rock and my Redeemer.[9]

David acknowledges his sin to the Lord. He knows that his heart is deceitful and that it contains many hidden sins, so he cries out for forgiveness. Any proper meditation on the law will have this effect. While we delight in the beautiful way of life set out in the law, and while we rejoice in the moral integrity that any obedience brings, yet the more surely we see the light of the law, and the more clearly we see ourselves by the light of the law, the more too we will see our failures. So David prays for the Lord's mercy and forgiveness for both known sins and hidden faults.

Having sought forgiveness, David prays that the Lord will keep him from willful sins, from being dominated by sin. This needs to be the prayer of us all. Like David, we are to pray that the Lord will acquit us of "great transgression."

The psalm ends with a prayer that David's own words and thoughts might reflect the loveliness of the Lord, just as the heavens speak out God's glory and the law unveils the beauty of his Redeemer's character. And how beautiful indeed is our Redeemer as we see his life described for us in the Gospels! The beauty of his righteous life is more glorious than the heavens.

David prays that he might be a third light making God known, that his thoughts and "words" (the same Hebrew term used for the "words" of the heavens in verse 4) would make known the one he calls "my Rock and my Redeemer." For David knows that the Lord loves him, that the Lord has forgiven him, and that the Lord will enable him to walk in the ways of his law. This is so for us today—God has redeemed us through the grace of his Son. Christ has acquitted us, making us innocent. And Christ will enable us to walk in his light, equipping us to reveal his beauty in our lives as we commit ourselves to obeying his commandments out of gratitude for his great love.

---

[9] Psalm 19:12–14, NIV.

Questions for Personal Reflection and Group Discussion

1. Have you come across teaching that declares, "We can be rich if we have faith; we can have good health if only we believe; we should have dominion over the world"?

2. How would you answer those who insist that if we have adequate faith then health, wealth, peace, and dominion will be ours? I had the distressing experience of being told that it was because of my lack of faith that my wife was laid up in bed with severe back problems. Eventually she needed two major back surgeries to correct the degeneration of two discs in her lower spine. How would you respond to someone who told you that your wife, husband, child, parent, or friend was sick because of your lack of faith, and that if you would only pray with sufficient faith, your loved one would most certainly be healed?

3. Are you familiar with the emphasis on the law that makes it primarily, if not exclusively, an instrument for convicting the believer of sin and exposing our need of Christ?

4. Are you familiar with the teaching that God has separate ways of dealing with Israel and the church? The most extreme form of this teaching is that there are two distinct peoples of God: (1) Old Testament Israel (and Jews today), saved by works of obedience to the law; (2) Gentile Christians, saved by faith in Christ. Thankfully, one rarely finds this extreme form. How would you respond to this teaching, whether in its milder or its strongest form?

5. Have you come across dispensationalist teaching that opposes law and grace as acutely as does the teaching of Darby or Scofield?

6. How would you respond to a friend who said that the law has no real benefit for the Christian life because the age of law is over and now we are living in an age of grace and no longer need the law?

14

Jesus Challenges
Additions to God's Law

In chapter 13 we looked at the way different traditions in Protestant-ism have understood the law. I need to add an important qualification. I have no wish to imply that the whole of each of the traditions I critiqued holds consistently to the view of the law I ascribed to them; nor do I want to imply that all believers in those traditions live by the inadequate views that have characterized those traditions.

Take, for example, my father-in-law, and the story of the offering of his firstfruits that I recounted in chapter 8. All his life he wor-shipped at a church in which he was never taught a high view of the law, a church whose theological tradition saw a sharp discontinuity between the Old and New Testaments, a church in which he had heard pastors teach that God has two different covenants for two different peoples: a covenant of law with the Jews and a covenant of grace with the Gentile church of this present age. He was a faithful member of a congregation where I doubt if he ever heard a sermon on the ethical implications of the Old Testament laws for Christians. Yet he loved to read the Word for himself. He was devoutly committed to living by the moral principles taught in the laws Moses gave to Israel, so much so that he designed for himself the lovely service of firstfruits that I described for you earlier.

In the same way, I know of Christians from holiness traditions, from Lutheran churches, and from strongly dispensationalist churches who delight in meditation on God's commandments. They do this because psalms, like Psalm 1, Psalm 19, and Psalm 119 teach them to love the law and to meditate on it, and because they see the Psalms as the Christian's primary devotional literature. Consequently, believers like this give their lives to living in obedience to the commandments of both the Old and New Testaments, no matter how strongly their churches may teach that the law has no positive place in the Christian life. The fundamental reason for this passionate commitment to the law among God's people of whatever tradition is simply that they are indeed God's people, not the people of a particular theological tradition, denomination, or church. They are the Lord's own treasured possession, his beloved in whom his Spirit dwells, his church, which he has promised to build all through this age and he has committed himself never to abandon.

As we think about a right view of the law, we do well to simply follow the lead of those Christians, from whatever tradition, who read Psalms 1, 19, and 119, and who, because they live by the Word, take delight in reading the law, in meditating on its precepts, and in seeing them as beautiful and liberating, and who then give their lives to following the requirements of the law every day in their homes, in their workplaces, and in all their relationships. Above all, we will not go wrong if we see the law as rooted in the loveliness of God's character, for the more we love the Lord himself, the more we will love his commandments. Such an approach will enable us to see the law as a friend and as a comforting guide and benevolent teacher—even when the law is convicting us of sin and leading us to Christ for forgiveness.

In chapter 13 I also briefly mentioned the problem of legalism: adding to God's law. To guide us in our reflections on this issue we turn to Jesus's teaching about the law recorded for us in Mark 7 and Matthew 15. This is an occasion in which Jesus's words are a response to the Pharisees and the teachers of the law.

THE PHARISEES ADD TO GOD'S COMMANDS

Jesus and his disciples are apparently at Gennesaret (Mark 6:53), close to the shore of the Sea of Galilee, and not far from Capernaum. A deputation from Jerusalem has come to check on Jesus—some perhaps to learn, others evidently to find fault. The discussion that takes place is triggered by someone in the deputation noticing that some of Jesus's disciples did not wash their hands before eating. We should be aware, of course, that their criticism of the disciples is not about hygiene but about ritual cleanliness. Notice how Mark keeps drawing our attention to the words "wash" (in its various forms) and "defiled."

> Now when the Pharisees gathered to him, with some of the scribes who had come from Jerusalem, they saw that some of his disciples ate with hands that were defiled, that is, unwashed. (For the Pharisees and all the Jews do not eat unless they wash their hands properly, holding to the tradition of the elders, and when they come from the marketplace, they do not eat unless they wash. And there are many other traditions that they observe, such as the washing of cups and pots and copper vessels and dining couches.) And the Pharisees and the scribes asked him, "Why do your disciples not walk according to the tradition of the elders, but eat with defiled hands?"[1]

Some background might help us as we think about these traditions of the elders, to which the Pharisees and the scribes referred. In the Old Testament law the priests were required to wash and to be ritually clean before taking up their duties in the temple, including their participation in ceremonial meals.[2] This washing was also required for the Levites who assisted the priests and who cared for the furnishings and utensils used in the tabernacle and temple worship. Washing was also required for many of the various vessels and implements used in the ceremonies.

By the time of Jesus some of the Pharisees had decided that it would be appropriate for laymen, too, to observe these laws. The Pharisees' motivation seems to have been their eager desire to be holy, to be "undefiled" and to be dedicated to God in all their lives. And so, in their zeal, they began to require that they and their fellow Jews be scrupulous about ritual washing before any meal. They created laws to define exactly how this should be done, laws governing necessary occasions, the manner of washing, and the amount of water. Mark, in his editorial or storyteller's comment, tells us that there were also

---

[1] Mark 7:1–5.
[2] Exodus 30:17–21; 40:30–32; Leviticus 8:5–6.

laws governing the ceremonial washing of various household articles. Again, the motivation for this seems to have been to take the laws about the articles used in the temple service and apply them to the articles in one's home, in order to demonstrate commitment to the service of God in all of one's life.

Before we criticize the Pharisees, which is easy enough to do at our distance in time and place, we might consider their intentions and motivations as they thought about their devotion and zeal to serve the Lord. We can imagine that their thinking might have proceeded in this manner: "It is not just the priests and the temple that are intended for the worship and service of the Lord. The Lord has told us that we are a kingdom of priests and a holy nation.[3] My life, my body, and my home are each also a temple of the living God. Just as the priests have a sign saying 'holy to the Lord,' I too will dedicate myself to him as one who is 'holy to the Lord.'" In addition they might have said: "We know that the Lord requires us to serve him in all of life, for there is no sacred/secular division for the people of God. So we will think of our homes as places of worship and service. Indeed, there can be no doubt that the Lord desires us to serve him in our homes; and so, what could be more honoring to God than to offer our homes, our furniture, our eating, and cooking utensils to the Lord and to set them apart for his service with the same kind of rituals that the Lord requires for the furnishings and utensils for holy purposes in the temples?" We should observe how faithful and godly these reflections on the law appear to be in both intention and understanding.

By the New Testament period these attempts to apply the law of God to every part of life had developed into a great body of rules. Some of these were written down, some were oral, and this body of rules, this collection of laws added to the law, was referred to as "the tradition of the elders." The Pharisees and teachers of the law saw the keeping of these rules as essential for true holiness and devout dedication to God's service. They required obedience in their own lives; and, in addition, the Pharisees and scribes devoted themselves to teaching these "traditions" and to imposing them on all their fellow Jews.

Before we simply dismiss this, we should notice that their mo-

---

[3] Exodus 19:6.

tivation seems originally to have been good. They wanted to apply the law to all of life. They desired to be "clean"—that is undefiled or wholly set apart to the Lord in everything they did. They wanted to ensure that they obeyed the law by making it more precise and more universal than it was in its original form. They wanted to be faithful in encouraging the service of God, recognizing that all God's people are priests before him. They knew that Moses taught that the whole people of Israel are a "kingdom of priests and a holy nation," so they appear to have reasoned that applying the laws for priests and vessels of the temple to the lives of all the "nation of priests" and all the "holy people" would be a demonstration of devotion and godly zeal in the service of the Lord. How could God fail to be pleased with such zealous worship and such careful application of his Word!

THE APPEAL OF RULES IN CONTEMPORARY EVANGELICALISM

Before we consider Jesus's response to the question of the scribes and Pharisees, and to their teaching and practice, we need to understand that something very similar exists in evangelicalism today. We live in a generation that has a passion for practical application, for in the United States we are a very practical and pragmatic people. We also live in a cultural setting that has put a very high value on technique: there has to be a set of simple rules or a method that will aid us to do things well. We want our pastors to tell us precisely how we are to live the Christian life; and how we might help ourselves and our children serve the Lord faithfully.

So, what do we do? We make God's moral laws more explicit, and we come up with practical techniques in order to apply his laws to our cultural setting. To aid our obedience we create lists of "how-tos" for the Christian life. Many seminars, books, and magazine articles, as well as much radio and television teaching and much preaching, are devoted to telling believers how to serve God more faithfully by following a list of rules governing their lives. The motivation seems good and thoroughly spiritual. We want to be wholly committed to serving God. We want to apply his law to our contemporary situation so that we know exactly what Christian obedience will be. We want to protect ourselves and our children from the world and its pressures. We want to be able to "see" what faithful discipleship means for us so that we can discern more readily our progress in the Christian life.

This embracing of rules is a particularly powerful tendency because much fundamentalism and some of us in every branch of the evangelical movement are dominated by a negative reaction to the secular culture. This negative reaction is vulnerable to the promise of security that legalism offers. All of us—and we feel this intensely for our children and young people—face strong pressure from the world to conform to its way of life. This is challenging to us in a cultural setting that appears to be departing ever further from God's commands. The pressure from the culture causes many of us to desire more detail than God gives in his law. We feel that we urgently need clear and specific application to our contemporary situation. We want a list of directions for life that will set us, and especially our children, apart from those around us, and we believe that this will create a safety net that provides security.

In addition, there is comfort in rules about the Christian life because it seems that by observing our rules, we will be enabled to measure our progress in obedience and in personal spiritual growth. We cannot see God, so we begin to believe that we need something we can see, and this seeing will help to ensure genuine spiritual devotion. We discover that there is a long history of teaching on spiritual disciplines, especially from Roman Catholic and Orthodox monastic movements, and these spiritual disciplines appear, for many evangelicals, to be the very helps we need to be able to see and to measure our spiritual progress. This fits in, once more, with the pragmatic nature of our culture, which teaches us that there must be a method, program, or technique to help us grow in piety and holiness. And so we develop sets of rules for spiritual discipline and personal piety.

To add to these pressures, we live in a celebrity culture. This has affected our churches very deeply. We find men and women who are heroes and heroines of the faith. We like to follow leaders who have found a way of practicing devotion and righteousness and who are very obviously mature and godly people. Sometimes these leaders, or we their followers, turn their way of life into a set of rules for discipleship thought to be a surefire means of growth in spiritual maturity, just as the leaders or heroes have seen.

If we add up all these elements, then perhaps we can begin to understand why we live in a time where evangelicals are constantly dealing with problems of legalism. One of the outcomes of adding rules to God's law is that people become negative to all laws. We will examine this problem later, but first we need to return to Jesus's reaction to the rule makers of his day.

JESUS'S RESPONSE TO THE RULE MAKERS

How does Jesus respond to all this seemingly well-intentioned teaching and practice? He makes a series of powerful criticisms to which we need to attend, both for ourselves and for our children, and for any context in which we are teaching young people or new Christians, who are most often susceptible to extra rules.

One additional introductory remark should be helpful. We find Mark including various comments to his account of this discussion between Jesus and the scribes and Pharisees. Mark's editorial comments are added for believers who read his Gospel. It is thought that Mark was writing down the gospel that Peter taught (so we are told by very early witnesses in the church), and that the congregations for which this Gospel was written were primarily made up of Gentile converts.

The question of how much of the Jewish law a believer was required to obey would have been a very important one for non-Jews. This was clearly an issue that troubled the first-century churches. Some Jewish believers in Christ insisted that Gentile converts, in order to be "clean"—that is, pure and holy—must obey the Jewish laws about purity. So given the setting in the churches for which Mark is writing his Gospel, Jesus's answer is of great practical importance.

We have the same challenge today. When there is a new convert from an unbelieving background, what will the church require of him or her? What music, movies, television shows, clothes, makeup, hairstyles, and so forth are allowable for the new believer? What rules will the young Christian be given to help him or her develop good Bible-reading and prayer habits?

How does Jesus respond to all this apparently well-intentioned effort to be zealous for God, this desire to help his people grow in devotion and holiness?

> And he said to them, "Well did Isaiah prophesy about you hypocrites, as it is written,
>
>> "'This people honors me with their lips,
>>> but their heart is far from me;
>> in vain do they worship me,
>>> teaching as doctrines the commandments of men.'
>
> You leave the commandment of God and hold to the tradition of men." And he said to them, "You have a fine way of rejecting the commandment of God in order to establish your tradition! For Moses said, 'Honor your father and your mother'; and, 'Whoever reviles father or mother must surely die.' But you say, 'If a man tells his father or his mother, "Whatever you would have gained from me is Corban"' (that is, given to God)—then you no longer permit him to do anything for his father or mother, thus making void the word of God by your tradition that you have handed down. And many such things you do."[4]

Hypocrisy

Jesus begins his response by quoting the prophet Isaiah and accusing the Pharisees and scribes of hypocrisy. The Greek word translated "hypocrite" means actor or player of a part. The Pharisees and scribes desire to be seen as acting purely and devoutly. One troubling element of such an approach is that people could very easily become more concerned with how they are seen than with the internal righteousness of their own hearts, more concerned with the outside appearance of spirituality than with inward devotion. This was certainly one of the problems with first-century Judaism, and this is also one of the problems today with all rules we make up for the Christian life. Our rules tend to focus on the outside rather than on the heart and inner motivations. God's law, in contrast, always points us to the heart and then sees the devotion of the heart as the motivating power for acts of genuine righteousness. (See, for example, the tenth commandment, which applies all the laws about my relationship with my neighbor to

---

[4] Mark 7:6–13.

the motives of the heart.) It is this problem that Jesus addresses in the Sermon on the Mount when he speaks not only of adultery but also of lust, not only of murder but also of abusive language and even of our hateful thoughts toward others.

Whenever the focus is on external spiritual practice and purity of life, this can readily decay into hypocrisy, for the outer appearance of spirituality can quickly replace the much more demanding inner devotion of the heart. This is the same criticism that many of the prophets leveled at the people of Israel: "Circumcise your hearts and not your foreskins"; "God does not delight in sacrifice . . . the sacrifices of God are a broken spirit and a contrite heart." When the focus of spiritual obedience is on the rules we design, or when we legislate our application of God's law to the details of people's lives, then we slip easily into going through the outer motions of obedience, and soon we become satisfied with the external appearance of spirituality rather than with a deep internal obedience.

Merely Human Rules

In Jesus's attack on the scribes and Pharisees, his second accusation is to charge them with raising human rules to the status of God's law. Jesus tells them (and us) that leaders err whenever they require of people what God has not commanded. This is true even if the leaders' intentions are zealous, protective, and apparently spiritual. This was certainly the case in first-century Judaism, where all faithful Jews were required to keep all the traditions of the elders, and it is still true in Judaism today, as well as in many Christian churches.

Think of all the laws among Christians about music, movies, books, clothing, devotions, church membership requirements, tithing, drinking, smoking—this list goes on. "But," you may be saying, "surely it is perfectly right for a church to require its members to tithe or to attend three meetings a week or to sign up for some kind of service?"

Many pastors and church leaders do indeed think such rules of membership are fine. However, we need to pay attention to Jesus's accusation. These teachings are but rules taught by men and therefore, Jesus says, they must not be made binding on the consciences of God's people. The apostle Paul teaches in his letter to the Colossians that, despite their appearance of wisdom, such rules for Christian living have no value in restraining the indulgence of the sinful nature.[5]

The most important point in Jesus's criticism is, however, not that such rules are ineffective in producing righteousness—though they are utterly ineffective—but that God has given us no authority to increase what he has demanded of his people. He is their Creator, we are not. He is their Lawgiver and Judge, we are not. They are his sheep and not ours. He purchased them for himself—and we did not. He knows them as we do not.

This is true even of our own children. God is their true Father, their true parent, and he is the only one who has the right to demand full obedience to laws that he gives. Our authority over others is always secondary and subordinate. It is "declarative rather than legislative"—to quote the Book of Church Order in the Presbyterian Church in America, the denomination in which I serve. Jesus insists that we do not have the right to make new laws binding on the consciences of other believers, no matter how good we believe our intentions to be.

Replacing God's Commandments with Ours

Jesus's third criticism strikes even harder. He declares that whenever we add our own rules to God's law, no matter what the original motivation, the effect will be to replace God's commandments with human rules—to jettison what God has required and instead insist on submission to our own laws. Notice Jesus's escalation of terms to describe the Pharisees' dismissal of the law in Mark 7: "leave"(v. 8), "rejecting" (v. 9), "making void" (v. 13), in the ESV. The NIV has "let go" (v. 8), "setting aside" (v. 9), and "nullify" (v. 13). We may protest that it is not our intention to abandon God's laws and replace them with our own; but Jesus's point is that this is inevitably the consequence of making up human rules and imposing them on God's people.

A challenging example may throw light on this problem. Many Christian rules about purity in our day are created for the specific purpose of preventing us, and especially our children, from being with those outside the church, for we want our children to be godly and not conformed to the world. Despite our good intentions, such rules

---

[5] Colossians 2:23.

produce a separation that is deeply disobedient to God's command for us. The Lord requires mercy toward unbelievers and gracious and generous relationships with them. Jesus prays for us that we will be in the world just as he was in the world.[6] He does not want us to replace his commands with rules about separation and purity that our own hearts devise to express the devotion we offer to him.

One of our Covenant Seminary graduates telephoned me one day with a very sad but very common illustration of this problem. He is the pastor of a church that is deeply committed to outreach in its community. The youth group was planning a pool party, both for itself and also to invite non-Christian friends. A sister church not far away heard about the planned party and asked to join them. The other pastor's wife came to speak to the young pastor about it: "We must have some ground rules for this party. The first of these is: no two-piece bathing suits for the girls. Teenage boys have raging hormones, so everyone must be decently clothed." My friend responded: "But if we have a rule like this, our young people, including my own daughters, will not be able to invite their non-Christian friends. Their friends would think we are crazy to have rules like that, and they would not come." The pastor's wife replied: "Your daughters ought not to have friends like that."

It is, of course, important to teach our children modesty in dress and other such matters. However, when we make rules like this, the immediate effect (often intentional) is to keep us, and especially our children, apart from the non-Christians around us. Jesus forbids this. He shows us another way—the way of both purity and love. We may find this difficult and even frightening, but Jesus promises us that he is praying for us, and for our children, as we follow him into the world in obedience to his example and command. And the Lord's command to his people, at whatever age, is that we are to love our neighbors and to show them mercy.

Voiding God's Commands: An Example

Jesus follows up his charge of nullifying God's laws by giving an example of this problem of ignoring what God desires when we focus on

---

[6] See Jesus's prayer for his church, for all of us, in John 17:15–19.

our rules. In Jesus's day a Jew could say his possessions were "Corban," that is, they were devoted to the service of God. This appears to be very thoughtful and truly spiritual, and to show a passionate dedication to honor the Lord—and this, no doubt, was the original intention. A faithful Jew could leave all he or she possessed to the temple or to the local synagogue by making this declaration. Individuals could still use their money and possessions for their own care and support as long as they lived, but at death the remainder would go to the temple for its upkeep and services.

This, of course, is exactly how a will works today. Once an individual's possessions were declared Corban, that declaration could not be revoked, and the dedicated property could be used for no other purposes, such as care for one's parents, even if the parents became elderly and sick and needed one's support. This was true whatever the motivation of the Corban declaration, whether it was from a sincere devotion to God or out of dislike of one's parents or anger with them. Whichever the avowed reason, the impact of the Corban promise was that the Pharisees, while alive and able to help their needy parents, were withholding support from them under the guise of devotion to the Lord. Jesus reminds his listeners that to honor (including to care for) one's parents is an absolute requirement of God and cannot be set aside for any reason. He adds the stern warning of the law that to dishonor one's parents makes one subject to the death penalty.

What parallels could we point to in our own time? One such parallel today might be a pastor or missionary saying, "I am devoted to the service of God's kingdom. God will take care of my children, for I am serving him first, and doing his work." This sounds very spiritual, but just like Corban, it is fundamentally disobedient to God's commandments.

A dear friend of ours experienced the consequences of just such a vow. When she was three years old, her parents set sail for India to be missionaries there. She was left in England with an aunt and had to stand on the dock in Southampton and sing "Count your blessings, name them one by one" as her parents disappeared across the sea. The next time she saw them was when she was twenty-three. This is an extreme example, but many pastors neglect their wives and children for the sake of the gospel, even though the apostle Paul tells us that if we neglect our own families, we have denied the faith and are worse than unbelievers.[7]

God desires that we love his law and submit ourselves to what he says. He does not want us replacing his prescription for our lives with our own. In the end such an approach is arrogant and presumptuous, for we imagine that we know better how to serve God than he knows. Let us determine to be content with his commandments!

Questions for Personal Reflection and Group Discussion

1. Are you surprised by the passionate nature of Jesus's denunciation of the laws that had the announced intention of helping God's people to know that they were all priests and holy to the Lord?

2. What might be some contemporary evangelical equivalents to the laws about ceremonial cleanliness?

3. How would you express in your own words the criticisms that Jesus makes about adding our own rules to God's commands?

4. What examples can you think of in which believers add to the commands of God? As you think about your own life, where have you been tempted to do this? (Again, I am aware that some of these questions will be very personally challenging and possibly difficult to discuss in public; so leading such a discussion needs to be handled with care.)

5. What motivations for creating new rules for our children and young people sound reasonable and appropriate to you? How would you respond to your own heart, and to others, as to why these rules might not be such a good idea?

6. What do you think would be some contemporary equivalents to the law of Corban, or devoting things to God and so ignoring or even disobeying some requirement of God's law?

7. Do you know examples of missionaries and pastors who have neglected their families for the sake of the way they understand their call to proclaim the gospel?

8. Are you convinced of Jesus's criticism of human rules? Which of his criticisms do you find most troubling personally, and which do you find most compelling?

---

[7] 1 Timothy 5:8.

15

JESUS'S ATTACK
ON LEGALISM

We are considering Jesus's passionate attack on the legalism of the scribes and Pharisees. We saw in the previous chapter that Jesus makes four basic critiques of their approach to righteousness.

1. *Hypocrisy.* Adding human rules to God's laws invariably shifts the focus to external behavior and therefore encourages pretense, the merely outward appearance of righteousness. God's law, in contrast, always addresses the heart and demands transformation from within, producing true righteousness.

2. *Human rules.* Jesus insists that all the rules the elders added to God's commandments were simply that: human rules rather than God's Word. Jesus's point is that God did not give the religious leaders the right to add to what God himself had required of his people. Even if we attributed to these teachers the best possible motives of service to the Lord and of passion for holiness, Jesus rejects all their rules and applications of the law as merely the "teaching of men."

3. *Replacing God's commandment with ours.* Whenever we add our own rules to God's law, regardless of our original motivation, the effect will be to jettison God's commandments and instead impose human regulations on God's people.

4. *Nullifying God's commandments.* Human rules invariably invalidate God's commandments. We looked at the example Jesus gives of Corban, offering one's wealth to the Lord presumably for the extension of his kingdom while failing to fulfill one's obligations to one's parents. Though some in Christian ministry neglect their

families for the sake of the gospel, Paul declares that they are worse than unbelievers and have denied the faith.

Jesus continues his denunciation of legalism in Mark 7 (and Matthew 15) by identifying the core of the problem.

Defilement Comes from the Heart

After delivering his passionate criticism of the teachers of the law and the Pharisees, Jesus calls the crowds to him to add a further commentary on his response, bringing them back to the original issue: "And he called the people to him again and said to them, 'Hear me, all of you, and understand: There is nothing outside a person that by going into him can defile him, but the things that come out of a person are what defile him.'"[1] Jesus's point is that the ritual washings imposed on the people of God by the Pharisees can never make a person "clean" before God. Indeed, nothing that enters a person or touches him or her on the outside can make a person unclean. Rather it is only what is within each individual that can make anyone unclean. All the rules the Pharisees and teachers of the law so carefully developed over the centuries; all the additions to the law they so painstakingly designed to help the people serve God more faithfully; all their attempts to apply God's law to every area of life in explicit detail—all of this human effort is a total waste and has no effect whatsoever on true purity and holiness.

These words of Jesus are revolutionary. It is no wonder that he is hated by so many of the religious leaders of his time, for these brief words completely undermine their authority over the people. He says in effect: "The teaching of the Pharisees and the scribes is absolutely worthless in helping you walk in God's ways. Their rules, their traditions, will not enable you to deal with the sin in your hearts."

Jesus Has to Repeat His Radical Words

The words of Jesus to the crowd are so shocking and so radically different from anything they have ever heard that even his disciples do not understand this "parable," as Mark calls it. In this context Mark is using the term to carry the meaning, not of a story, but of a riddle or

---

[1] Mark 7:14–16.

a dark saying. The disciples themselves are so influenced by the teachings of first-century Judaism that they do not grasp the meaning or implication of what Jesus says to the crowd. So Jesus has to give further explanation of what appears to the disciples to be a new, strange, difficult, and thoroughly confusing teaching.

> And when he had entered the house and left the people, his disciples asked him about the parable. And he said to them, "Then are you also without understanding? Do you not see that whatever goes into a person from outside cannot defile him, since it enters not his heart but his stomach, and is expelled?" (Thus he declared all foods clean.) And he said, "What comes out of a person is what defiles him. For from within, out of the heart of man, come evil thoughts, sexual immorality, theft, murder, adultery, coveting, wickedness, deceit, sensuality, envy, slander, pride, foolishness. All these evil things come from within, and they defile a person."[2]

This teaching of Jesus is so very different from what the disciples are used to hearing and thinking and from the way they have been living their whole lives that only later do they truly understand the meaning of his words, as Mark makes clear by his comment in parentheses: "Thus he declared all foods clean."

The first time Jesus says these words to the crowds, the disciples simply fail to understand him, so Jesus has to repeat his statement to them in private. He makes it clear to them that he is declaring all food clean, setting aside the food laws of the Old Testament and not just the rules of the Pharisees. The biblical laws about diet and defilement had been given to keep Israel distinct in all of life from the pagan nations around them. Because Jesus is himself the Lawgiver, he declares with absolute authority that the time of Israel's separation from the nations is now over. With Jesus's coming a new day has dawned, a day for people in every part of the world to worship God in spirit and truth. Jesus makes the same point in his conversation with the Samaritan woman: worship will no longer be in Jerusalem alone, or at the temple, but will be offered in every nation by those who come to know him.[3]

---

[2] Mark 7:17–23.
[3] John 4:20–24.

In addition to declaring all foods clean, Jesus insists that the food and defilement laws were never intended to make the people think that food and ritual can make you morally clean or unclean. This was not their purpose. The Old Testament itself makes this point repeatedly. Think, for example, of the refrain, "Circumcise therefore the foreskin of your heart"[4] or, "The sacrifices of God are a broken spirit; a broken and a contrite heart."[5] Circumcision and the sacrifices were intended by God to be an outward expression of an inward commitment of the heart; they were not themselves the true expression of devotion to the Lord. Without love from the heart these outward expressions were worthless. David's prayer of confession to the Lord in Psalm 51 expresses this understanding with absolute clarity.

In this element of Jesus's teaching, first to the crowd, and then to the disciples, he is saying nothing new when he declares that it is only what is in the heart that can make us clean or unclean morally. And he is not bringing a revolutionary, radically different teaching when he concludes that, therefore, uncleanness cannot be removed by laws about food or ritual washing or any other external rules. While this teaching of Jesus was not in fact new, it certainly appears new to the disciples, and this makes the words of Jesus very challenging for them to understand and accept, so deeply were they shaped by centuries of interpretation and of religious practice.

The Example of Peter and the Home of Cornelius

To help us realize how difficult this teaching is for Jesus's listeners, we can look, for example, at Acts 10 and read there about Peter's struggle with visiting the home of a Gentile and eating "unclean" food. It is only after a personal invitation, after several visions, after the appearance of an angel, and after direct commandments from God—commandments given in the face of Peter's rejection of the vision in which the voice of God challenges Peter to eat unclean food—that we see Peter prepared to enter the house of an unclean Gentile. And even when Peter has arrived at the home of Cornelius, a God-fearing Gentile, Peter recounts his wrestling with the teaching of Jewish law that he ought not to be

---

[4] Deuteronomy 10:16.
[5] Psalm 51:17.

there: "You yourselves know how unlawful it is for a Jew to associate with or to visit anyone of another nation, but God has shown me that I should not call any person common or unclean."[6]

Peter finally grasps what Jesus said to him long before, beside the Sea of Galilee, recounted for us in Mark 7. That is when Peter heard Jesus say that nothing external to a person, nothing entering a person physically, could make that person unclean. This meant that all the Jewish laws about food (some given by God and many more added by men over the centuries) and all the laws about not visiting the homes of Gentiles were to be set aside as having no impact on a person's purity. Only looking back many years later at Jesus's words in this discussion recorded in Mark 7 did the disciples finally understand what Jesus meant, and what a transformative impact faithful obedience to his teaching would have on their lives, particularly their relationships with Gentiles.

Gentiles to Find a Home in the Church

One more point should be added here: it is evident, from the editorial comments that Mark adds to Jesus's discussion of the traditions of the elders that Mark is seeking to help his Gentile readers know that Jesus himself is already thinking about their place in the church even before his death and resurrection. His teaching is designed as a rebuke to the Pharisees and teachers of the law for their adding to God's Word. And his teaching is also designed to ensure that Gentiles will be able to enter the church as full members without their having to become Jews first, and without their being required to observe the ritual and food laws of scrupulous Jewish members of their churches. This was to become one of the most contentious issues in the first-century churches.[7]

Jesus, the Lord of history, was teaching the church of the future in Mark 7, as well as communicating the truth to the people present on that day, for Jesus knew how bound the Jewish people were to their rules for holiness and purity. He knew that the legalism of Judaism would create barriers for his disciples in reaching Gentiles; and he

---

[6] Acts 10:28; see also Galatians 2:11–16 for another example of Peter's difficulty in keeping Jesus's teaching in his heart and then living faithfully according to that teaching.
[7] See the epistles to the Galatians and the Colossians and also 1 and 2 Timothy, as well as the extensive discussions about this issue in the book of Acts.

knew that this legalism would produce all sorts of problems of fellowship between Jewish and Gentile believers in the churches. Indeed, Jewish legalism became an idol that took the place of God himself in the hearts of many of the people of Israel in Jesus's day.

Jesus's words are still difficult for the church today. We are sure it is wise and spiritual to add to God's commandments, to make them contemporary, to have outward measures of inward obedience. Jesus rebukes us for this. He has not given us the right or authority—as parents, teachers, or pastors, or simply as individuals seeking to serve him—to make our own rules in addition to the laws he has given us once for all. Disobedience in this regard is one of the most serious weaknesses of the evangelical church today. We feel so threatened by the world that we feel we must add to God's Word, but Jesus forbids us!

Yet, we often ignore his passionate denunciation and so we make our endless rules about what a Christian can see or read or listen to, what a believer is to wear or may eat or drink. However, Jesus tells us that any such rules will do nothing to make us genuinely holy or protect us from sin. Tattoos and ear-piercing, coloring one's hair, wearing it in spikes or ringlets, or any such external cultural practices will not hinder a person's spiritual growth or moral maturity, and avoiding these things will not help, simply because they all affect the outside of a person, rather than the heart. The same is true with rules about books, movies, music, and so on. Again, the rules we design for spiritual purity and maturity are legion, yet they have no spiritual value. In truth, they are spiritually damaging rather than spiritually helpful.

We need to think about the effect that ignoring Jesus's teaching in Mark 7 has on the outreach of the church, as well as the damage done inside the church.

THE PROBLEM OF DETAILED RULES

If our idea of being a Christian emphasizes detailed records of rule keeping as a precise account of our purity, we end up with a long and exacting list of things to do in order to be a godly person. Like the Pharisee, who said to the Lord, "I fast twice a week; I give tithes of all that I get,"[8] we will itemize our spiritual accomplishments as we pray, "Lord, I read my Bible every day; I pray for thirty minutes; I attend church twice on Sunday and prayer meeting on Wednesday evenings; I tithe faithfully," and so on. Jesus, however, is unimpressed by such devotion. Instead, the Lord tells us that we have neglected the more important matters of the law, and we have substituted our ideas of what being spiritual or righteous is in place of the things God regards as central and requires of us when we come to know him: "Woe to you, scribes and Pharisees, hypocrites! For you tithe mint and dill and cumin, and have neglected the weightier matters of the law: justice and mercy and faithfulness."[9]

Legalism is ugly and has no power to attract unbelievers to the truth. If our focus is on our rules for holy living, then unbelievers will not see true Christianity either in our words or in our lives. The Scriptures teach us that the attractiveness of the faith to non-Christians resides to a large degree in our practicing justice, mercy, faithfulness, and love. Jesus makes this very clear in his teaching of his disciples. See, for example, his words about love and unity being attractive to the world, or his call to us to be light and salt to the world.[10]

Legalism Separates Us

Legalism encourages separation and drives unbelievers away. Our character is thought to be demonstrated by the company we keep rather than by the quality of our lives. We develop a kind of safety-in-numbers mentality, and we become more concerned with ourselves and our purity than with the needs of the world around us. Jesus reminds us that the heart of the law is mercy, and that sinners need mercy. Jesus was constantly criticized by the Pharisees and the teachers of the law because he delighted to be friends with and to eat and drink with sinners, tax collectors, and prostitutes. In response to these criticisms Jesus showed, both by his own example and by his teaching, that the people of God are called to extend God's grace to those trapped in sin, not to keep apart from them.[11]

---

[8] Luke 18:9–14.
[9] Matthew 23:23.
[10] Matthew 5:13–16; John 13:34–35; 17:20–21, 23.
[11] Matthew 9:9–13; 11:19; Luke 7:39; 19:7.

Both in Jesus's time and in ours, many of the rules thought to make us pure have as a central purpose to keep us apart from sinful people, to keep our children away from sinful children, and to keep them out of sinful homes. We teach our children to shun "worldly" people, rather than to show them mercy. Then when they grow up, we wonder why they find evangelism so difficult.

In other words, the rules we adopt have the effect of undermining the desire to love, serve, and communicate the gospel to unbelievers. Our rules undermine the believer's ability to relate to non-Christians in a comfortable way. We make ourselves so culturally different that we feel out of place with non-Christians, and non-Christians feel uncomfortable with us. Yet the things that produce this discomfort and displacement are not the marks of genuine righteousness and godliness, but are, in effect, simply external cultural differences. And even where the differences between Christians and the world are not merely external cultural practices but the contrast between real purity of life and genuinely sinful patterns—even then, our calling is to be merciful, just as Jesus was, and to delight in being friends with those around us, just as Jesus has come to us in love and friendship.

Legalism Undermines Authority

Legalism fosters rebellion against parents, against schools, against churches, and ultimately against God. Whenever we add to God's Word, we immediately increase the likelihood of resistance to our authority. Take the example of a required chapel service, or the insistence on attendance at a certain number of church meetings, or compulsory devotions, or obligatory spiritual disciplines. God does not force us to adore him, and we cannot compel a person to worship our Lord. If we try to make worship obligatory, we will produce either spiritual arrogance or superficial observance and a resistant heart.

Any believer who is seriously committed to reaching out with the gospel of Christ will know from experience that some of the most difficult people to reach are those who have rebelled because of the overly legalistic homes in which they were raised, or because of membership in churches that impose all sorts of unscriptural demands. The sinful nature responds with rebellion even to the requirements of God's beautiful commandments.[12] It responds even more negatively to those obligations imposed by humans in authority.

Where a church is characterized by legalism, unbelievers will resist the Christian faith even more, because they will assume there is nothing in the church for them. Even if they are by nature rigid people who cannot live without strict structures and are attracted by the rules, they will join with hearts closed to the truth and will participate in church life with no understanding of the grace that is the very heart of the gospel. It is surely in such a context that Jesus says that Pharisees and legalists make converts who are twice as much children of hell as they are themselves.[13]

Legalism Replaces the Gospel with Worldly Religion

Fundamentally, legalism is worldly, though it claims to be true religion. This is the point that the apostle Paul makes in his letter to the Colossians when he is addressing the problem of the rules imposed on Gentile believers by the Judaizers.[14] All other religions, including many unfaithful versions of the Christian faith (the only exception being true Christianity), are basically rule-oriented and require the practice of particular moral and spiritual disciplines so that their devotees will, through the carefully ordered life, find their way to God. Because of this, all other religions lead to a mentality of salvation and spiritual life—however these may be defined—as coming about through human effort.

Basically—and I write this as respectfully as I can—all the religions of this world are forms of works-righteousness, systems of human effort devised to search for and to please God. But Christians are to make known the one message that is different, the message that alone can save and transform.

Christ did not come to bring religious devotion or spiritual discipline or even an ethical code (though a life of devotion and moral beauty will come as fruits of knowing him). Rather, Jesus came to substitute his moral perfection for our moral failures and to bear our

---

[12] Romans 7:8–11.
[13] Matthew 23:15.
[14] Colossians 2:8, 20.

deserved penalty by his death on our behalf. Life, godliness, spirituality, and goodness come to us only as we hold out to him the empty hands of faith and as we begin to love him in response to his love for us. Any other message should be anathema to us, for it is a different gospel. This is the precise criticism that the apostle Paul makes of the false teachers in the churches of Galatia, who were requiring new converts to keep the laws of Judaism.[15]

Legalism Breeds Pride

When we read the Gospels, we discover that Jesus's harshest words are reserved for the legalists. Why does Jesus say such challenging things to these designers of rules who are passionately committed to being as explicit as possible about the requirements of detailed obedience to the Lord? The reason for the severity of Jesus's criticism is this: the most damaging problem of human rules is that we can keep them, simply because they are our rules, because they aim for the outside, and because they give us a set of actions to perform in the practical details of our daily lives. We can record our obedience to our rules in our own hearts, to one another, and to the Lord. We can measure our righteousness and feel good about ourselves (or despondent about our failures to keep things God did not command). Legalism produces self-righteousness and pride because we can keep our rules about food and clothing, books and movies, times for prayer, amounts given, services attended, and the like. Anyone can keep these rules with a little determined effort—anyone, whether a believer in Jesus or not.

God's law, when properly understood as aimed at our hearts, does not produce self-righteousness and pride. The reason God's law does not is that we cannot keep it. Not one of us has ever loved God with his or her whole heart, soul, mind, and strength. We have not loved our neighbor as we love ourselves. Not one of us has lived a day without pride, or anger, or greed, or selfishness. No one has a life that is always and everywhere characterized by justice, mercy, and faithfulness. It is impossible to be self-righteous when we look into God's perfect law.

Jesus is so hard on the legalists because their pride in their knowl-

---

[15] Galatians 1:6–9.

edge of their laws and in their ability to keep them is an obstacle to faith. His passionate denunciation has the purpose of humbling them. As he says to them on another occasion, "If you were blind, you would have no guilt; but now that you say, 'We see,' your guilt remains."[16]

Pride creates a heart that is hard to penetrate, eyes that refuse to see, ears that are closed. Jesus's harsh words arise from his commitment to break through their arrogant obstinacy. Later in Matthew's Gospel we find an even more damning indictment of the teaching and the lives of the Pharisees and scribes than the one in Matthew 15 and Mark 7. In Matthew 23 Jesus pronounces his seven terrible woes on the teachers of the law and the Pharisees. But even there, at the end of that shocking condemnation of their service, Jesus reveals his desire to save them. His words of love, longing, and distress are some of the loveliest words in the Gospels: "O Jerusalem, Jerusalem, the city that kills the prophets and stones those who are sent to it! How often would I have gathered your children together as a hen gathers her brood under her wings, and you were not willing!"[17]

When we read in the book of Acts that a great number of the Pharisees eventually came to faith, we know that the Lord's severe words bore their fruit in time; for he did, at last, gather many of those reluctant, proud, self-righteous, and obstinate people to himself.

The problem we face is this: When could it ever be appropriate for us to speak to people with the severity of Jesus? This is a very difficult question to answer, for unlike the Lord, each one of us has a Pharisee in our own hearts, a Pharisee who needs regular rebuke. We all struggle with pride and self-righteousness. We all try to hold at a distance the true demands of the law of God so that we will not be so readily condemned. We resist these wounds from our friend, the law, because we feel more comfortable congratulating ourselves on our shallow righteousness than we do when the law exposes our sins.

This sad reality of our own inner lives should mean that our severity toward the self-righteous and the legalists must always be tempered by compassion borne of our own failings in these matters. Our severity should also always be tempered by the agonized prayer of Jesus,

[16] John 9:41.
[17] Matthew 23:37.

quoted above. Is our denunciation of self-righteousness and legalism motivated by our own pride that we are not like the self-righteous Pharisees of our time and we are not legalists? Or is our denunciation of these obstacles to the gospel motivated by a passion for truth and by compassion for our present-day Pharisees?

Having made these necessary qualifications—we still must sit at Jesus's feet and recognize that all legalism is an implacable enemy of the gospel of grace. And we need to be prepared to fight against it, rather than bow to it or allow it to govern the life or outreach of our churches. Indeed, we may regard it as a principle: the more legalistic a church is, the less genuine outreach there will be. Attacking legalism is necessary to bring about the salvation of the legalists themselves by humbling them before the Lord, before his truth, and before his grace. Attacking legalism is also necessary in setting people free from the rules that the legalists impose upon them. We are to proclaim liberty: "For freedom Christ has set us free; stand firm, therefore, and do not submit again to a yoke of slavery."[18] This proclamation of liberty from legalism is one of the great friends of true proclamation of the gospel, both to the church and to the world.

Questions for Personal Reflection and Group Discussion

1. Are you truly convinced by our reflections on Jesus's criticisms of human rules?

2. Have you noticed how legalism so readily produces rebellion in children and young people (as well as adults!)?

3. Can you think of examples where rules we create keep Christians apart from unbelievers?

4. Do you see how all our rules are aimed at the outside and at things we have to do to measure up to a standard we personally set, or some Christian leader sets for us?

5. Is it clear to you that rules appear to enable us to measure our spiritual progress and that this is one of the reasons why they are so attractive to us, especially when we think of trying to help young Christians to grow in their Christian faith and life?

---

[18] Galatians 5:1.

6. Is it also clear to you that the problem with the appeal of rules is that because they make presumed spiritual progress measurable, they necessarily create either self-righteousness and pride or self-condemnation and despondency?

7. Do you see the sharp distinction between legalism and God's law: that God's law aims at the heart and at transformation from the inside out, and so produces humility and dependence on God's mercy and power, rather than self-righteousness and pride?

8. Where do you find yourself resisting God's law and its friendly wounds that expose your sin while substituting the rigors of God's law for the much easier requirements of our rules for the Christian life?

16

Rules for the
Family and Church?

In our past two chapters we saw how passionately Jesus attacked the legalism of the Pharisees and the teachers of the law. Their laws were not God's commandments for his people but were merely human rules. God had not given the leaders of Israel the right to make new legislation, nor has he given the leaders of the church the right to make new laws for Christians.

We saw too that all human rules aim for merely external practice and so encourage hypocrisy. Human rules emphasize the appearance of spirituality and a superficial righteousness, rather than the deep obedience from the heart at which God's law always aims.

In addition, Jesus insisted that human rules about holiness and the service of God always have the effect, even if unintentional, of nullifying God's commandments. Likewise, the rules Christians adopt today that seek to keep believers, especially young believers, apart from non-Christians often undermine God's call to show mercy to the sinful and broken people around us.

Jesus's criticism also focused on how sin works in our lives: all true defilement comes from within our hearts. Consequently, all the rules about appearance or about what we eat, drink, wear, read, listen to, or watch will never bring the fruit of true righteousness into our lives. We saw how neither the crowds nor the disciples understood this point, and so Jesus had to repeat it. This teaching was bewildering even to the apostles, whose thinking about righteousness was shaped by the centuries of emphasis on laws about food, about defilement by the world, and about purity through separation from the Gentiles, the Samaritans, and any others considered unclean.

All these teachings from Jesus were revolutionary to his contemporaries and are revolutionary for us today.

THE WOMAN AT THE WELL

A few examples from the Gospel records will help us further understand how deeply ingrained this attitude was regarding separateness and purity. Our first example comes from the encounter between Jesus and the woman at the well (John 4). The meeting begins with Jesus asking her for a drink of water. This seems a natural and unsurprising request to us. But the text draws our attention to the astonishment of the woman: "The Samaritan woman said to him, 'How is it that you, a Jew, ask for a drink from me, a woman of Samaria?'"[1] The woman's astonishment comes because she realizes that Jesus is breaking his culture's customs and laws by asking a Samaritan, and a woman, for a drink of water (v. 7).

In reflecting on this seemingly ordinary request, we should note that Jews did not drink or eat from containers used by Samaritans. Rabbi Eliezer taught, "He that eats the bread of the Samaritans is like to one that eats the flesh of swine"[2] (and we know, of course, that the Jews were forbidden to eat pork). Yet Jesus breaks his people's social customs, in fact the Jewish law of the time, when he asks the woman to use her container to draw water from the well for him. No Jew has ever requested food or drink from her before. Jesus does not even have something of his own from which to drink, something purified by Jewish law. He will have to drink from a vessel she has handled. She is amazed because she is aware of the extraordinary nature of his request. She understands that Jesus is defiling himself, that he is making himself ritually unclean, by what he is proposing to do.

We should notice also how John draws attention to her astonishment that Jesus is talking to a woman, as well as to a Samaritan. No man has ever before addressed her as a social equal. The disciples, too,

[1] John 4:9.
[2] *Mishnah*, Shebiith 8:10.

214 DELIGHTING IN THE LAW OF THE LORD

are surprised to find Jesus talking with a woman when they return (v. 27). This surprise shows how little they know him! All through the Gospel accounts we see Jesus treating women as equals, calling women to faith and to discipleship, teaching them the truth, and commissioning them for service in his kingdom.

Jesus sets aside the usual barriers that would keep him apart from the woman at the well. He ignores social custom, even Jewish law, in order to reach out to her. In the eyes of the Pharisees and teachers of the law, and of all devout Jews at that time, Jesus would be making himself ceremonially unclean. He would pollute himself by drinking water she has drawn for him from a container she has touched. Jesus sets aside these laws because they are not God's laws, but merely human rules, the traditions of the elders, imposed on God's people for many years by the Pharisees and scribes. For Jesus, only God has the authority to impose his laws on his people. To Jesus such laws are rubbish, and neither he nor any other Israelite is under any obligation to obey them.

ZACCHAEUS, THE TAX COLLECTOR

A second example comes with Luke's account of Jesus's inviting himself to the home of Zacchaeus, a chief tax collector.[3] When we turn to this story in Luke's Gospel, we read that the whole crowd of people present, not just the Pharisees and scribes, is deeply critical upon hearing Jesus tell Zacchaeus that he wishes to eat at Zacchaeus's table and then seeing him head off to Zacchaeus's house. The people despise the tax collectors because they work for the occupying Roman army. In addition, they despise them because most of them are corrupt and dishonest. So the people grumble out of hatred for men like Zacchaeus, who enrich themselves at the expense of their compatriots and collaborate with the enemy.

Despite all this, and despite the grumbling of the people, Jesus delights in the opportunity to spend time with Zacchaeus and honors him by gracing him with his presence at a meal in his home. Zacchaeus responds to this amazing invitation with joy:

---

[3] Luke 19:1–10.

[Jesus] entered Jericho and was passing through. And behold, there was a man named Zacchaeus. He was a chief tax collector and was rich. And he was seeking to see who Jesus was, but on account of the crowd he could not, because he was small of stature. So he ran on ahead and climbed up into a sycamore tree to see him, for he was about to pass that way. And when Jesus came to the place, he looked up and said to him, "Zacchaeus, hurry and come down, for I must stay at your house today." So he hurried and came down and received him joyfully. And when they saw it, they all grumbled, "He has gone in to be the guest of a man who is a sinner."[4]

We do not know all that happens on this day, for Luke has compressed the day's events into a few short verses. However, it is clearly understood by everyone present in the crowd that Jesus is received by Zacchaeus and that the two of them head off to Zacchaeus's home for a meal and a lengthy visit.

The reason for the crowd's complaints and criticisms is that Jesus's actions are totally unacceptable, even outrageous. There is more than hatred because of the close relationship with the Romans and the financial corruption. Indeed, what happens is remarkable, for in going to Zacchaeus's home to eat, Jesus is breaking not only the social customs, but also the religious and moral laws of his time by becoming a guest and eating in the home of a sinner, a man with an unclean profession. Jesus is making himself socially, ritually, morally, and religiously unclean by going to Zacchaeus's home. He is polluting himself just as if he had gone to the home of a Samaritan or a Gentile.

To try to understand this reaction, recall the subsequent words of the apostle Peter when he goes to the home of the Gentile Cornelius. A devout and God-fearing man, Cornelius gives generously to the poor and is held in high honor by the local Jews in Caesarea. Yet, on entering Cornelius's home, Peter says to those present, "You yourselves know how unlawful it is for a Jew to associate with or to visit anyone of another nation."[5]

It was against the laws of Judaism to enter the home of any Gentile, even a devout and generous God-fearer. What Jesus is doing on this

[4] Luke 19:1–7.
[5] Acts 10:28.

216 DELIGHTING IN THE LAW OF THE LORD

occasion is much worse than what Peter later finds both difficult and unlawful. Zacchaeus is considered as unclean as any Gentile because of his profession and his daily interactions with the Romans. To the minds of many Jews, to eat with Zacchaeus is even more "unclean" because he is a Jew who is constantly defiling himself. In addition, he is viewed as a notorious public sinner.

Jesus sets all this custom and law aside, for it is not God's law. These laws were designed to foster and maintain religious and moral separation and purity. But regardless of the intention of such laws, regardless of the motivation of separation and purity, Jesus sets them aside as merely human rules; for these rules were created by the leaders of God's people rather than by God, and so Jesus refuses to be bound by them.

In addition to this problem of their origin, these laws also prevent God's people from being obedient to their Lord's command to practice hospitality to strangers, to be merciful and gracious to the alien (that is, Gentiles), and to be kind to the sinful, the needy, and the poor. There are many such laws in the Mosaic legislation. God's people are required to invite the aliens (Gentiles) to eat with them at the times of festival so that the Gentiles could experience the kindness of God.

Sadly, it is true that such people—strangers, aliens, sinners, the needy, and the poor—are always, in every human society, regarded as outcast and unclean. But these laws about socially acceptable behavior and maintaining purity by separation are a moral offense to God, who calls his people to precisely the opposite way of life: to be a people characterized by the mercy, compassion, and grace that he has shown to them. Think again of the example of Boaz and his kindness toward Ruth. Ruth was an alien, a Gentile, and yet Boaz, in obedience to God's law, invited Ruth to come and eat with him and his harvesters and provided drink for her. By Jesus's day, Boaz would have been regarded as making himself "unclean" by his association with Ruth.

THE WOMAN WHO WASHED JESUS'S FEET

A third example from the Gospel narratives is Luke's account of the sinful woman who washed Jesus's feet with her tears and dried them with her hair.[6] The fact that Jesus allows the woman to come so close

---

[6] Luke 7:36–50.

to him and to touch him in such a personal and intimate way makes Simon the Pharisee question whether Jesus can truly be a prophet from God. We may imagine Simon's inner response this way: "If Jesus is prepared to have such a sinner get so close to him, then it is obvious that either he does not know what kind of a person she is or, if he does know what kind of a person she is, he is not committed to righteousness. If either of these is true, then I have to conclude that Jesus cannot be a prophet from God."

In Simon's view, those who know God, and who therefore pursue righteousness, know sin when they see it, and, even more importantly, they keep themselves apart from such sinners. Simon believes that association with sinners makes one unclean before God; his credo is that one is contaminated by the company one keeps. Jesus, however, teaches us that he came into the world precisely because people are sinners and therefore need mercy and compassion, both from him and from us his disciples.

RETURNING TO THE PROBLEM OF DETAILED RULES

This brings us back to problems with legalistic human rules. As we noted, detailed rules appear to give us the ability to measure and to record our growth in godliness, devotion, purity, and righteousness. We think that we, others, and the Lord can see how devout we are. However, Jesus is utterly unimpressed by such records of righteousness. In the Sermon on the Mount he calls his disciples to recognize their spiritual poverty, not to parade their acts of righteousness before the world.[7] This too was revolutionary to Jesus's contemporaries and it is revolutionary for us.

We observed the related problem that legalism separates us from unbelievers and drives them away. Legalistic rules have no power to attract unbelievers but feed contempt for those whom unbelievers see as self-righteous and rigid rather than as demonstrating the beauty of true holiness. We become characterized by our cultural differences as Christians rather than by the justice, mercy, compassion, and faithfulness that love for Christ ought to produce in us.

We saw too that legalism undermines the authority of God by

---

[7] Matthew 5:3; 6:1–18.

increasing the likelihood of rebelliousness in the hearts of children, young people, and indeed all believers. Such human rules also undermine submission to God's law because any kind of law becomes an offense to the person who is subjected to a life in which leaders dishonor God by lording it over others.

Furthermore, the apostle Paul teaches us that all legalistic rules about spirituality are worldly because the heart of all other religions is our searching for God, our offerings to God, our attempts to make our lives acceptable to God. But true religion is found only in the gospel of Christ, who gave himself up for his people so that we might give ourselves back to him in love and gratitude.

Finally, Jesus insists that the observance of human rules produces pride. The great attraction of human rules for spiritual devotion and holy living is that we can keep our rules and so feel proud before God, proud before each other, and proud before the world. This pride is deadly. It keeps us from knowing our utter dependence on Christ and from knowing the poverty of our spirituality and our righteousness. All faithful teaching of God's law will produce humility in our hearts because our sin is exposed and we are driven to our knees to seek the mercy and forgiveness of Christ.

It may seem that I have belabored these points by repeating these problems with human rules. However, I am persuaded that this is necessary. Human rules about spiritual devotion, about personal purity, and about holiness are a powerful enemy of the gospel of Christ—an enemy that keeps returning to trouble the church in every generation. That is why Jesus's teaching was revolutionary to his contemporaries, and it is revolutionary for us today.

NO RULES ALLOWED?

Having attacked legalism as strongly as I can, I recognize, of course, that we need to have some rules or structures in our families, our youth groups, our churches, our ministries, and our schools. We cannot do without rules altogether; Scripture and common sense teach us that things must be done decently and in order,[8] so we recognize that for practical reasons some rules are necessary.

---

[8] 1 Corinthians 14:40.

Especially in our responsibility for our own children, or if we are given responsibility for the children or teenagers of other people, then we must fulfill that calling with great care. In such settings we recognize that we are accountable for ensuring that the guardianship of moral behavior and wise oversight of relationships and daily habits are always in place.

In addition to this moral responsibility, it is obvious that in the life of any church or school or ministry we need to know when services, classes, study and work times, or meals are to be observed and how they are to be run. Life is full of details such as this, for in any human setting we need some structures for things to run smoothly. Yet we need to remember that families, schools, ministries, churches, or even summer camps are not businesses or military units where efficiency and order are fundamental. Sadly, some homes, churches, and ministries are run more like businesses or military units. However, efficiency and order are not their essential characteristics. Rather, love, service, respect, honor, and self-sacrifice are the essential characteristics of families, churches, and ministries of every kind.

Recognizing this, we ought to keep rules to an absolute minimum, rather than, as is often our automatic response, coming up with another rule whenever a problem arises. So how are we to think about our rules and our structures to avoid the risk of coming under the condemnation of Jesus and of the Word of God? I do not want to hear the Lord's rebuke on the day of judgment: "Jerram, why did you impose these rules on the consciences of your sons when you were a father, on the consciences of the members of my church when you were a pastor, on the consciences of your students when you were a seminary professor? I gave you no such authority!"

In our seeking to be wise about rules, the most important issue will be to remember the nature of the laws that God has revealed to us in his Word. God's law is a marvelous gift that promises freedom, blessing, and life to us as we commit ourselves to obey it out of love for Christ and in humble dependence on the Spirit. We think so positively about God's commandments because submission to them brings maturity and beauty into our lives. In contrast, the legalism of

220 DELIGHTING IN THE LAW OF THE LORD

human rules, which so often plagues the people of God, brings bondage, immaturity, and rebellion into our homes, churches, schools, and ministries.

God's law reflects his character. His law reveals what human life is to be like as we live in a way that reflects the image of God and so become more fully human. His law teaches us what it means for us to love God and to love our neighbors. His law aims for the heart, not the outside. His law encourages growth in moral wisdom as we seek to walk in the Lord's ways and to apply the inner meaning of the law to every aspect of our lives. So, how are we to proceed as we design the few rules that may be necessary?

DESIGNING GOOD RULES

1. First of all, we will require obedience to God's commandments. If, for example, we are running a youth ministry or a camping trip, we will have to do all that we can to ensure that young people are not sleeping together, that they respect other people's property, and that they do not lie to their leaders or to one another or gang up against other children. These are not human rules; they are the commandments of the Lord. We are answerable to their parents for the time children and young people are under our care, so we must both teach God's law and have structures in place that will help to make sure that his laws are obeyed. Even then, we must always seek to help those under our responsibility understand why God's commandments are for their good.

2. When it is needful to have human rules in addition to God's commandments, we should learn from God's law, for it expresses his character and is designed for our nature, and so everything in it has a reason that can be explained. His commandments define what it means to be human, and so they are meaningful. In the same way, any rule we adopt for the life of home, church, or any other Christian institution must be explicable very easily. If it does not make sense, a rule should not be there. It ought to be possible to explain why a particular rule is needed in order that our humanness may flourish.

3. We do not need, nor should we have, arbitrary rules that are there just for the purpose of being obeyed. Unfortunately many books

on family life teach precisely the opposite: that it is essential to put rules in place just to show who is in charge, or to impose them simply as a display of our authority over young people. But God's rules are never arbitrary or merely for the purpose of displaying his authority over us. They are always for bringing the good life into being.

4. God requires that we teach explicitly that any human rules for church and family life are not the law of God, and so they are not moral absolutes. Therefore they must not be made binding on the consciences of people in the same way as we seek to make God's words binding on the conscience. We have to distinguish constantly between God's laws and our rules so that church members and children are never in confusion about this issue. The Presbyterian Church in America Book of Church Order reminds us that our authority as church leaders is declarative, not legislative.[9] Christian leaders and parents often make mistakes at this point; but we must resist this tendency if we desire to be obedient to the Lord.

5. The above point reminds us that God's law must be taught far more frequently and clearly than any rules. We need to ask ourselves regularly, what are we teaching our children, our young people, and our members? This is especially true for Christian schools and youth ministries; but it is also true for parents. Far too often our rules about the details of life or our programs for keeping things running smoothly become more important than the weighty matters of the law: justice, mercy, and faithfulness. Jesus, however, reminds us that it is these weighty matters of his law that must be kept central in our teaching and practice.[10]

6. Love is central in everything, and love must be kept in the center when we make our rules. Paul says that all the laws there are can be summed up in one: "Love your neighbor." He writes:

> Owe no one anything, except to love each other, for the one who loves another has fulfilled the law. For the commandments, "You shall not commit adultery, You shall not murder, You shall not steal, You shall not covet," and any other commandment, are summed up in this

---

[9] Many denominations and churches have such statements on their books, but, sadly, this wisdom is frequently ignored.
[10] Matthew 23:23.

word: "You shall love your neighbor as yourself." Love does no wrong
to a neighbor; therefore love is the fulfilling of the law.[11]

In the same way that God's commandments about human relationships
serve the law of love, so our rules must serve the law of love. We adopt
them for practical reasons, so that in the family, in the church, or in
the school we might better serve human relationships. Of almost any
rule in our homes we need to ask, is this particular rule here so that
we might love one another better? If any rule hinders this purpose,
then it should not be in place.

7. In contrast to the unchanging nature of God's commandments,
our rules must be flexible. We need to ask ourselves regularly: Do
these rules continue to serve the purpose for which we adopted them?
Are they damaging relationships if we insist on continuing to apply
them? Too easily rules we have in place become the context for a
power struggle between people rather than a means of meeting human
needs. Once a human rule no longer serves the purpose for which it
was adopted, it needs to be summarily abandoned.

8. God's commandments encourage growth in wisdom and in maturity as believers seek to apply his law to every aspect of their lives.
Think of the story of Boaz. He is clearly a man who spent his days
meditating on God's commandments, thinking about the way those
commandments called him to imitate the generosity and kindness of
God, and then asking himself what it would mean for him to treat well
those who worked in his fields and to meet the needs of aliens, widows, and orphans who came into his life. The desire for true obedience
to any of God's commandments will produce this life of meditation,
prayer, and wise application. We need to ask whether our human rules
are having this same maturing effect on the lives of people. Too often
human rules exist for the purpose of telling young people precisely
what we want them to do, rather than for the purpose of helping them
to grow in wisdom and personal maturity. Such rules need to be set
aside, for the whole point of childhood is to move into adulthood, not
to remain in permanent dependence on the commands of others. As
teachers at a seminary, my colleagues and I have to ask ourselves this

[11] Romans 13:8–10.

question over and over again: Shall we require this student to observe this rule, or shall we let him or her make a choice, live with the consequences, and mature in the process?

9. We should never be satisfied with bare obedience. Christ says to us, "If you love me, . . . keep my commandments."[12] In the same way, our desire should be always that church members, children, and young people in youth ministries or in schools should be obeying out of love, rather than out of fear of punishment, mere duty, or simply because we are bigger and stronger than those under us, or because we have the power to enforce obedience. For anyone in authority, if there is only obedience rather than glad obedience out of love, we know that resentment and grudging submission will be the consequence.

10. We need to discipline far more seriously for disobedience to God's commands—stealing, lying, gossip, unkindness to others—than for the breaking of human rules about attendance, homework, clothing, makeup, cleanliness, tidiness, music, books, and the like. This is an area where families, youth groups, and Christian schools often make mistakes. If we discipline for minor offenses against our rules and fail to discipline for the major offenses of unkindness, social exclusion, untruthfulness, or abusive language, we will communicate utterly false views of what is truly significant in human life. This dishonors the Lord by replacing his laws with ours, and produces lives that are content with moral standards of very questionable value.

11. Our discipline is to be modeled on God's discipline of us. He disciplines us out of love, not out of anger. His discipline is always for our good; it is not an exercise in arbitrary power, nor is it an attempt to prove he is in charge. Rather, he disciplines us to produce the peaceable fruit of righteousness.[13] Can we say the same about the discipline that we impose on our children, our students, our youth, or our church members?

12. We are stewards and servants of our children, young people, and church members. God is their Lord and Father. All responsibility is given to us that we might help others to come to the full realization of who is their true Father and Lord. So with our children at home and

---

[12] John 14:15.
[13] Hebrews 12:5–11.

with young people in schools and youth ministries, our desire should be to give them ever more freedom as they mature, so that they will learn to walk in love for God and in obedience to their heavenly Father. The rules must be removed and those who have been under their tutelage must learn to be discerning for themselves, even though this may mean making mistakes. Our heavenly Father has given us the parable of the prodigal son (or the lost sons) to remind us of the freedom he gives us in order that we might learn to freely love and obey him.[14] "For freedom Christ has set us free; stand firm therefore, and do not submit again to a yoke of slavery."[15]

I will close this discussion with a reminder of the context of all our exercise of responsibility for children or young people or members of our churches. The parable of the lost sons teaches us that God, who is the perfect Father, only has ungrateful and rebellious children; he has children all of whom resist him, yet we are children that he continues to love, that he pursues, and that he delights to welcome back home.

When (not if) our children, our young people, our students, or our members go through times of ingratitude or rebellion, we ought not to presume had we done everything just right, or done something differently, or had better rules in place, then there would have been no trouble. Do we believe that we could have been more successful parents or overseers than our heavenly Father if we had adjusted something here or there? He is perfect; we are not. There are no perfect parents, other than the Lord. There are no perfect teachers, pastors, and ministry leaders. We all need and can receive the grace and mercy of God every moment of our lives.

The resistance—or even, for a time, rebellion—of our children, our young people, our students, or our members does not mean that we should cut them off; nor does it mean that the Lord has finished with them, any more than our struggles, our sins, and our periods of doubt or lack of faith mean that the Lord has finished with us.

> If we say we have no sin, we deceive ourselves, and the truth is not in us. If we confess our sins, he is faithful and just to forgive us our

---

[14] Luke 15:11–32.
[15] Galatians 5:1.

sins and to cleanse us from all unrighteousness. If we say we have not sinned, we make him a liar, and his word is not in us.

My little children, I am writing these things to you so that you may not sin. But if anyone does sin, we have an advocate with the Father, Jesus Christ the righteous. He is the propitiation for our sins, and not for ours only but also for the sins of the whole world.[16]

Questions for Personal Reflection and Group Discussion

1. Are you truly convinced by our reflections on Jesus's criticisms of human rules? I ask this question once more because Jesus's teaching on this issue is truly radical.

2. How many of the cultural habits and rules about Christian purity we adopt today have a purpose or effect of preventing believers from being friendly, merciful, and gracious to those outside the church or those who are disobeying God's commandments? Try to think of rules that do this, even if this is uncomfortable for you as a parent, or as a teacher, or as someone subject to such rules.

3. Do you agree that we ought to be able to explain the reason for and the value of any rules we adopt as furthering the flourishing of our humanness? Can you think of good examples of rules that serve our human flourishing?

4. Do you agree that our rules are not to be arbitrary or simply about the exercise of our power or control over our children, young people, or members?

5. How important is it that any rules we adopt should serve the law of love and so help the development of human relationships in our families and churches? Do you know of examples of rules that do the opposite and that damage human relationships?

6. Do you know of examples where human rules have been taught and imposed as strongly as, or even more forcefully than, the commands of God?

7. What do you think of my proposal that all our human rules, simply because they are human, must be flexible, and that we should be ready to abandon or change them whenever it is wise?

8. Would you add any other guidelines about human rules to this chapter's proposal of twelve? (Please send them to me via Crossway.)

---

[16] 1 John 1:8–2:2.

17

JESUS APPLIES THE LAW

Our reflections on Jesus's passionate attack on legalism led us to think about what place human rules ought to have in our lives. We recognized that any imposition of human rules and structures has to be educated by God's law. Any parent understands that little children need all kinds of rules and structures simply for their own safety. In addition, we understand that very often with a young child there is no opportunity to explain why we have a particular rule or why we have to demand instant obedience of them. A very small child does not know enough about the dangers in the world to be able to comprehend all our reasons for requiring him or her to do what we say. Think, for an obvious example, of refusing to allow a two-year-old to cross the road without holding a parent's hand; or not letting that same child help with putting wood on an open fire, or remove a sheet of cookies the child has helped prepare from a four-hundred-degree oven. Authority, order, obedience, and rules are clearly essential in any such setting. The same is true in many other aspects of daily living with people at every stage of life.

However, even in such a setting it is needful that we who are parents know that our commands are not arbitrary but are rooted, like God's law, in love, in the flourishing of human life, in safety, and in wise reasons. As the child grows, we remove many of the regulations that are necessary in the early stages of life, and we need to be able to give excellent reasons for those that remain. Long before a teenager leaves home for college, he or she has to be helped by parents to mature to the point where wise and sensible decisions can be made rather than foolish and destructive ones. This can happen only when the rules of childhood are replaced with personal freedom.

The book of Proverbs addresses this need to grow in practical wisdom. Most of the proverbs are not laws but rather examples of prudence that comes from maturing moral wisdom. Our homes, too, should ideally be places of close relationship and wise instruction where children can grow into moral maturity. The legalistic mentality that plagues many Christian homes and so many churches of every kind is the enemy of such growth into moral wisdom. Instead of steady development into maturity, young people are given rules, some of which have an appearance of wisdom, and many of which are arbitrary, imposed on every area of their lives. Significant numbers of such rules have the result of preventing young believers from being gracious, merciful, and kind to those outside the church; and all such rules deserve the same passionate rejection that Christ pronounced on the rules of his day. The central requirements of God's law are set aside in the interests of protection, purity, and separation from the world, and this should be an anathema to us.

I will never forget one of our sons inviting a fifteen-year-old friend to come and stay with us for the weekend. The young man was delighted with the invitation until he learned that I am a pastor. His response was, "Don't tell your father I am an atheist; if he finds out, he will hate me and not let me come to stay in your home." My son assured him that I am not like that. However, this sad story reveals how widespread such views are. What a tragedy that this would be the expectation of a young non-Christian concerning all those who represent Christ and who teach of his love! Lord, have mercy on us, and incline our hearts to hear your Word.

At its very heart the legalistic mentality betrays a lack of trust: trust in our children and, above all, trust in the Lord. He most certainly knows better than we do what is wise and needful for our children. Do we believe that the good life comes from listening to our Creator and Redeemer? He calls us to trust him, rather than to be afraid of the world and, in our fear, to design our own means of protection from its influence. He also calls us to trust our children as he trusts us; and he calls us to remember that he trusts us even though we are all aware that we are not entirely trustworthy.

I am often amazed when I think of all the responsibilities the Lord has given me. I ask myself, "Does he really know me?" Of course he does! He, in his grace, understands that we will only grow into his likeness as he gives us tasks that seem to us rather more than we can handle. The same is true for our children. We have, at some point, to allow teenagers to drive, even though we know perfectly well that these young men and women have no true understanding of the power of the machine we put into their hands, of the damage they might do to themselves and others, or how they might deal with all the possible challenges they might face. Wisdom only arises from gradually expanding freedom and steadily growing experience.

As we think back on Jesus's attack on legalism, we should notice that we, in fact, looked at only two or three places in the Gospel accounts where Jesus teaches on this problem. There are many more such passages, some of them even more passionate in their dismissal of the teaching of the scribes and Pharisees than the one we studied in Mark 7. The strongest of these passages is Matthew 23, with its seven woes against these teachers. We should notice that these attacks on legalism are one of the primary ways in which Jesus unfolds the true nature of God's commandments. However, we will leave this particular aspect of Jesus's teaching and move to consideration of other ways in which our Savior presents the law of God.

WHAT MUST I DO?

In an earlier chapter we looked at Jesus's encounter with the teacher of the law who came to question and to challenge our Lord's fitness to teach.[1] We noted how Jesus teaches the law by telling a story, one that reveals the beauty of righteousness and opens to his hearer the inner meaning of God's commandments. On that occasion Jesus tells the parable of the good Samaritan as an exposition of the command to love one's neighbor as oneself. Several of Jesus's parables have this kind of reflection on the inner intent of the commandments. I have mentioned the example of the parable of the prodigal son or the lost

---

[1] Luke 10:25–37.

sons. This story is not primarily an exposition of laws about relationships between fathers and sons, but it certainly has much to teach us about parental love and about filial obedience.

As we consider other ways that Jesus teaches the law, or uses the law to communicate the truth to the people around him, we will look at Luke 18:18–27. This is another account of a man who asks Jesus, "What must I do to inherit eternal life?"

Who is the questioner on this occasion? Luke describes him as "a certain ruler,"[2] and as the conversation with Jesus unfolds, we also learn that he is wealthy. Two other Gospel accounts add a little more information about him. Matthew tells us that he is a young man.[3] Mark adds that he ran up to Jesus.[4] "A rich young ruler" is how Christians have usually described this man. By "ruler" Luke probably means that he is a ruler or "elder" of the synagogue, for Luke uses a similar word to describe Jairus.[5] It is possible that even though he is young, this man is already a member of the Sanhedrin (the central body of elders over the people of God); but most likely he is an elder of his local synagogue. In our setting today he would be a youthful elder in a church.

We can easily imagine this young man. We all know men like him: bright, fit, prosperous, successful, gifted in leadership, eager to learn and to serve, earnest and well-meaning. He is evidently an upright, outstanding, respectable, and decent man. He is the kind of man we would be proud to have as a brother or a friend; or if you are older, like me, he is the kind of man you would be proud to have as a son or a son-in-law. Luke gives this account of their meeting:

> And a ruler asked him, "Good Teacher, what must I do to inherit eternal life?" And Jesus said to him, "Why do you call me good? No one is good except God alone. You know the commandments: 'Do not commit adultery, Do not murder, Do not steal, Do not bear false witness, Honor your father and mother.'" And he said, "All these I have kept from my youth." When Jesus heard this, he said to him, "One thing you still lack. Sell all that you have and distribute to the

[2] Luke 18:18, NIV.
[3] Matthew 19:22.
[4] Mark 10:17.
[5] Luke 8:41.

poor, and you will have treasure in heaven; and come, follow me." But when he heard these things, he became very sad, for he was extremely rich.[6]

It is clear that this man's question is sincere, for there is no suggestion that he is testing Jesus or simply wanting to engage in theological debate, as was true of the Bible scholar. This young man is being genuine in his respect when he addresses Jesus as "Good Teacher." Mark adds for us the detail that the young man runs up to Jesus and falls on his knees at Jesus's feet to ask his question, "What must I do to inherit eternal life?"[7]

Just as in the story of the expert in the law, this encounter raises the question, why does Jesus not answer him? In this situation it seems even more troubling, for here is a man who is eager to know the answer to his question, not someone playing games or showing off his knowledge. Why does Jesus not tell him how to inherit eternal life? For those of us who are Christian believers, how would we likely respond if such an earnest young man were to ask us such a question? We would be out with our Bibles in a moment, stumbling over our words in our eagerness to tell him how to be saved. We might want to share with him a clear summary of the gospel, such as the Four Spiritual Laws, or the Roman Road.

On reflection, we can fairly readily understand why Jesus does not answer the insincere teacher of the law who asks a similar question, but why not this serious young man? He is sincere. He is eager to know, so eager that he has run up to Jesus and fallen on his knees before him. He genuinely respects Jesus. Mark even tells us that Jesus "looked at him and loved him."[8]

We wonder what is going on, for the truth is that many Christians are troubled by this story and by what Jesus says to the young man. Is Jesus driving him away? Is he teaching him salvation through good deeds? Is he telling him that he will get to heaven by giving up his wealth? I have heard sermons that have understood the passage this way, sermons in which there is no message of salvation by grace, but

---

[6] Luke 18:18–23.
[7] Mark 10:17.
[8] Mark 10:21, NIV.

only a challenge to be obedient to God's commandments and to be prepared to give away one's wealth.

Jesus's Response to the Young Man's Question

We can be certain that Jesus is not teaching this young man salvation by good works; nor is he encouraging him to try to inherit eternal life by giving money to the poor. So what is Jesus saying to him? To understand what Jesus is doing we need to look with care at this conversation.

As he does in so many of his encounters with people, Jesus responds to the young man's question with a question of his own. On this occasion Jesus adds a couple of statements to his question: "Why do you call me good? No one is good except God alone. You know the commandments: 'Do not commit adultery, Do not murder, Do not steal, Do not bear false witness, Honor your father and mother.'"

Jesus's question is in itself fascinating, and again some Christians are troubled by it. When Jesus asks, "Why do you call me good?" is Jesus denying that he is good, and is he suggesting that the young man should doubt Jesus's goodness? Of course not! The question is intended to disclose the heart and mind of this young man; and even more, its purpose is to help the young man understand his own heart and mind. Jesus is eager for him to reflect on what it means to be called good. Jesus does not ask the young man directly, "Are you good?" or "Am I good?" Rather Jesus replies with a less direct question, "Why do you call me good?" Then he explains his question with his first statement, "No one is good except God alone." What is Jesus getting at here? There is a lot for this young man to think about in Jesus's brief response. If we reflect on it, we can see four questions within Jesus's words:

1. "What is true goodness? Do you understand what it means to describe someone as good?" We throw the ascription of goodness around very lightly; but we need to ask ourselves if we have truly thought about what we mean when we give someone such a character assessment.
2. "What are the consequences of recognizing that only God is good?" The theological affirmation that Jesus makes here is this: true goodness is found in God alone. Given this, what does that mean for any ordinary person who does not measure up to this goodness of God?

3. "Why are you calling me good? If you truly see me as good, then who am I? I do not deny that I am good, but rather I ask you to reflect on who I must be if I am indeed good." The question is, in fact, an indirect claim to divinity by Jesus as the necessary consequence of acknowledging that he is truly good.

4. "What about you? If you understand what goodness is, then is it possible for you to claim to be good? But if you recognize that you are not good, then, what are the consequences? How could there be anything that you could *do* to inherit eternal life?"

After his question and affirmation that only God has true goodness, Jesus helps the young man further by summarizing the second table of the law. (The first part, or table, of the law is about our relationship with God; the second part is about our relationships with each other.) "You know the commandments: 'Do not commit adultery, Do not murder, Do not steal, Do not bear false witness, Honor your father and mother.'"

What Jesus desires to do with his summary of the law about human relationships is to get the young man thinking about his failure to keep these commandments. Jesus is encouraging him to see that he is not truly good. He may be a decent young man if he compares himself with other people around him; but if he compares himself with God, the one alone who is truly good, then he cannot claim goodness, for he is not good like God. He will have to come to the realization of the apostle Paul, "All have sinned and fall short of the glory of God."[9] Any true and deep understanding of these requirements of the law will have the effect of convicting the young man of the poverty of his goodness. As we have seen in earlier chapters, all faithful reflection on the law will have this convicting consequence, for this is one of the gracious purposes of the law.

THE YOUNG MAN'S ANSWER

How does this young man answer? As a leader of God's people, the young man, of course, is familiar with the second table of the law and its summary of what it means to love our neighbor as ourselves. He not only knows this outline of the law but, as a faithful and regular

---

[9] Romans 3:23.

worshipper at his synagogue, has spent his life trying to devote himself to observing these commandments. And so he responds: "All these I have kept from my youth." He is clearly not aware of the vast gap between his own "goodness" and the true goodness of God. He has not yet understood the full meaning of these commandments, which are so simple to learn and even appear easy to be obeyed, at least externally. His understanding of the law is shallow, for he does not yet see that each of these commandments demands purity of the heart. The tenth commandment makes this clear by applying the rest of the commandments to the heart: "You shall not covet."

The commandments this young man has committed himself to observing since he was a boy mean the following: Adultery is not just the outward act but lust of the eyes and mind. Murder is not only refraining from killing someone, but hatred, scorn, and despising another—even calling someone a fool. Theft is not merely the stealing of someone's property, but covetousness toward property, reputation, ability, or anything else that belongs to another. False testimony is not simply telling falsehoods in court to harm another, but any failure to tell the truth about my neighbor and any failure to speak well of my neighbor—so that all gossip and any words intended to bring discredit on my neighbor or to make me appear better than my neighbor are also forbidden by this commandment. What does it truly mean to honor one's parents? It certainly means that we are to treat them with respect, whether they always deserve it or not, but it also means to love, care for, and serve them when they need our help and support. And so it is with every other commandment: we cannot claim to have kept them until we have understood and fully obeyed the full measure of what these commandments require of us.

The young leader of the synagogue has not begun to reflect upon the full extent of the righteousness that the law of God requires, and so he is unaware that he is not a good man. He is oblivious to his true state: that he is in desperate need of the forgiveness of God. He knows that he is not a murderer, that he is not an adulterer or fornicator, that he is not a thief, that he has never testified falsely about anyone in court, that he has been respectful to his parents in word and deed. Consequently, he believes himself to be a decent, honest, faithful, and

God-fearing man. By claiming goodness for himself, he misses entirely the point of Jesus's statement that only God is good. The young man's reply says, in effect, "I am good, too, for I have obeyed the law."

JESUS'S REPLY TO THE YOUNG MAN'S CLAIM OF VIRTUE

What does Jesus say in response to this claim of goodness? Jesus does not simply contradict him with words such as: "You are quite wrong. You have not kept these commandments. You are not good. You need forgiveness." It is noteworthy that Jesus does not refute the young man's claim of goodness with a direct statement, for example, "You are a sinner; you deserve judgment."

Such an approach is what preachers of the Word often do, especially in evangelistic meetings; and we seem to think that the louder and more vehemently we say this sort of thing, the more strongly people will be convicted. This is also what we feel we should do in personal conversations with non-Christians. We feel that the way to convict unbelievers of sin is to have the courage to come out with direct statements: "You are a sinner. You need to repent and believe the gospel!" It is of course true that all people are sinners and that they need to repent and believe the gospel. But Jesus does not take this approach. Instead, Jesus tries once more to help the man see the true state of his heart. "One thing you still lack. Sell all that you have and distribute to the poor, and you will have treasure in heaven; and come, follow me."[10]

Jesus asks him to give up his wealth, to give it to the poor, and then to return and follow the Lord. Why does Jesus say this to him? Again, many believers are troubled by these words. Is Jesus teaching salvation by distributing one's wealth? Once more, *no!* The young man has failed to see that he does not understand the requirements of the second table of the law, and that he has no sense yet of his moral poverty. By bringing up the man's wealth, Jesus is returning him to the law and its requirements. But this time Jesus wants him to reflect on the first table of the law, the commandments about worshipping and serving God alone—in particular the commandment against idolatry.

By his challenge to give up his wealth Jesus is asking the young

---

[10] Luke 18:22.

man: What has the place of priority in your heart? You think you are obeying the commandments and are therefore good. But ask your heart where its devotion lies. Whom do you worship in truth? Or, perhaps, what do you worship? What do you live for? What shapes your choices day by day: is it the Lord, or is it your money? The young man knows that the law commands him to love and to serve God alone, and, of course, he thinks that he does love and serve God alone. So what is Jesus telling him or seeking to help him to understand?

1. Jesus desires to expose the young man's devotion to his wealth, to turn his eyes to look into his heart where he will see not only love for God, but also love for money. What does the man's heart treasure? In the Sermon on the Mount Jesus makes it plain that it is impossible to love both God and money.

2. Jesus wants this leader of God's people to realize that he lacks true righteousness toward God and toward his neighbor. He thinks that he is keeping the commandments about loving one's neighbor, the second table of the law. But Jesus wants him to reflect more deeply on these commandments: Does he, in fact, love the poor as the law of God demands? Is it not true that when he sees the poor, he often closes his heart against their need of his help, rather than giving generously to them? The apostle John teaches us that if we close our hearts against our neighbor who is in need of our help, then the love of God has no place in us.[11]

3. Is his treasure on earth, or is it in heaven? Is he genuinely seeking eternal life, the life of the heavenly kingdom, or is his present comfort the thing that means the most to him? What governs the choices he makes: life now, or the life to come? This is precisely what Jesus teaches in the Sermon on the Mount. There Jesus charges us to lay up treasures in heaven, where moth and rust do not corrupt and where no thieves break in and steal; we are to do this rather than devote our time to thinking about how we can make our own lives more comfortable and financially secure, for that is simply laying up treasures on earth.[12]

4. Jesus also claims to be the one the young man should love and serve. Jesus says, in effect: "Forsake everything else in your life and

---

[11] 1 John 3:16–18; see also James 2:15–16.
[12] Matthew 6:19–21.

follow me. I am indeed good, as you say, and that means that I am God, and therefore you should forsake your riches to serve me alone." Jesus is claiming to be the Lord God, Creator of heaven and earth and the Judge and Lawgiver of the whole human race. Serving Jesus alone, serving God alone—this is what the whole law is teaching, for the Old Testament law summarizes all its commandments with these words: "You shall love the Lord your God with all your heart, and with all your soul, and with all your mind, and with all your strength."

These are challenging words to this young elder of the synagogue, and so he goes away sorrowful. Jesus has spoken to his heart at last. The man is beginning to understand that he is not, after all, quite so good as he has always thought. But he is not yet ready to reveal the secrets of his heart to Jesus and then to acknowledge his need.

Jesus wants him to come to the point where he can say: "I see now that I have not kept the commandments from my youth. In fact, I see that I have not kept them one single day of my life. There is nothing I can do that will qualify me for entrance into the kingdom of heaven. My heart is torn between devotion to God and to my wealth. I know that I am a selfish man—sometimes kind to the poor, but far more often kind only to myself. My treasures are mostly here on earth. How did you see into my heart? How are you able to tell me everything I ever did? Lord, help me!" This is the cry that should have come from his sorrowing heart. But he is not there yet; and so we want to ask, is this the end of the story? Hasn't Jesus just driven him away?

We cannot be certain of course, but it is very probable that the young elder of the synagogue came back to Jesus later. The early church identified the rich man who provided a tomb for Jesus's body, after his crucifixion, with the young man of this encounter with Jesus. We will find out for sure one day, but it seems likely that Jesus's revealing of the secrets of the man's heart did begin to draw him to the love that Jesus showed for him. If this was indeed the man, then one day we can ask him how long it was before his worldly sorrow of that day was turned to a godly sorrow that led him back to Jesus and to repentance and faith.

What was impossible for this rich young man to do, that is to enter the kingdom of God, was possible for Jesus. What is impossible for any rich man, or indeed for any man or woman, is to enter the kingdom of God by one's own virtue and deeds. But this is what the kingdom of God is all about: the resolution of this impossible problem. God has done for us, in Jesus, what is impossible for us to do. Jesus has fulfilled every requirement of the law, in our place, by the moral perfection of his life. Jesus has met all the sanctions of the law for us by his death on the cross. Jesus comes to us in his love and in the perfection of his holiness and leads us to conviction by exposing our failures to keep the law's demands. Having humbled us and made us aware of our need, he calls us graciously to trust him and to follow him.

In this encounter between Jesus and the rich young ruler we see played out in dramatic form the story of the life and conversion of every one of us. We also see how the law is to be used to lead people to the conviction of sin and to faith in Christ.

Questions for Personal Reflection and Group Discussion

1. Did you grasp the point about the difference between proverbs and laws? Proverbs are expressions of mature wisdom; laws are God's absolute requirements for human life. Proverbs are prudent reflections on the application of the commandments. Laws are direct statements of how we must live. Does this distinction help you to think about the kind of moral teaching, rather than the imposition of human rules, we need to have in our families and in our youth groups?

2. It is clear that the rich young man did not understand the deep righteousness that the law requires. How deep is your understanding of the commandments? Do you truly think of them as commands from God that require purity of your words and thoughts as well as of your actions? It might be helpful here to go through the second table of the law, commandment by commandment, asking your own heart this question.

3. Have you in the past found this story of Jesus's encounter with the rich young ruler somewhat confusing? Have you been troubled by the words that Jesus says to this man?

4. Jesus asks a very challenging question: What governs the choices that we make? What is the treasure of our hearts? Ask yourself: What is my treasure: is it my present comfort, security, and happiness, or is it the life to come? Am I saving up treasures in heaven, or merely spending and saving treasures on this earth? (Again, this is a difficult question to discuss in a group. It might

be wise to spend several minutes in personal prayer and reflection about this issue, asking the Holy Spirit to reveal to us the devotions of our hearts.)

5. John Calvin said that our hearts are idol factories. What about the idols of your heart? If you were to meet Jesus today, what question or challenge might he bring to you that would send you away sorrowful? Have you ever forsaken any idol to follow Jesus?

6. Do you understand that each one of these questions is so difficult that we can only answer: "Lord, this is impossible for me to do; you must change my heart, Lord, or else I will die without ever knowing you, or ever serving you; I cannot save myself!"?

18

Jesus Shows
Amazing Grace

In the previous chapter we reflected on the way Jesus used the law to challenge "the rich young ruler," the young and wealthy synagogue elder who came to honor Jesus and to ask him how to inherit eternal life. Just as with Jesus's encounter with the expert in the law who asked the same question, we saw how Jesus did not answer the question directly. Instead, he took both of these men back to the law. This raises a fascinating and challenging question: when is it appropriate for us to use the law when we are presenting the Christian faith to people, and when is it appropriate simply to proclaim the good news of eternal life and salvation through Jesus?

To remind ourselves of the issue, let me briefly review what Jesus did with the young man. First, he challenged him to remember that God alone is truly good and righteous. Second, he reminded him of the second table of the law, our duties to our neighbor. In response the young man claimed to have obeyed these commandments from his youth. With this claim he revealed his lack of understanding of the full requirements of the law and also of his own lack of compliance with the law. Third, Jesus turned to the first table of the law with its call to love God above anything else in life, and by doing this Jesus revealed the idolatrous love of wealth in the young man's heart. Such treasuring of money undermines our obligation to love God with our whole heart, mind, soul, and strength, and also undermines the call of the second table of the law to love our neighbor as ourselves.

Jesus expounded the law to this young man because he wanted him to come to the point where he could say: "I see now that I have not kept the commandments one single day of my life. Nothing I can do will qualify me for entrance into the kingdom of heaven. My treasures are mostly here on earth. Lord, help me!" This is the cry of a sorrowing heart.

We saw in an earlier chapter that this same attempt to teach the law and so expose sin was precisely what Jesus was doing in his encounter with the expert in the law. Jesus told the parable of the good Samaritan to that man to expound the second table of the law and to reveal to the expert how far short he was falling from fulfilling the law. He might know the Scriptures well enough to have deep theological discussions or to prove how well trained he was in the law. But he had never applied the deep requirements of the law to his own heart or seen his complete failure to measure up to the righteousness that the law requires.

So far, then, we have looked at two examples of Jesus's proclaiming the law. In this chapter we will examine an occasion in Jesus's ministry where he does not proclaim the law, but instead simply reveals his amazing grace. It is a story we looked at briefly above, the story Luke tells of Jesus going to the home of Zacchaeus. Because this particular episode is recorded only in Luke's Gospel, we may assume that Zacchaeus is one of the eyewitnesses whom Luke searched out and interviewed as he was preparing to write his Gospel.[1] There are many lovely things to note as we study this story, but most of all we will focus on the honor, respect, and grace that the Lord showed to this despised man.

> [Jesus] entered Jericho and was passing through. And behold, there was a man named Zacchaeus. He was a chief tax collector and was rich. And he was seeking to see who Jesus was, but on account of the crowd he could not, because he was small of stature. So he ran on ahead and climbed up into a sycamore tree to see him, for he was about to pass that way. And when Jesus came to the place, he looked

---

[1] Luke 1:1–4. In this passage Luke tells his readers about the research he has done in compiling his Gospel and about the eyewitnesses whom he has interviewed. We must presume that Luke managed to find Zacchaeus and interview him about his extraordinary day with Jesus.

up and said to him, "Zacchaeus, hurry and come down, for I must stay at your house today." So he hurried and came down and received him [Jesus] joyfully. And when they saw it, they all grumbled, "He has gone in to be the guest of a man who is a sinner." And Zacchaeus stood and said to the Lord, "Behold, Lord, the half of my goods I give to the poor. And if I have defrauded anyone of anything, I restore it fourfold." And Jesus said to him, "Today salvation has come to this house, since he also is a son of Abraham. For the Son of Man came to seek and to save the lost."[2]

Jesus's Knowledge of Zacchaeus

First, we note that Jesus knows this man and even knows his name. Though he has clearly never met Zacchaeus before this occasion, he knows him out of all the other people in Jericho on that day, out of all the other people in Palestine at that time, and out of all the other people throughout history. You may respond, "But of course Jesus knows Zacchaeus! Jesus is the eternal Son of God."

However, in the incarnation the Son's divine nature is veiled for much of the time. That is why Luke tells us that as a child Jesus grew in wisdom as well as stature.[3] But from time to time—when he stilled the storm, when he walked on the water, when he showed his disciples a vast catch of fish (and Peter, overwhelmed by his sudden sense of the divine majesty of Christ, cried out "depart from me, for I am a sinful man"),[4] when he turned water into wine to help the wedding celebrations, when he was transfigured before his disciples, when he called Zacchaeus by name—on these occasions we see that truly in Christ the whole fullness of the godhead dwelled bodily.[5] So it is here: Jesus is passing along the road through Jericho, and there are great crowds of people. But out of all those people, Jesus sees this one man, and he knows him. He knows who he is and he knows his name; he sees into his heart and he sees there a desire to know who Jesus is.

---

[2] Luke 19:1–10.
[3] Luke 2:52. The incarnation is a mystery and a wonder to us. How could it be that the infinite and eternal second person of the Trinity came to dwell in a finite human person? He was fully God and fully man at every moment of his life (and continues to be!). Yet he chose not to cling to his divine power. Rather, we see his majesty veiled through much of his earthly life.
[4] Luke 5:8.
[5] Colossians 2:9.

ZACCHAEUS'S EAGERNESS

Zacchaeus is so eager to see Jesus that he climbs into a tree to see over the crowd because he is short. His small stature is the one thing about Zacchaeus that every child knows from Sunday school. The tree that he climbs is called, in our English Bibles, either a "sycamore" (ESV) or a "sycamore-fig" (NIV). Botanically the tree described is neither a sycamore nor a fig, but has leaves similar in shape to the leaves of sycamore and fig trees. The advantage for Zacchaeus's purpose is that this kind of tree often has branches growing out horizontally from the main trunk, beginning low down, so it would be easy for even a small man to climb, even a small man wearing a full-length robe. Zacchaeus is so intent on seeing Jesus that he clearly is not interested in preserving his dignity. The wealthy and powerful (and he was very wealthy and very powerful) do not usually behave like small boys and climb trees before the watching world.

BEHOLD, ZACCHAEUS!

The Greek text draws attention to Zacchaeus: "Behold, there"—or we might say, "Take note of"—"a man named Zacchaeus. . . . He was a chief tax collector and he was rich." There is a careful emphasis that highlights this particular person, an emphasis that reflects the way in which Jesus meets him and singles him out, not because of his wealth, as if that made him worthy, and not because of his profession as a tax collector, as if that makes him a man of importance who deserves Jesus's attention, but simply because Jesus desires to meet him. The Lord sees past the social exterior to find the searching heart and the dignity of this man. He recognizes that he is one who bears the image of God and who is a unique and precious person, and he sees Zacchaeus's eagerness to learn more about him; so Jesus calls to him by name and says to him, "Zacchaeus, hurry and come down."

AN UNUSUAL DINNER INVITATION

One of the more remarkable aspects of this encounter is Jesus's request to be entertained by Zacchaeus in his home for the rest of that day. Just as with the Samaritan woman, Jesus is eager to receive what

Zacchaeus can give him, so he invites himself to Zacchaeus's home for a meal: "Zacchaeus, hurry and come down, for I must stay at your house today."

We might be tempted to say, "Well! That is rather a presumption, a bit of a cheek, inviting yourself to the home of someone you have never met." So we need to ask what is happening here. Why is Jesus inviting himself into the home of a complete stranger? Zacchaeus would not, and could not, invite a Jew, and especially a Jewish religious leader, into his home, for no self-respecting Jew, and certainly not any rabbi, or teacher of God's Word, or synagogue leader in that day, would ever consider accepting such an invitation. No such person would dream of ever visiting the home of such a man as Zacchaeus; it would be even more unthinkable than going into a Gentile's house. So, because Zacchaeus cannot invite him, Jesus invites himself, much to Zacchaeus's amazement, and to everyone else's as well.

As we see in the story of the woman at the well, Jesus delights in showing his need of what others can give to him. Especially he does this with people who are despised and regarded as social and moral outcasts. So it is on this occasion.

We should notice the reaction of the people. It is not just the Pharisees and the teachers of the law who criticize Jesus on this occasion, but everyone in the crowd; they all grumble and murmur about it: "He has gone to be the guest of a sinner." And Jesus does this gladly. With Zacchaeus, with the Samaritan woman, with the prostitute, Jesus gladly receives their acts of kindness. There is nothing more honoring or dignifying that Jesus can do for Zacchaeus than what he does, inviting himself to be Zacchaeus's guest.

HATRED OF ZACCHAEUS

Here is a man who is hated by people. Why? He is a tax collector, and not just that, but a chief tax collector. He and all those in his profession are despised by people for all sorts of reasons. He works, not for our Internal Revenue Service (whatever hard thoughts you may harbor about them when you complete your tax returns each April), but for the Romans, for the occupying army of the Jews' loathed oppressors. These tax collectors are not paid by the Romans for their work, and so they have to collect enough for their own salary as well. Consequently, this is a system that leaves plenty of room for greed and abuse. Zacchaeus, the head of the whole district's tax collection, has become very rich at his job. (It is quite likely that chief tax collectors required bribes from their subordinates or from anyone who desired to work as a tax collector.) He is a man with great power and with a position that has opened the door to great wealth. Zacchaeus is what the Chinese today call a "man-eat-man" capitalist.

In many of our cities we have one or two corrupt politicians, and a few dishonest business people who are always lining their own pockets at other people's expense. To understand the attitude of the crowd to Zacchaeus, we should try to imagine the very worst of these. Picture this greedy and corrupt person collaborating with whomever we hate most passionately, such as a terrorist responsible for the deaths of many innocent people. This is how the Jews of Jesus's day thought of the Romans and of their fellow Jews who collaborated with them.

The Romans were brutal tyrants, not some pleasant occupying force seeking to bring peace and stability to the region. They gained and held their power by acts of terrible ferocity. In Gaul (present-day France) alone, during the time of Julius Caesar, just a few decades before Jesus's birth, the Romans had slaughtered two million people as they brought Gaul into their empire. For a New Testament example of this brutality we can look at Luke 13. We are told there that Pilate had his soldiers massacre a group of Galileans so that their blood was mingled with the blood of the sacrifices they were offering at the temple.[6]

This is why the people grumble: they hate men like Zacchaeus, both for their greed and for their collaboration with the enemy. Despite all this, and despite the response of the people, Jesus delights in the opportunity to spend time with Zacchaeus and honors him by gracing him with his presence at a meal in his home. Zacchaeus responds to this amazing invitation with joy: "He hurried and came down and received him joyfully." We do not know all that happened that day, for Luke has compressed the day's events into a few short

---

[6] Luke 13:1.

verses. However, it is clearly understood by everyone present in the crowd that Jesus is received by Zacchaeus, and that the two of them head off to Zacchaeus's home for a meal and a lengthy visit.

OUTRAGEOUS SOCIAL BEHAVIOR

The reason for the crowd's complaints and criticisms is that Jesus's actions are outrageous. What happens is remarkable, for in going to Zacchaeus's home to eat, Jesus is breaking both the social customs and the religious and moral laws of his time: he is becoming a guest and eating in the home of a sinner, a man with an unclean profession. Jesus is making himself socially, ritually, morally, and religiously unclean by going to Zacchaeus's home. And we noted earlier, he is polluting himself just as if he had gone to the home of a Samaritan or a Gentile.

To try to understand this reaction, think once more of the words of the apostle Peter when he goes to the home of the Gentile Cornelius. Cornelius was a devout and God-fearing man who gave generously to the poor and was held in high honor by the local Jews in Caesarea. Yet Peter says to those gathered in Cornelius's home, "You yourselves know how unlawful it is for a Jew to associate with or to visit anyone of another nation."[7] What Jesus is doing on this occasion is much worse. Zacchaeus was considered as unclean as any Gentile because of his profession and his daily interactions with the Romans. In addition, he is viewed as a notorious public sinner.

JESUS IGNORES SOCIAL CUSTOMS AND HUMAN RELIGIOUS LAWS

Jesus sets aside merely human laws designed to foster and maintain religious and moral separation and purity. Regardless of the intention of such laws, these rules were created by the leaders of God's people, not by God; they were part of what was called "the tradition of the elders."

Such laws also prevent God's people from being obedient to their Lord's command to practice hospitality to strangers, to be merciful and gracious to the alien (that is, Gentiles), and to be kind to the sinful, the needy, and the poor. Of course it is true that strangers, aliens, sinners,

---

[7] Acts 10:28.

the needy, and the poor are regarded as outcast and unclean in every human society. But these laws about socially acceptable behavior are a moral offense to God, who calls his people to precisely the opposite way of life: to be a people characterized by the mercy, compassion, and grace that he has shown to them.

SEEKING AND SAVING THE LOST

These social barriers mean nothing to the Lord Jesus in his passion to save the lost, for that is why he came into the world. He says so in this account: "The Son of Man came to seek and to save the lost." Jesus did not come into the world to keep himself apart from sinners; nor to demonstrate that his life was socially acceptable. Rather, he came in fulfillment of the promise of the Lord made in Ezekiel 34:

> For thus says the LORD GOD: Behold, I, I myself will search for my sheep and will seek them out. . . . I will seek out my sheep, and I will rescue them . . . . I myself will be the shepherd of my sheep, and I myself will make them lie down, declares the LORD GOD. I will seek the lost, and I will bring back the strayed.[8]

By quoting this promise from Ezekiel, Jesus is announcing both his divinity and the purpose of his coming. He is making the claim that he is the "Lord GOD" (*Yahweh*, God's personal name); he is the true shepherd of his people, the one who will seek and save the lost.[9] God's passionate desire and purpose, which is revealed both in the Old Testament and in the coming of the Christ, is to seek and to save those who are lost, those who have strayed from him and from his ways. This is, of course, the condition of each one of us. In his sight, all of us are unclean and outcast because of our failure to love him and because of our flagrant disobedience to his commandments. Yet he sets aside his moral and religious outrage, not counting our sins against us, but rather counting them against himself, when he comes to seek and to save us who are lost without him. He calls us to have

---

[8] Ezekiel 34:11–16.
[9] Jesus also refers to the prophecy in Daniel 7:14, the promise of the coming Son of Man. This is Jesus's favorite title for himself, used more than eighty times in the Gospels. Son of Man is a title that captures both Jesus's humanity, for it means, literally, a human, and his divinity, for in the Daniel passage the Son of Man has divine power, glory, and honor, sharing the throne and rule of God eternally.

fellowship with him and to be his friends. That is why he goes to Zacchaeus's home to eat and to visit there, in utter disregard of the custom and law of his day.

JESUS AND SINNERS

Jesus's going to a sinner's home should cause us to think carefully about the way Jesus relates to sinners. He does not keep his distance from them, the way the Pharisees and teachers of the law do; nor does he preach condemning sermons at sinners, as do the Pharisees and teachers of the law. If Jesus were to conform to their practice of devotion to God and to their understanding of moral purity and separation, the religious leaders would not be outraged by his behavior. What is so shocking and unacceptable to them is that Jesus desires to have intimate fellowship with sinners. He visits with them. He sits down and eats with them. He invites them to the homes of his friends and disciples.[10] He goes gladly to their homes, even inviting himself to be their guest, just as he does with Zacchaeus. He welcomes sinners joyfully, and, in return, sinners welcome him joyfully.

"Intimate fellowship with sinners"—these are shocking words to many of us. However, that is exactly what it meant for Jesus to go to Zacchaeus's home. That is what it meant when Jesus went to the home of Matthew (who had also been a tax collector) and when he shared a meal with many tax collectors and sinners there.[11] Eating with people and visiting with them in their home are seen all through the Bible as the marks of intimate fellowship. And, of course, it has been seen this way in almost all human societies. Many of the Old Testament sacrifices end with a fellowship meal in the temple, signifying God's love for and acceptance of the person who has come to make their offering. God invites us to his table in the Lord's Supper to be his well-beloved guests. One day we will sit with the Lord and eat at his table at the Marriage Supper of the Lamb.[12] Eating together, being at home together—these imply love and personal fellowship. And because of these, Jesus's behavior is considered scandalous. Such a commitment

---

[10] See Matthew 9:9–10 as an example of this.
[11] Matthew 9:9–13.
[12] Luke 12:37; Revelation 19:9; see also the parable of the great banquet, in Luke 14:12–24.

to have intimate fellowship with sinners is still considered scandalous by many Christians today.

GRACE AND REPENTANCE

To the expert in the law and to the rich young ruler Jesus proclaimed the law. But with Zacchaeus, instead of this proclamation of the law we see Jesus simply treating the despised tax collector with wonderful grace by entering his home and being entertained there. It is, of course, this lovely grace, this mercy and respect, this honor and love that lead Zacchaeus to repentance. We are not told at what point in Jesus's time in his home Zacchaeus makes his amazing statement about giving half of his goods to the poor and paying back four times those he has defrauded. Perhaps it is at the end of their meal together, for the text says that Zacchaeus "stood" to say his remarkable words of repentance. Clearly Zacchaeus and Jesus are reclining together at table, sharing a meal, and then at some point Zacchaeus stands up to give his remarkable testimony.

But at whatever time of their day together this takes place, what Zacchaeus proposes to do is beautiful. The law requires that if one has defrauded someone, then one should repay, plus twenty percent.[13] If one stole something outright and already consumed what was stolen, then one should repay either four or five times the value of what was stolen. One would have to pay only double the value if, for example, a stolen animal was still alive and in the possession of the thief. If the person realized the guilt of his theft or any other such sin and openly confessed the wrong, then the penalty is restitution plus twenty percent, just as in the case of fraud.[14]

What is the point of giving all these details about the penalty for various forms of fraud or theft? It is simply this: Zacchaeus is so deeply moved by the grace of Jesus that he chooses to regard his defrauding as the very worst kind of theft. This deep sense of sin and desire for full repentance is what takes place in the heart when any person meets the Lord and sees him in his moral perfection and marvelous grace. When a person sees the Lord as he truly is, then

---

[13] Leviticus 6:5.
[14] Exodus 22:1–5; Numbers 5:6–7; 2 Samuel 12:6.

that person also sees himself or herself with a clear vision of the seriousness of his or her sin. When we meet the Lord in his glory, we see our sin in all its ugliness, rather than minimizing it. If we think about the rich young ruler and the expert in the law, it is clear that neither of them understands the divine nature and moral perfection of Jesus, for if they were to understand, then both of them would come to immediate repentance, as Zacchaeus does when Jesus comes to his home.

This is what happens to Zacchaeus. His clear sight of his sin leads to a passionate desire to make amends and to do what is right and pleasing in the eyes of the Lord. What Zacchaeus does is wonderful to read. He is overwhelmed by the grace and love of Christ, and so generosity flows from his heart. There are very few people in this world who joyfully give away half of their possessions to the poor, and who are so deeply committed to making restitution for the wrongs of their past life. But that is Zacchaeus. His stated intentions are so overwhelmingly generous that even some of the commentators suggest that we should not take them literally. But such a response is absurd. We must presume that Luke is recounting things that Zacchaeus has told him years later about what the repentant tax collector said on that day he had Jesus in his home, and also what he went on to do.

I know of people who have had just this same kind of extraordinary response to coming to know Christ. Indeed, in the kingdom of God, such a response ought not to surprise us. What the Lord has done for us is inexpressibly generous and kind. Why should we be reluctant to believe that this inexpressible grace has such lovely consequences in the lives of some who receive it?

One example is a dear friend of mine who is now with the Lord. When she was a young woman, her wealthy parents both died and left her, their only child, a large inheritance. She was so overwhelmed with the responsibility of being the steward of so much money that her reaction was to cry out to the Lord for help. Instead of becoming a "flapper" (what wealthy young high-society women were called at that time) in London and spending her fortune wildly, this young woman became a believer in Christ and dedicated her life to serving him in gratitude for his grace in saving her and in helping her to use her wealth wisely. As a young heiress she went to India to serve the poorest of the poor, working with Amy Carmichael at Dohnavur Fellowship, a wonderful ministry devoted to saving young girls from abandonment or temple prostitution. An accountant friend back in England gave the money away to various ministries as she directed him. I could tell much more of her story, but this brief account helps us to see that the transformation of Zacchaeus's attitude to his wealth is just one of the Lord's many victories over the pursuit of mammon in the lives of those he redeems.

SALVATION HAS COME TO THIS HOUSE

When he hears Zacchaeus's words of repentance, Jesus declares "salvation has come to this house, for this man too is a son of Abraham." Salvation comes to dwell in Zacchaeus's house. From then on, his home would be a place of love, generosity, and grace, in place of the corruption and greed that had been present before.

This is the way others should be able to describe our homes, places in which salvation dwells. We need to ask ourselves, "In what way is salvation known to be dwelling in my house?" In some small way we, like Zacchaeus, are to show the grace that God has shown us: God's response to our sin is grace, the grace of Jesus Christ. Our response to that grace is to show love and gratitude toward others.

A SON OF ABRAHAM

Jesus declares that Zacchaeus, too, is a son of Abraham. God promised to be the God of Abraham and his descendants after him. Zacchaeus, even though he was a Jew, a literal descendant of Abraham, was just as lost as any Gentile. However, Jesus came into the world with the explicit purpose of seeking and saving the lost sheep of Israel. Through meeting Jesus, Zacchaeus becomes a true son of Abraham, sharing not only literal descent from the first patriarch, but also his faith. From that point onward Zacchaeus becomes a man whose life and words show others the seeking and saving grace of Jesus, the grace that sought him out and found him. He becomes a man who obeys the law from the heart—though Jesus never proclaimed the law to him.

Questions for Personal Reflection and Group Discussion

1. Do you find it troubling that Jesus proclaimed the law to people who were worshippers of the Lord and who were devoted to obedience to the law (people like the rich young ruler or the expert in the law)?

2. Do you find it troubling that Jesus did not proclaim the law to Zacchaeus or to other obvious sinners (like the Samaritan woman of John 4)?

3. What application of Jesus's proclaiming the law to churchgoers and not proclaiming the law to sinners could we make today?

4. What aspects of Jesus's encounter with Zacchaeus are most interesting and remarkable to you?

5. What kind of people do you think might be contemporary equivalents, in your own city or in your country, of a man like Zacchaeus?

6. In the story of Zacchaeus we see the love of Christ bringing this man to a beautiful repentance. Do you concur that only this kind of love, this grace, has the true power to bring repentance? Or do you feel, secretly, that it would be more appropriate to condemn wicked people like Zacchaeus and "beat up" on them in order to bring about true change? In other words, in the privacy of your heart do you think Jesus was too soft on really serious sinners?

7. In this story the repentance of Zacchaeus is truly beautiful. Have you thought of repentance as beautiful? Can you think of other examples of repentance that reveal its true beauty? Your answer may include biblical examples or ones from other literature or from life.

8. This is a private question for personal meditation and prayer: What is there about your life personally, and what takes place in your home, that demonstrates to the world that salvation has come to make its dwelling at your house?

19

LESSONS FROM JESUS'S
TWO APPROACHES

In the previous chapter we looked at Jesus's inviting himself to the home of a corrupt and greedy man, the wealthy chief tax collector, Zacchaeus. We noted how differently Jesus treated Zacchaeus from the way he responded to two men who considered themselves faithful and obedient worshippers of the Lord. Jesus proclaimed the law to the expert in the law and to the rich young ruler, but not to Zacchaeus. Instead, we see Jesus simply treating Zacchaeus with wonderful grace by entering his home and being entertained there. This lovely grace, expressed in mercy, respect, honor, and love, brings Zacchaeus to repentance and to a deep obedience to the requirements of the law.

How can we apply such examples from Jesus in our own lives and in our own communication of the gospel? We might even ask whether it is ever appropriate for us to follow Jesus's example in this regard. To attempt to answer these questions we need to reflect a little further on the contrasting responses of those three men to Jesus. Zacchaeus did not seek to contend for his righteousness with Jesus or to justify himself, unlike the expert in the law. Zacchaeus did not claim to have kept the law from his childhood, unlike the rich young ruler. Instead, he looked back at his life and he saw his sin for what it truly was: a heinous offense in the sight of God, and now heinous to his own heart also. Thus Zacchaeus's words: "Behold, Lord, the half of my goods I give to the poor. And if I have defrauded anyone of anything, I restore it fourfold."[1]

---

[1] Luke 19:8.

We see in Luke's account that Zacchaeus chooses to do far more than the law requires. He acknowledges that he has defrauded some of those from whom he has collected taxes. His fellow Jews have to give Zacchaeus whatever he demands. They cannot refuse because he has the power of the Roman army behind him. The penalty of the law for such cases of fraud is to return the amount of the defrauding and add 20 percent to that sum.

Instead of obeying this base requirement of the law, Zacchaeus is so deeply moved by the grace of Jesus that he chooses to regard his defrauding as the very worst kind of theft, a crime that requires a fourfold repayment. Zacchaeus understands that his life of greed and defrauding is a terrible sin against the Lord and against the people whose money he has taken to enrich himself. Zacchaeus does not say: "Well, I only defrauded people, after all. I was just a bit greedy." He is appalled as he looks back at his life. He has no desire to minimize his years of corrupt and ruthless treatment of his fellow Jews. He acknowledges, to his own heart, to the Lord, and to anyone else present, that he is desperately sinful.

This deep sense of sin and desire for full repentance is what takes place in the heart when a person truly meets the Lord and sees him as he is in his moral perfection and marvelous grace. This is what ought to happen to us. When we meet the Lord in his glory, we should see our sin in all its ugliness, and we should propose a restitution for our sins that is far greater than the base requirements of the law.

Zacchaeus is honored by Jesus, most especially because he realizes that Jesus knows all about him. Jesus knows his name, his profession, his greed, his life of corruption, and his selfishness. Yet Jesus desires to sit at his table, to eat his food, and to enjoy his company for many hours. Zacchaeus has never before been treated with such grace and generosity. His sin begins to burn within his heart, and he has to respond to the grace of Christ who is reclining in his presence. Jesus's merciful and gracious presence leads Zacchaeus to this passionate desire to make amends and to do what is right and pleasing in the eyes of the Lord. His heart is filled to overflowing with the generosity of Jesus to him, and so generosity flows from his heart: generosity to the poor and to those he has defrauded.

Notice how very different from this are the responses of the rich young ruler and the expert in the law. Neither has a deep sense of his own sin, for neither has recognized the true righteousness of God or the glory and grace of Jesus. This is so, even though both could see and hear this glory and grace right before their eyes and ears. After all, Jesus honored them both with time and with careful attention. He treated them both far more graciously than they deserved. He looked at the rich young ruler with love and treated him with love. He responded to the insincerity and pride of the teacher of the law with grace. Imagine being a person who comes to Jesus with a cold and haughty attitude and with a desire to prove Jesus's inferior understanding. And yet, consider the patience and love that Jesus showed this man to invest the time, the effort, and the imaginative gifts to create the parable of the good Samaritan! If we are honest, we should be able to see that this kind of remarkable patience and kindness is the way the Lord treats us every day of our lives.

Zacchaeus realizes the grace that Jesus shows to him. His response is to see the wickedness of his past life. From then on he loves Jesus, the Lord, with his whole being. His first deed of faith is to give away a huge portion of his wealth. He begins to try to love his neighbor as himself, to make more than full restitution for the wrongs he has done and to give half of his possessions to the poor immediately.

In contrast, neither of the other two realizes that Jesus is the Lord; nor do they realize how gracious Jesus is to them. Neither of them is prepared to love Jesus, the Lord, with his whole being or to love his neighbor as himself. So Jesus proclaims the law to these two men to try to bring them to a realization of his glory and their sin, so that they might turn to him for grace. But the one went away still trying to justify himself, and the other went away sorrowful because of his great wealth. Zacchaeus, however, became a man who obeyed the law from the heart, though Jesus had never proclaimed the law to him.

This contrast in responses to Jesus demonstrates that, yes, there are people to whom we ought to proclaim the law. But before delving further into that question, there are some additional lessons we do not want to miss from this encounter with Zacchaeus. At the heart of them is a restatement of what it means to be a Christian in this world: our calling today and every day is to show to the lost world and to our lost neighbors the seeking and saving grace that we have received from the One who came to seek and to find us.

LEARNING FROM JESUS

Issues of Human Dignity and Shame

What are we to make of the criticism that the Pharisees and scribes often make of Jesus, and the criticism that the whole crowd in Jericho makes of Jesus when he heads off to Zacchaeus's home for a meal? These reactions to Jesus bring to our attention an issue of fundamental importance. Everyone present is criticizing Jesus for the company he keeps, for his table fellowship with "sinners." There is also, of course, an explicit criticism of the tax collector Zacchaeus and others like him. Zacchaeus is characterized simply as a sinner. In the minds of those who consider themselves godly or righteous, "sinner" sums up people like Zacchaeus. They see nothing else but his sin, and so they dismiss him.

One of the temptations that we face in every age is to view the people around us in a judgmental and dismissive way. This person is dismissed as a "philanderer"; this one as "homosexual"; this one as "a humanist"; this one as "a liberal"; this one as "a Jehovah's Witness"; this one as "a Hindu." We can all add to the list.

If we look into our own hearts and try to be honest about the people we dismiss with a single word of description, we will observe that we mix together all sorts of different issues, just as did the Pharisees of Jesus's day with their rejection of association with "Gentiles, Samaritans, tax collectors, and sinners." We dismiss people on the basis of race, gender, class, social status, wealth, job description, culture, personal lifestyle, outward appearance, and sinful practices we find offensive.

One of the most striking things about Jesus is that he never seems to look at people in this kind of way; he does not reduce anyone to one characteristic in order to dismiss that person. You might object that Jesus refers to the scribes and Pharisees and other religious leaders as "vipers," "blind guides," and "whitewashed tombs." These examples, however, are rather different, for their purpose, as we saw in an earlier chapter, is to humble the arrogant hearts of the self-righteous who are confident that they are in good standing with God.

Before we look at the issue of our dismissal of sinners, we need to consider the way Jesus deals with the other kinds of summary judgments that we so easily make of people. An important lesson we can learn from Jesus is to look beyond the exterior appearance of people. Racial, religious, cultural, and gender barriers that divided his society were set aside by Christ as if they did not exist at all (think of the Samaritan woman in John 4). Indeed, they did not exist for him, for he was the Creator of all the people on both sides of each of these barriers. In addition, he was the Savior of the world, the one who came into the world to redeem people from every cultural and racial group, from both genders, from all religious backgrounds, and from every possible cultural or social difference that existed in his day.

Can we see through such differences to each person's abiding glory as a bearer of God's image? Can we move beyond seeing racial and cultural diversity as problems and see them instead as part of the glory of our humanity? The God who made us all delights in variety, and so should we. Just as each sunset is different from every other sunset, indeed is different every moment of each sunset that God has designed, just so, each person in this world is unique. We worship a God who loves diversity.

In addition, of course, as the Savior of the world, he came to seek and to save sinners, and everyone from every cultural and social background is a sinner in the eyes of Christ and needs his love desperately. Jesus was able to see the human dignity of each person he encountered, even where that dignity was expressed in a cultural form very different from his own human culture as a Jew, and even where that dignity was deeply damaged by moral failure, as was true of the Samaritan woman, and as was true of the sinners and tax collectors like Zacchaeus. With sinners, Jesus sees their dignity, and he also is filled with compassion regarding their sin.

Jesus's encounters with Samaritans, with Gentiles, with tax collectors, and with the sinners of his day are a model and a challenge to every Christian in our day. Are we able to look beyond the outside of a person, past the surface matters of racial, religious, economic, cultural, gender, and educational differences, and most of all, past the presence of the terrible reality of particular sins, idolatries, and false beliefs? Will we persevere in seeing people's dignity as God's image bearers through all the cultural differences we encounter? And will we persevere in seeing their dignity even through the disfigurement of sin? And will we respond with the mercy and compassion of Christ, rather than with condemnation and dismissal?

This is very challenging for us—to see beyond the sin that disfigures a person and to treat him or her with the respect that God's creation of that person in his likeness demands. Are we willing to value each individual we meet as Jesus did, and as he still does, for he values each of us as having inestimable worth?

Two films from the 1990s make this point. *Dead Man Walking*, a true story of a man on death row for murder and rape, describes how this man becomes a believer through a nun, his counselor as he awaits execution. What is remarkable about this story is that the nun is able to look beyond the horrible crime the man has committed to see his human dignity. It is her recognition of his underlying worth, her realization that he is a person made in God's image, that leads to his conversion. The nun's willingness to look past his sin makes her a wonderful example of imitating Jesus's treatment of the sinners of his day.

Another film that illustrates this principle is *Paradise Road*, a movie set in a Japanese prisoner of war camp during World War II, and also a true story. In this film the heroine is a missionary. Along with several other women, she is captured by the Japanese and spends several years in the POW camp. There she endures severe mistreatment and suffering at the hands of the guards. Again, what is most powerful about the film is the way this believer in Jesus is able to see the dignity of each person in the camp, including the guards who abuse the women so terribly.

Turning back to the Gospels, we see many occasions when Jesus shows respect, gentleness, and grace toward unbelievers. The living Word is simply practicing for us in a perfect way what he tells us through his apostles elsewhere:

Always be prepared to give an answer to everyone who asks you to give the reason for the hope that you have. But do this with gentleness and respect.[2]

Let your conversation be always full of grace, seasoned with salt, so that you may know how to answer everyone.[3]

A troublesome question arises for us at this point. If Jesus is so clear both in his example and in his teaching, why do so many of us Christians have such a problem with practicing his command? The way we treat unbelievers in their sin is one of the major problems that the evangelical church has today. We may be tempted to ask the question that many people, even leaders of churches and ministries, have asked me: "How can we respect people or be gentle and gracious with them when they are living in sin (like Zacchaeus)? Surely it is impossible to respect people who break God's commandments by living in open sexual sin or by practicing other behavior that God's Word clearly condemns? Some of these people are even teaching others to disobey God's commandments or believe false ideas! In such situations respect, gentleness, and grace are inappropriate and impossible. These people reek to heaven!" This expression "they reek to heaven" was used by a professor of Old Testament when I was asked to give a lecture to a seminary faculty on what I teach in apologetics and outreach.

Two examples will suffice to illustrate a sadly flawed understanding of what it means to bear a good testimony to Jesus. One person told me how, that day at work, she criticized her fellow employee for the soft porn novels sitting on her desk. She told the woman that they were offensive to her because she was a Christian. I asked what effect this had. She replied that the woman told everyone else in the office about it during the coffee break and, the next day, asked the Christian to remove the Bible from her desk because this coworker found it offensive. All the Christian's coworkers started avoiding her or moving away when she came near.

I urged her to go back and apologize to the woman for the utterly inappropriate words of condemnation and criticism that she used and

---

[2] 1 Peter 3:15, NIV.
[3] Colossians 4:6, NIV.

to ask for the forgiveness of the woman, explaining that what she did was a complete misrepresentation of Jesus. She agreed that this was the right way to move forward, and was later delighted to report that the woman forgave her readily. Moreover, a fruit of the Christian's apology and confession of misrepresenting Jesus was that she was able, for the first time, to have some valuable discussions with the woman and with other people in her office.

A sadder example came from a young man who started working at a garage. On the first day he was deeply upset by the "girlie" posters prominently displayed in the work area. So he denounced the posters to the other men. He told them how offended he was, and he gave them a stern lecture about sexual purity and God's condemnation of lustful thoughts. By the next day the men had obtained some far worse posters, with explicit pornographic images, and tacked these to the walls. The young man immediately resigned his position. He told me this story as something of which he was proud. He had been a good witness to Christ, and then he had been persecuted for righteousness' sake.

Both of these believers had been taught to behave this way toward unbelievers and sinners. Both were confident that what they did was a faithful testimony to Jesus and to the truth of the gospel. Both stories raise the question very acutely, how are respect, gentleness, and grace possible in a world of such sin?

Our first answer brings us back to the foundational teaching of the very first chapter of the Bible in which we are taught that all people bear the image of God. The definition of what it means to be human is that we have been created in the image and likeness of God. He is infinite and we are finite. But he is personal, and so also are we, infinitely precious persons made to be like him and bearing the worth of that likeness.

But the question arises, can we continue to affirm human dignity when it is horribly defaced by sin? In Psalm 8 David answers this question by first raising a question of his own:

When I look at your heavens, the work of your fingers,
the moon and the stars, which you have set in place,

> what is man that you are mindful of him,
>> and the son of man that you care for him?
>
> Yet you have made him a little lower than the heavenly beings
>> and crowned him with glory and honor.
> You have given him dominion over the works of your hands;
>> you have put all things under his feet.[4]

God has given us such great dignity as those who are made in his image, that, as the psalmist says, even God himself is mindful of us. If the perfectly holy God can respect and be mindful of the glory of our humanity, how much more should we, who share the sin of everyone around us, respect the divine image in all those we meet? The apostle James also reminds us of this very fact when he rebukes his readers for failing to show honor for their fellow human beings. James's simple point is that it is dishonoring to God to disrespect anyone made in the image of God: "With the tongue we praise our Lord and Father, and with it we curse men, who have been made in God's likeness. Out of the same mouth come praise and cursing. My brothers, this should not be."[5]

In an earlier chapter we saw how the great Reformed theologian John Calvin wrote that we are ruined statues on which we can still trace the outlines of our former glory. J. R. R. Tolkien described us as having still the "rags of the lordship" that once was ours, and as a minted "image blurred of distant king."[6] Francis Schaeffer said that we are "glorious ruins." Our task, then, is to see what is beautiful and true—the traces, the outlines, the rags of lordship, the blurred image, the glory still present in the lives of obviously sinful and difficult people.

In addition to seeing the glory of our neighbors as those who share God's image with us, we should also see them as sinners in need of Christ's forgiveness. We cannot ignore sin, but when we see their sin, we see them as those who, precisely because they are sinners, are in need of the forgiveness of Christ. This again is the example that Jesus

---

[4] Psalm 8:3–6.
[5] James 3:9–10, NIV.
[6] J. R. R. Tolkien, *Mythopoeia*.

shows us as he meets Zacchaeus and as he eats with him in his home. He shows respect for Zacchaeus's dignity as a person he has made, and he shows gentleness and grace toward Zacchaeus as a sinner in need of his love. This is, after all, the very reason why Jesus came into this world. He did not come for the healthy, but for the sick, because all of us are sick. He did not come for the righteous, but for the sinners, because all of us are sinners.[7]

This brings us to another important issue. Christ showed love and grace to sinners even though he was perfectly holy. It is different for us, for we are not perfectly holy; so why should we think that it is ever appropriate for us to refuse to show love and grace to sinners? When it comes to sin, we all stand on a level playing field. Before God, our sin makes us all equals. The only way we can approach God is to acknowledge our unworthiness before him.

This acknowledgment of the fellowship of sinners is the only appropriate way for us to approach others, whoever they are, whatever they have done. We are one with them in human dignity, and we are one with them in human shame. The face of each one of us is covered with the shame of our sin. This means that we are never in a position to look down on other people, no matter how serious their sin, their idolatry, or their false belief. If we despise, rebuke, and condemn the people around us, we must likewise despise, rebuke, and condemn ourselves.

The Challenge to Our Own Hearts

The grace that Jesus shows to sinners is very challenging to us. We are not to compare ourselves with other people; nor are we to think of ourselves as more righteous, and of others as more obviously sinful. We are to compare ourselves only with God in his absolute moral perfection, goodness, justice, mercy, and love.

This will become clearer to us as we mature as Christians. The more we delight in God's law and grow in the true knowledge of God, the more deeply aware we become of the gap between the Lord's holiness and our own lack of holiness. The more clearly we see the purity

---

[7] Matthew 9:12–13; see also Matthew 11:19 and the parables of Luke 15 that Jesus tells when he is criticized for the company he keeps.

of the Lord, the more acutely we see the absence of purity in our hearts and in our thoughts. If I still think of others as the sinners and think of myself as good, then it is clear that I know God very poorly, if at all; and I certainly do not understand his law well.

But when I begin to know him and come before him as he is, then the moral differences between me and other people become insignificant. Before him my own sins loom large and ugly, just as they did for Zacchaeus. Kneeling at his feet I know my dependence on his mercy and the hopelessness of my position without his forgiveness.

Kneeling before Jesus

When I am on my knees before Jesus, I begin to look with kindness and grace on others, however awful their sin, for I no longer think of myself as being better than they are. Rather, my own sins become very clear to me, and truly heinous, so that when I look at others, I see that we share the bond of a common plight and a common need for God's unmerited favor. If my heart does not have compassion and sympathy for the broken lives of other people, then I must conclude that my knowledge of my own sin, my awareness of my own need for mercy, and my amazement at the love that Jesus has shown for me are merely superficial.

THE SCHOOL OF THE LAW

This reflection on our fellowship in sin and our common need of grace brings us back to our main questions: Should our own communication of the gospel follow Jesus's examples in his encounters with the expert in the law, the rich young ruler, and Zacchaeus? And if so, when? We might express these questions this way: What about "showing and telling" the good news of grace to some while we send others to preparatory school? By the expression "sending some to preparatory school," I mean this: Jesus sends the expert in the law and the rich young ruler to school by challenging them to see the full demands of the law of God.

With many people, the law of God—what God demands of us—must be communicated before they are ready to hear the gospel of God's grace in Jesus. We might describe the law as preparatory school because a challenge such as "You should obey these commandments and do these good deeds" is certainly not yet the good news of the forgiveness of sins. Proclaiming the gospel is: "There is nothing you have done that can make you acceptable to God; acknowledge your guilt and need and receive the forgiveness on the merits of Christ and his sacrifice for sinners"—this is the good news.

The good news is for those who know they are sinners, and preparatory school is for those who do not. "School" is, of course, a biblical image, for Paul likens the law of God to a guardian, or pedagogue, who has the purpose of leading the people of Israel to the school of the law in order that they might come to faith in Christ.[8] Zacchaeus already has been instructed by the pedagogue; he is deeply aware of his sin, so he receives the good news of the gospel of grace. The expert in the law and the rich young ruler have failed to understand the instructions of the pedagogue, and so they are left with the challenge to love God more fully and to love their neighbor better than they do. They are returned to the school of the law for further instruction.

So when should we give the good news, and when should we send someone off to school? To which people should we give only the law for the present, and to which should we give the good news at once? These may seem like strange questions, a new way of thinking, perhaps absurd or even heretical. However, there are many examples of Jesus doing one or the other in the gospels. The expert in the law and the rich young ruler are both assigned tasks and sent away to go and obey the law. They are sent back to school, for their earlier attendance has not yet produced the fruit of conviction, repentance, and dependence on the grace of God for salvation. The lessons of the law had fallen on deaf ears.

As I mentioned earlier, many of us find these examples problematic. It does not disturb us that the expert in the law is sent away to learn what it truly means to love God and to love his neighbor, so that he might discover that he too is a sinner in need of mercy. We do not like him because he is clearly arrogant and self-righteous; so we feel comfortable with the way Jesus treats him. But we find it more troublesome that Jesus also sends the rich young ruler away with a set of commandments to obey; we find it troublesome because he is

---

[8] Galatians 3:24.

someone we like, someone who claims to be, and seems genuinely to be, seeking God and also seeking eternal life. Perhaps this troubles us because we see ourselves all too easily in this man, and we think he is just fine. In addition, we are made uncomfortable by Jesus's challenge to this young man to give away his wealth and then follow Jesus. We all want to believe that we can keep whatever wealth we have and still follow Jesus.

This also disturbs us because we want to say: "Surely! Everyone needs the good news of forgiveness and grace. People should not be left hanging in limbo, trying to please God by keeping his commandments, when we all know that nobody will be saved that way! Why not tell everyone the good news and forget about the law? And if not everyone, whom should we first send to the preparatory school of the law?" I will try to answer this question in our next chapter.

Questions for Personal Reflection and Group Discussion

1. Do you find the story of Jesus and Zacchaeus offensive in any way? Before you quickly respond *no!* try to imagine a similar scene today. How might you react, and how might the people of your church react, if a dirty and unshaven homeless person, or someone obviously suffering with AIDS, or a prostitute, or a known drug pusher, or a gang member, or a corrupt politician, or a ruthless businessman came into a church meeting, and your pastor immediately invited him to go out for dinner, leaving everyone else sitting there in amazement to figure out what just happened?

2. As you think about your own city and community, who are some of the more obvious, public "sinners"? How difficult do you find it to look beyond their sin and see their human dignity? Please use specific and actual examples.

3. Do you have favorite books or movies like *Dead Man Walking* or *Paradise Road* that illustrate the point of showing respect and grace to sinners?

4. What aspects of the law of God keep you humble and aware of your constant need for the forgiveness and mercy of Christ?

5. Did you understand the image of the law as preparatory school? Was it helpful or confusing?

6. Who do you think needs to be sent to the school of the law? And who do you think should simply have the gospel shown or told to them? Again, try to think of particular examples of people you know.

20

TO WHOM OUGHT WE TO SHOW AND TELL THE LAW?

We have begun to answer the question of how we can follow Jesus's example in using the law. We turn now to the issue of who are the people we should take to the school of the law, and who are the people to whom we should immediately give the good news of redemption through Jesus. In making this difficult decision, we find help once more in thinking about the way Jesus behaves and the message he gives to different kinds of people.

THE SINFUL WOMAN AT THE HOME OF SIMON

In the story of Jesus going to the home of the tax collector Zacchaeus, we found how Jesus caused offense by the kind of relationship he was prepared to have with a sinner. We find the same kind of response in the story that Luke records in chapter 7 of his Gospel, about a dinner in the home of Simon the Pharisee. On that occasion a sinful woman enters the house, kneels at Jesus's feet, washes them with her tears, wipes them dry with her hair, and then anoints his feet with precious ointment. Here is Luke's account:

> One of the Pharisees asked him [Jesus] to eat with him, and he went into the Pharisee's house and reclined at the table. And behold, a woman of the city, who was a sinner, when she learned that he was

reclining at table in the Pharisee's house, brought an alabaster flask of ointment, and standing behind him at his feet, weeping, she began to wet his feet with her tears and wiped them with the hair of her head and kissed his feet and anointed them with the ointment. Now when the Pharisee who had invited him saw this, he said to himself, "If this man were a prophet, he would have known who and what sort of woman this is who is touching him, for she is a sinner." And Jesus answering said to him, "Simon, I have something to say to you." And he answered, "Say it, Teacher."

"A certain moneylender had two debtors. One owed five hundred denarii, and the other fifty. When they could not pay, he cancelled the debt of both. Now which of them will love him more?" Simon answered, "The one, I suppose, for whom he cancelled the larger debt." And he said to him, "You have judged rightly." Then turning toward the woman he said to Simon, "Do you see this woman? I entered your house; you gave me no water for my feet, but she has wet my feet with her tears and wiped them with her hair. You gave me no kiss, but from the time I came in she has not ceased to kiss my feet. You did not anoint my head with oil, but she has anointed my feet with ointment. Therefore I tell you, her sins, which are many, are forgiven—for she loved much. But he who is forgiven little, loves little." And he said to her, "Your sins are forgiven." Then those who were at table with him began to say among themselves, "Who is this, who even forgives sins?" And he said to the woman, "Your faith has saved you; go in peace."[1]

Simon's Thoughts about Jesus

As we noted in an earlier visit to this passage, the fact that Jesus allows the woman to come so close to him and to touch him in such a personal and intimate way prompts Simon the Pharisee to ask whether Jesus can truly be a prophet from God. Simon must have thought: "If Jesus allows such a sinner to get so close to him, then obviously he does not know what kind of a person she is, or he is not committed to righteousness. In either case, Jesus cannot be a prophet from God." In Simon's view, those who know God, and who therefore pursue righteousness, know sin when they see it, and more importantly, they keep themselves apart from such sinners.

---

[1] Luke 7:36–50.

The Sinful Woman's Love for Jesus

What do we know about the woman who comes to kiss Jesus's feet? She is described in the NIV simply as one "who had lived a sinful life." It is almost certain that she is a prostitute or someone who has lived a very loose life sexually. She is clearly aware of her sinfulness and is burdened down by it. She probably thinks of herself as someone whose whole life is subsumed by the description "sinner." She is accustomed to being ignored and despised by those who attend the synagogues and temple as worshippers of God, and by those known publicly as righteous people, in particular the preachers, the Pharisees, and teachers of the law. These self-styled leaders of God's people have made sure that she, and everyone else, knows that she is a sinful woman.

However this sinful woman has also heard of Jesus, and she has heard that he is apparently a preacher with a difference. She has heard that he welcomes sinners and eats with them, as numerous examples in the Gospels recount for us, and so she comes to honor him with a jar of expensive ointment and to give to him all of the devotion of her heart. As Jesus reclines at the table, his feet behind him, she comes and washes his feet with her tears, wipes them dry with her hair, kisses them repeatedly, and pours perfume on them from an alabaster jar. She does this, we presume, with tears that are a mixture of repentant sorrow and joy from his welcoming of her devotion.

Do we know her name? This is an interesting question. Some parts of the church have identified this woman with Mary of Bethany, the sister of Martha and Lazarus, whom we read about in several other parts of the Gospels, and who anointed Jesus at Bethany a few days before his death. Those who take this view believe that Mary anointed Jesus on two or even three occasions, so overwhelmed was she by his love for her despite her life of sin. Other parts of the church have proposed that there were three different women who anointed Jesus during the course of his ministry. I think it most likely that there was simply one woman, Mary of Bethany, who was responsible for each of these anointings of the Lord.

If indeed Mary of Bethany is the sinful woman in Simon the Pharisee's home, then we must assume that Luke has not given us her name, out of respect for her and because of his recognition that, even in the church, there are many who will never acknowledge that a notorious sinner could ever truly change, especially a woman guilty of flagrant sexual sins. Yet Mary of Bethany became a woman of great significance in the early church, so much so that Augustine called her "an apostle to the apostles." Even today, almost two thousand years after these events, there are evangelical theologians and commentators who insist that Mary of Bethany, Mary who is honored and praised by Jesus, Mary who sits at his feet to be taught by the Lord, and Mary who is chosen to be one of the first witnesses of Jesus's resurrection could not have once been a prostitute.

If this is what many people think in our day, then no wonder that Luke conceals her name when he tells us the beautiful story of her first meeting with Jesus. I find it astonishing that anyone who truly understands their own sinfulness, anyone who believes that Jesus died to bear their judgment and shame, would be troubled that the Lord redeemed a prostitute, transforming her by his grace and then calling her to be a leader of his people. Such an attitude is not far from the thoughts in the heart of Simon in this story, and such an attitude reminds us of our discussion in our last chapter about all of us being on level ground before the cross. Here I will simply quote the words of the apostle James: "For whoever keeps the whole law but fails in one point has become accountable for all of it."[2]

Jesus's Response to the Sinful Woman

Jesus responds to the woman and to Simon in very different ways. Jesus gladly receives the devotion that the woman offers him, for he understands that her extraordinary gesture of love comes from a heart overwhelmed by an awareness of her sin. She has come to him—come weeping about her sin, come to wash his feet with tears of repentance, come to kiss his feet with a heart full of gratitude, come to anoint his feet as an indication of her love in response to his glad acceptance of her.

This sinful woman understands that Jesus is receiving her with love despite her sin—indeed, *because* of her sin. For, as we learned in

---

[2] James 2:10.

the account of Jesus and Zacchaeus, the reason Jesus came into the world was "to seek and to save the lost."[3] He came and loved people because they are sinners in need of his love.

This woman has no doubt that Jesus knows she is a sinner, for everyone knows it. She has no doubt that she needs his forgiveness and grace. She understands that he is giving her his full acceptance without any word of disapproval or condemnation, without even a demand for public and explicit repudiation of her sin. He does not ask her to stand up and give a verbal disavowal of her past life; nor does he insist that she give a testimony of her intention to live purely in the future. He does not suggest that her display of devotion is too emotional, that it is distasteful to him in any way, or that it is inappropriate in its intimacy. There is nothing about his response to her that would indicate the slightest hesitation about his welcoming wholeheartedly what she does.

Does this mean that her act of devotion earns her forgiveness? No! Her washing of his feet, her wiping them, her kissing and anointing them—all this comes from a grateful heart. And Jesus delightedly accepts her gift. Hers is not a work to earn his love, but rather a response to his love, a response pouring out of her grateful heart. As the apostle Paul says, "Faith work[s] through love."[4]

The truest sign of genuine faith in Jesus is love for him, love that is founded on, or rooted in, his love for us. Therefore, to her as someone responding to Jesus's grace and love, he pronounces the good news of forgiveness and salvation. He commends her for her faith, and he sends her away with the peace of God in her heart. She is overwhelmed by his love and his acceptance of her, and so she pours out her gifts accordingly.

Jesus's Response to the "Righteous Man"

Jesus tells Simon a simple story about gratitude for cancelled debts. Two men owe debts, one a large sum and the other a much smaller amount, about a tenth of the first. The larger one is equivalent to five hundred days' wages (let's say, two years' salary). In other words, this

---

[3] Luke 19:10.
[4] Galatians 5:6.

debt is almost impossible to pay off. The other is a debt equivalent to fifty days' wages, still a significant amount, but not an impossible debt. However, in this case the debts are both cancelled as neither can pay what he owes.

This is true of course of our sins: whether we are guilty of "big sins" or what seem to us "little sins," none of us is in a position to pay off our debts to God. As the psalm teaches, not one of us can pay the ransom price for his or her own sins, or for the sins of another.[5]

Jesus finishes the story with a question: Which of the debtors will love the moneylender more? Simon of course replies that the one who has the bigger debt cancelled will love his benefactor more. Yet he still does not see how the story applies to the situation right before his own eyes.

Despite the simplicity and clarity of the story, Jesus does not tell Simon directly the good news of forgiveness and eternal life. Instead he rebukes Simon for not showing more devotion. Simon has failed to show Jesus the marks of honor expected of a genuinely welcoming host, the acts of love that Simon should have performed when Jesus entered his home, had Simon any sense of who this guest was. Simon should have been overwhelmed that Jesus distinguished the Pharisee by coming to recline at his table and to eat in his home. He should have known how deeply indebted he was to Jesus as the only one who could forgive him for his sins. But Simon knows nothing of all this, and so he does not welcome Jesus appropriately.

Appropriate Honor for a Distinguished Guest

Simon has no idea of the true nature of Jesus. If he had understood that Jesus is the Messiah, the Son of God, he would ask one of his household servants to wash Jesus's feet when he arrived for dinner; better still, he would have welcomed him by washing Jesus's feet himself. Toward the end of his ministry, Jesus himself took the task of the lowliest servant when he washed the feet of his disciples. He did this both to express his commitment to serve them and to show them the kind of service one should gladly give to those one honors and loves.[6]

---

[5] Psalm 49:7–9.
[6] John 13:1–20.

Simon should have welcomed Jesus with a kiss when Jesus entered his home if he were truly pleased to see him. This is a custom of the culture, but Simon has not greeted Jesus this way. A good host would honor a distinguished or loved visitor to his home by anointing his guest's hair with oil, but Simon fails to do this. In contrast, the sinful woman anoints Jesus's feet and showers them with kisses—and in doing so, demonstrates her awareness of the honor that is due to Jesus. She will not presume to anoint his head or kiss his cheek, for she sees herself as unworthy, and so she anoints his feet and kisses them. In other words, she does far more than is required of a good host.

Simon does far less than the laws of hospitality require, and far, far less than the law's call to love God with one's whole heart, mind, soul, and strength, for he has no true idea of who Jesus is. He invites Jesus that he might make a skeptical assessment of Jesus's credentials. Simon does not know that Jesus is the Savior, the Messiah, the Lord, God in the flesh. He does not realize the kind of love, devotion, and honor that ought to be given to Jesus. Even less does Simon have any clear idea about his own true status before God; he has no understanding of the reality of his own sin. He is quite unaware of the place of humble supplication that would be his if he were truly aware of his own need and sin, or if he had a true and deep knowledge of God.

How Much Have We Been Forgiven?

We should notice Jesus's remarkable words to Simon: "Therefore I tell you, her sins, which are many, are forgiven—for she loved much. But he who is forgiven little, loves little."[7] The sinful woman is deeply aware of her moral need before God and before Jesus, and so she pours out her love upon Jesus in passionate thankfulness. The self-righteous man, on the other hand, does not think that he needs to be forgiven anything, and so he offers Jesus no thanks for the Lord's presence in his home, no love, no devotion. He has no true sense of his own sin. He might say in prayer, "Lord, I know I am not perfect," but Simon is not aware of his desperate need for the forgiveness and mercy of God. And so it does not enter his mind that Christ, who is reclining at his table, is the one who has come into this world to forgive sinners. Jesus,

---

[7] Luke 7:47.

present in his home, is God's provision to make a way to show mercy to all whose lives fall short of God's perfect standards of righteousness. Simon is ignorant of this, whereas the prostitute understands it.

For the sake of the sinful woman, and also for the sake of Simon and the other guests, Jesus declares openly to her, "Your sins are forgiven." He also says, "Your faith has saved you; go in peace." With these words Jesus makes an open declaration of his mission from God, his identity as the Messiah, and his divine nature. Only God can forgive sins. Only God can declare that someone will inherit salvation and be welcomed into his eternal kingdom. Only God can see into the heart of a person and observe with complete assurance the presence in that heart of saving faith. Only God can send someone away with the certainty that this person is at peace with heaven. The sinful woman leaves, but she departs as one who has now received, through faith, the righteousness of God. She is, as Martin Luther said, *simul justus et peccator*—at once justified and a sinner. Knowing that she is a sinner, she by faith is fully justified, declared to be righteous, by the Lord.

On the other hand, Simon, the supposedly righteous man, is still a sinner who is trapped in his sin, unaware of his need for forgiveness, and so not justified. He does not know that he also is unrighteous, unclean before God, without true knowledge of God, without forgiveness, without salvation, and without the peace of God. Simon is left to ponder the significance of the story about debts and who it is who owes little or owes much. Simon is left to reflect on what he perceives to be a strange and distasteful encounter between Jesus and the sinful woman. He is left to wonder who Jesus is that he should claim to be worthy of such honor as Simon's guest; who Jesus is that he should openly forgive sin; who Jesus is that he should declare the woman to be saved and assure her of the peace of God. Simon is left to think about his own standing before God: is he, after all, truly a righteous man?

Above all, Jesus wants to drive Simon to the point where he will begin to understand that he too is a sinner, that he too needs forgiveness, that before God he is in debt, just like the woman. But for the present, Simon gets no good news. The sinful woman receives the good news of forgiveness, but not Simon, the righteous man. For the righteous man there is only more law, more challenge to treat the Lord as he deserves, to honor him with wholehearted devotion. Simon is sent back to the school of the law, the law that he thinks he understands so well.

True Righteousness

We are being shown by Jesus's example and by his teaching that true righteousness, truly knowing God, truly being a follower of Christ does not mean despising sinners or separating ourselves from them. Although it is very widely taught among evangelical Christians today that this is precisely what Christian faith means, according to Jesus himself, truly believing him and being his disciple means welcoming sinners. The Pharisees taught personal separation from sinners, just as so much of the Christian church today teaches separation from sinners, but it is clearly evident that this is not what Jesus taught and lived.

Remember the story I recounted earlier of the pastor, the pool party, and the woman who said, "Your daughters should not be friends with girls who wear two-piece bathing suits"? This same pastor has found that the people who are uncomfortable with the outreach of their church are often "mature Christians" who start coming to the church when they move into the area. At first they find the worship uplifting and glorifying to the Lord; they are pleased by the solid biblical teaching; they enjoy the fellowship and the spiritual vitality. But many of them leave after six months because they are afraid their own children will be polluted by the kind of non-Christian young people who attend the service and the youth group.

Some may respond that consorting with sinners is one thing for adult, mature believers, but our children need to keep separate. However, there are two problems with this response. First, if children or young people are taught all their lives to stay away from "sinners" because they are unclean and polluting, it is very difficult to try to break that habit when those young churchgoers become adults. It is even more difficult for young people with such a background to change their way of thinking, the way they see the world, and their attitude toward unbelievers.

The second problem is even more serious. There is only one kind of true Christian obedience, and at its heart that obedience requires being merciful and compassionate to sinners, of whom any and every believer needs to be able to declare, "I am the foremost."[8] It is this message of grace to us and to our children, and of mercy to others, that we are called to teach our families and the young people in our churches.

When Jesus is told that holiness means that sinners should be kept away, his response is that he came into the world to save sinners. In obedience to Jesus and in imitation of his example, every Christian, no matter what age he or she may be, is called to be gracious and gentle to sinners, to befriend sinners, and to show them the mercy of Christ.

WHAT ABOUT THE NEED TO CONDEMN SINNERS?

What about the issue of condemning sinners, of "blasting them with the fear of judgment," of exposing their sin, rebuking it and insisting on a demonstration of repentance and a changed life before we welcome them to the celebration of the good news of the gospel? Unhappily, sometimes we are taught not only that we are to separate ourselves from sinners, but also that we are openly to condemn their behavior and to challenge them with the requirements of God's law. In other words, we are taught, both by precept and by frequent example, to send the sinners to the school of the law. I know a pastor who had charges brought against him by some members of his congregation for not preaching sermons directed at unbelieving sinners to make them feel guilty.

Another story makes the point even more clearly and even more sadly. While I was in seminary, one of my fellow students was invited to preach a series of revival meetings at a nearby church. One evening he stopped to get a meal at a local fast-food place before the service. This was in the late sixties, and he met some young people who were arrayed in typical hippy style of the time: long hair, beards, colorful clothes, beads, no shoes. They had a good conversation together, and the group asked my classmate where he was going and why he was dressed up in a suit, white shirt, and tie on a weekday evening. He

---

[8] 1 Timothy 1:16.

told them about the service at which he was going to preach, and they asked if they could come. He was delighted and so they walked together over to the church.

The church's pastor was waiting at the door to welcome people. But when he saw the "hippies" he told them politely that they would have to go home, change their clothes, and put on shoes. They could not come to the revival service "looking like that." Of course they did not return. The message they received was essentially this: "Unless you clean up your life, and your appearance, you are not welcome to this church or to God. We Christians want nothing to do with you until you change, for you offend us, and you might contaminate us or our children." Jesus's treatment of sinners and his message for sinners were very different.

THE LAW FOR THE "RIGHTEOUS"

Indeed, Jesus, unlike us, preached the school of the law to those who seemed closest to God, those who already had extensive knowledge of the truth, those who valued God's law and taught it, and those who seemed committed to living in obedience to God's commandments. This brings us back to the question, who are the people to whom we ought to show and tell the law?

First, it may well be that we ourselves, and any of our own fellow church members who are confident that we are serving God zealously, ought to be challenged with God's commandments, rather than hearing the gospel over and over again with little true understanding. For all of us, grace can become something on which we presume. The lack of a sense of accountability to God that is so prevalent in our culture is almost everywhere present in our churches. Many of us in the church have very little idea of the requirements of God's law. We are a generation of whom it can be said, "There is no fear of God before their eyes."[9] Consequently, we have little idea of our true need for forgiveness. Therefore, we also have little appreciation for the work of Christ.

The sad truth is that we live at a time when, in the church, there is widespread ignoring of God's standards for our sexual lives, and there is moral laxity about our financial dealings. In many other areas

---

[9] Psalm 36:1.

of life we follow the pattern of our culture, rather than being obedient to God's commandments. Indeed, we may say that one of the great weaknesses of evangelical churches today is a serious failure to teach thoroughly the requirements of God's law. Instead, we have countless humanly devised rules about what Christians ought to do or ought not to do—rules about movies not to see, music to avoid, books that must not be read; rules about clothing, drink, public and private behavior; rules about church attendance, membership requirements, and tithing on gross or net income. These rules we design for ourselves, our children, and our church members will never produce righteousness, though they may have the appearance of wisdom. Nor will these rules produce the humility before God that is at the heart of the Christian life. We have already dealt with this problem of legalism, so no more needs to be said here on that subject.

Instead of those rules, what we all need in our churches is to be taught what it means to love God with all our hearts, souls, minds, and strength, and to love our neighbors as ourselves. We need to be taught God's commandments about showing mercy and sacrificial love to those in need, about faithfulness in the home and the workplace, about justice and integrity in our business practices, about righteousness and generosity in the use of money. In other words, what we need in our churches is serious exposition of the kind of righteousness that God and his laws demand.

Wherever there is little serious exposition of the school of the law of God, people end up with a devalued understanding of the good news of the gospel. Like Simon the Pharisee, we who think we have been forgiven little love little! But the law, properly expounded, because it is so beautiful, exposes the ugliness of our sin. Without understanding of the law we have no sense of our own sin, and therefore we have no sense of our need for Christ. All of us need to hear the law of God taught frequently and powerfully, so that we may be convicted of sin and come to understand our continuing need of Christ.

Second, we should show and tell the law to anyone who is a member of religious groups that commit themselves to living by the laws of God and who see their obedience as foundational to their expectation of eternal life. This will mean expounding the school of the law to churches that are moralistic or legalistic, to Jehovah's Witnesses, to Mormons, to Orthodox Jews, to devout Muslims—to anyone who believes that their way of life makes them acceptable to God, anyone who is self-righteous. Also, perhaps we should communicate the law to many of our cobelligerents in the culture war, those who claim to be on the side of family values and who choose a conservative lifestyle—particularly if these people are arrogant about their way of life and critical of everyone else. The school of the law is for the proud. Its purpose is to humble them before God so that they may see their need of his grace, mercy, and the forgiveness that comes only through Jesus.

In addition when we do communicate the law, either to the "righteous" or to the "sinners," we need to make sure that, rather than beginning with the condemnation of sin, we expound the beauty of righteousness. Think of Jesus telling the parable of the good Samaritan. He is upholding the beauty of righteousness, the beauty of the law. This is a far more powerful means by which the Holy Spirit convicts people of sin and their need for forgiveness. In seeing the loveliness of what God intends for human life, people become aware of how deep the damage is that they have done to themselves by ignoring God's commandments in favor of what will give them pleasure.

I remember preaching on God's design for sexuality and marriage at the wedding of one of my sons. Several of his closest friends from high school flew to England to be at the wedding. None of them were Christians and none of them were accustomed to attending church. They had all been sexually active since high school. One of them, a very handsome young man, had had many sexual encounters and at that time was having an affair with one of his college teachers, a married woman. After the service he came up to me to talk. "Jerram," he said, "I feel like such a total jerk! I have been using women to satisfy my lust without any respect for them, without any care for them. I have been thoroughly selfish and I am completely ashamed of myself. I am going to stop this and try to live chastely from now on until I get married. Thank you for showing me what a wonderful gift sex is and for challenging me to use this gift rightly." In my sermon I had said nothing to try to make anyone feel condemned or guilty. That is not the preacher's calling at a wedding! Rather, I had simply tried to teach

278 DELIGHTING IN THE LAW OF THE LORD

on the beauty of God's design for sexuality and marriage, on the loveliness of chastity and fidelity, and on the destructive nature of indulging one's sexual desires without commitment.

TEACHING THE LAW TO CHILDREN

I am often asked about teaching the law to our children. I think that for all of us, both children and adults, stories that reveal righteousness in its beauty and the ugliness of sin are very helpful. These can be stories from Scripture, like the true story of Boaz and Ruth, or they can be the parables Jesus tells, like the good Samaritan or the prodigal son; or they can be other well-told stories that communicate moral truth in a powerful way.

Let me give some personal examples: I have taught a class on Jane Austen several times at Covenant Seminary. I will never forget the response from one of the women in the class to our reflections on *Pride and Prejudice.* We had been thinking about the domineering and arrogant behavior of Lady Catherine de Bourgh and the crushing impact she had upon her own daughter. The woman in the class said to me that she had seen herself in Lady Catherine. She too was a strong woman with decided opinions and very articulate in expressing them, confident of her understanding of exactly how Christians should live. She said to me: "I am so thankful for this book and for our discussions in this class. Without this I would have crushed my daughter as Lady Catherine crushed hers." She wept as she said this, for the story had exposed her sin in a way that challenging her directly about her behavior could never have done.

Another personal story: One time when we were driving 850 miles to the Upper Peninsula of Michigan with one of our sons, his wife, and their children, we listened to a wonderful unabridged reading of *The Secret Garden* by Frances Hodgson Burnett. Many readers will be familiar with this classic story, which recounts the rebirth and transformation of an overgrown garden and of two completely neglected children who have become self-centered, demanding, and sour-natured. It also tells of the renewal of two adults and the restoration of relationships.

Our grandsons, who were five and two at the time, listened to this story with rapt attention. They were shocked by the behavior of the children in the story. For a couple of years afterward all we had to do if one of them misbehaved was to mention "the young Rajah," and our grandsons would immediately stop their demanding, complaining, or other problematic behavior. We have also found, both with our sons and with our grandchildren, that the books by Laura Ingalls Wilder have greatly helped us think about the nature of marriage, family life, service, love, respect, obedience, and many other aspects of moral beauty.

In a children's literature class that I teach at the seminary, when we were studying *The Secret Garden* one of the mothers reminded me of how her husband had come to me for advice on handling a difficult phase that two of their daughters were going through at the time. I recommended reading *The Secret Garden* aloud as a family and suggested that this would give plenty of opportunity for discussion about many issues of behavior—and, of course, about the beauty of the forgiveness and newness of life that come to us through Christ's atoning death. She told me with tears of joy how helpful the reading of this book had been to their family life.

I can remember having the most wonderful discussions about righteousness, moral failures, and the substitutionary work of Jesus with our three sons when we read *The Lion, the Witch and the Wardrobe* as a family. Reading about Edmund's betrayal of his brother and sisters, about the quarreling between the children, and about the many other moral issues addressed in that book was a great help in our confronting our own family issues, a great help in leading us to confession and repentance, and a great help in teaching us the beauty of the gospel of Jesus's sacrifice for us. It is only as our children and we, their parents, see our sin clearly exposed to us by the law that we develop a growing appreciation for the love of Christ.

Questions for Personal Reflection and Group Discussion

1. What is your response to the story of Jesus at the home of Simon the Pharisee?

2. Think back on your life and ask yourself when you were most acutely conscious of the wonder of what Christ has done in forgiving all your failures. Was it when someone told you how bad you were? Was it when you became aware of how damaging to yourself and others your sins were? Was it when you un-

derstood the righteousness of God more fully? Was it when you were inspired by a story of moral beauty and then saw your own failures in comparison? Or was it some other time and some other way? God uses many means to convict us of sin and to reveal his mercy to us, so I am not suggesting that there is one right answer to this question.

3. Are there people in your life from whom you are prepared to hear challenges? Or, to put this question another way, is there anyone you know to whom you are prepared to listen when they challenge you about your sin? If there is, what are the characteristics of this person, and what kind of a relationship do you two have that makes you willing to listen?

4. Why do you think we so readily hit on the notion that the best way to convict people of their sin is simply to attack them, to accuse them of their wrongdoing, and then command them to repent?

5. What books and movies have you found helpful in teaching your own heart about righteousness and especially about areas where your own life needs to change? Have you had experiences yourself like the one I described from the study of *Pride and Prejudice*?

6. What books and movies have you found helpful in communicating to children the beauty of the law and the loveliness of God's mercy?

21

THE LAW OF GOD AND OUR SECULAR SOCIETY

By this point, I trust that every reader has become convinced of the preciousness of God's law for believers. Every Christian should be able to rejoice with the psalmist:

> The law of the LORD is perfect,
>   reviving the soul.
> The statues of the LORD are trustworthy,
>   making wise the simple.
> The precepts of the LORD are right,
>   giving joy to the heart.
> The commands of the LORD are radiant,
>   giving light to the eyes.[1]

We know from Scripture, and it ought to be evident from our own personal experience, that walking in obedience to God's law brings freedom, blessing, and gladness into our lives. We rejoice that God is good, just, upright, and pure. We rejoice that this holy God has created a moral universe where there is a sure and eternal distinction between good and evil. We rejoice that this morally righteous God has made us to be finite reflections of his infinite being and that, as a consequence, we are created to imitate him in his goodness. We rejoice that even though we are sinners, Christ has fulfilled the demands of the law for us where we have failed to obey our Creator, Lawgiver, and Judge. We

---

[1] Psalm 19:7–8, NIV.

rejoice that as those redeemed by his perfect life and by his offering himself up to death in our place, we are now called to love his law and to be revived by his Spirit as we commit ourselves to obeying his commandments. We rejoice that our Father has promised that through the intercession of his Son, by his Spirit's power and as we offer ourselves to him as living sacrifices, he will day by day renew us into his likeness in true righteousness and holiness.

This delight in the law leads us to a new and challenging question: Should Christians try to bring God's law to bear on our secular society? This question raises many others: Does God's law apply to unbelievers? Why would an unbeliever want to obey God's law? Surely unbelievers need the gospel and not the law. Won't improving society make people forget their need for Christ? What right do we have as Christians to influence society if we accept the doctrine of separation of church and state? Why would unbelievers listen to the views of a Christian about the laws of our society? Is this truly part of our spiritual calling as believers? These are important questions, and I am sure readers could add many more of their own to this brief list.

I will begin to answer these questions by presenting a theological framework for our reflections.

1. *Scripture everywhere teaches us that this is God's world and that all creatures and all peoples owe their origin to him.*

> The earth is the LORD's, and everything in it,
>   the world, and all who live in it.[2]

The claim that this earth and all who live in it are created by God and owe their life to him remains true no matter what people believe about the existence of God, what they believe about who or what God is, and whether they acknowledge him or not as their Lord and Savior. This is still God's world. Despite the reality of the fall, despite the power of Satan at work in inciting humanity to rebellion, this universe in which we live is God's and everything we see in the universe around us declares this to be the case.[3]

2. *God did not simply create all things that exist and then sit back to let the*

---

[2] Psalm 24:1, NIV.
[3] Psalm 19:1–4; Romans 1:18–21.

world go its way (the view of deism); rather, he continues to uphold the world in its ongoing life and order. Of the beloved Son, Paul writes: "By him all things were created, in heaven and on earth, visible and invisible, whether thrones or dominions or rulers or authorities—all things were created through him and for him. And he is before all things, and in him all things hold together."[4] The author of Hebrews declares of Christ that "he upholds the universe by the word of his power."[5]

3. *God has such love for all this creation and for the whole human race, despite our rejection of him, despite our refusal to worship him, despite our ongoing disobedience, that he continues to care for and provide for all of created reality because he has made a covenant with the human race and with the whole created order of this earth.*

> Then God said to Noah and to his sons with him, "Behold, I establish my covenant with you and your offspring after you, and with every living creature that is with you, the birds, the livestock, and every beast of the earth with you, as many as came out of the ark; it is for every beast of the earth. I establish my covenant with you, that never again shall all flesh be cut off by the waters of the flood, and never again shall there be a flood to destroy the earth." And God said, "This is the sign of the covenant that I make between me and you and every living creature that is with you, for all future generations. I have set my bow in the cloud, and it shall be a sign of the covenant between me and the earth. When I bring clouds over the earth and the bow is seen in the clouds, I will remember my covenant that is between me and you and every living creature of all flesh. And the waters shall never again become a flood to destroy all flesh. When the bow is in the clouds, I will see it and remember the everlasting covenant between God and every living creature of all flesh that is on the earth." God said to Noah, "This is the sign of the covenant that I have established between me and all flesh that is on the earth."[6]

This passage is full of repetition: "I establish," "covenant," "sign," "never again," "every beast," "all flesh," "every living creature," "I will remember," "between me and you," "the bow in the clouds." These repetitions underline God's total commitment to the promise that he

---

[4] Colossians 1:16–17.
[5] Hebrews 1:3; see also Psalm 104.
[6] Genesis 9:8–17.

makes. He reveals an everlasting covenant with us and with every crea-ture of the earth. These words about the everlasting covenant that the Lord makes with all that lives are the foundation for the doctrine we usually refer to as common grace, or what John Calvin termed "general grace"[7] and I delight to call the general kindness of God.

This doctrine of common grace has been neglected in many churches of almost all theological traditions. However, from time to time in the history of the church this conviction of God's general kindness to this earth, to its creatures, and especially to the human race has been celebrated. The theologian who celebrated this doctrine most powerfully was Calvin, and he did this in a particularly beautiful manner, for he had a deep and thorough biblical understanding and a writing style of extraordinary elegance and clarity. Indeed, it would not be inappropriate to think of Calvin as the theologian of the cov-enant of common grace.

Some may be surprised that I use the language of the covenant when referring to this doctrine of common grace. When we think of the covenant, we usually begin with a theological discussion about the nature of the covenant that God made with Adam and Eve at creation.[8] Or more often we begin with God's covenant with those he has called to himself through the blood of the covenant fulfilled in Jesus's death on our behalf.

However, the first time in the Genesis text that we find explicit reference to a covenant is when God makes his covenant after the flood with all of creation. This covenant is not made only with those whom God calls to himself, those who put their trust in him and walk in his ways. This covenant is made with the whole human race and with every living thing.[9] God covenants not to destroy the earth again, but to uphold the seasons and to make provision for every creature on the earth including the human race. The rainbow is the sign of God's commitment to this promise.

A remarkable feature of this covenant is that God makes his prom-ise and guarantees it no matter what happens. He holds himself to

---

[7] John Calvin, *Institutes of the Christian Religion*, ed. John T. McNeill, trans. Ford Lewis Battles (Philadel-phia: Westminster, 1960), 2.2.15.
[8] Hosea 6:7 refers to Adam transgressing the covenant.
[9] Genesis 8:16–17, 21–22; 9:1–3, 7–17.

his promise regardless of the response of those who are the recipients of the promise. This commitment to care for all his creation is celebrated in the Psalms, especially Psalms 104 and 145. Psalm 104 describes God as the one who is not only the original Creator, but also the present ruler of the whole universe, the one who governs the seasons and who orders the physical structures of this earth and who provides for every living creature. Psalm 145 rejoices in these same themes of God's continuing covenant with creation. In this psalm we should notice the way in which the psalmist uses God's personal name, *Yahweh*, the "Lord," as he writes about his love for all creatures and all people on earth:

> The Lord is good to all,
>   and his mercy is over all that he has made. . . .
> The eyes of all look to you,
>   and you give them their food in due season.
> You open your hand
>   and satisfy the desire of every living thing.
> The Lord is righteous in all his ways
>   and kind in all his works.[10]

Everywhere we look on this earth we observe both the majesty of the Creator and the wonder of his commitment to give richly to all that he has made. In addition to seeing God's love for all creatures displayed around us, we see his even deeper commitment to us as human beings.

> You cause the grass to grow for the livestock
>   and plants for man to cultivate,
> that he may bring forth food from the earth
>   and wine to gladden the heart of man,
> oil to make his face shine
>   and bread to strengthen man's heart.[11]

> The Lord upholds all who are falling
>   and raises up all who are bowed down.[12]

---

[10] Psalm 145:9, 15–17.
[11] Psalm 104:14–15.
[12] Psalm 145:14.

Jesus also encourages us to know of God's generous care for us when he speaks about the heavenly Father's provision for all creatures, and he urges us, therefore, not to be anxious about what we eat or what we wear, nor to seek after these things as the Gentiles do, but to trust our Father and seek his kingdom and his righteousness:

> Look at the birds of the air; they do not sow or reap or store away in barns, and yet your heavenly Father feeds them. Are you not of more value than they? . . .
> See how the lilies of the field grow. They do not labor or spin. Yet I tell you that not even Solomon in all his splendor was dressed like one of these.[13]

Lest we are tempted to respond to this last point, "But, surely, God cares only for those who are his children through faith," Jesus sets aside this thought with his assertion of how deeply committed God is to serving and caring for even those who are his enemies. Jesus calls believers to imitate God in his care for the wicked as well as for those who obey him:

> Love your enemies and pray for those who persecute you, that you may be sons of your Father in heaven. He causes his sun to rise on the evil and the good, and sends rain on the righteous and the unrighteous.[14]

> The Most High . . . is kind to the ungrateful and the evil. Be merciful, even as your Father is merciful.[15]

And Paul appeals to the pagans who want to offer sacrifices to him and Barnabas by reminding them that God constantly gives them good gifts:

> We also are men, of like nature with you, and we bring you good news, that you should turn from these vain things to a living God, who made the heaven and the earth and the sea and all that is in them. In past generations he allowed all the nations to walk in their own

---

[13] Matthew 6:26–29, NIV.
[14] Matthew 5:44–45, NIV.
[15] Luke 6:27–36, particularly 35–36.

way. Yet he did not leave himself without witness, for he did good by giving you rains from heaven and fruitful seasons, satisfying your hearts with food and gladness.[16]

4. *The Lord cares for the human race, including all unbelievers; and in addition he rules the histories of every nation on this earth because all nations belong to him.* In his address to the Athenians on Mars Hill, Paul refers to this rule of God over history, as well as his upholding of human life and his nearness to all people. God's rule over history and the other ways that he cares for this world, Paul says to the Athenians, are evidences of God's desire to be searched for and known. He even declares that their own thinkers are aware of these truths:

The God who made the world and everything in it, being Lord of heaven and earth, does not live in temples made by man, nor is he served by human hands, as though he needed anything, since he himself gives to all mankind life and breath and everything. And he made from one man every nation of mankind to live on all the face of the earth, having determined allotted periods and the boundaries of their dwelling place, that they should seek God, and perhaps feel their way toward him and find him. Yet he is actually not far from each one of us, for

"in him we live and move and have our being";

as even some of your own poets have said,

"For we are indeed his offspring."[17]

God governs history, resisting the proud pretensions of our race just as he did at the Tower of Babel.[18] He deposes tyrants and brings down the rulers of nations in order to draw people to himself. See, for example, the account of the judgment of Nebuchadnezzar in the book of Daniel.[19] In our own time we can think of the overthrow of the former Soviet government and the liberation of the peoples of central and eastern Europe, as well as the remarkable growth of the

---

[16] Acts 14:15–17.
[17] Acts 17:24–28.
[18] See Genesis 11.
[19] See Daniel 4.

churches there in the years after 1990. Even the terrible massacre in Tiananmen Square in China had the effect of causing many Chinese people to turn away from their rulers in disgust and to start asking questions that led them eventually to faith in Christ. In each of these situations we see God ruling history to draw people to himself and to turn them to righteousness.

It should be our prayer that even the brutality of Islamic radical militants will be used by God to cause many Muslims to turn away, sickened by these appalling acts of terrorism, and to find their hope in Jesus Christ. Indeed, this is happening all over the Muslim world today, just as it happened under Islamic fundamentalism in Iran with the number of Christians there growing from thirty thousand in 1989, at the time of the Islamic Revolution under Ayatollah Khomeini, to over 350,000 today. Our hope as Christians is that no matter how the Devil or wicked rulers may rage, God will rule history for the sake of the advance of the gospel of Christ.

Christ rules the nations and all of human history in behalf of the gospel and for his church.[20] Christ has not given the nations up completely to unbelief, idolatry, and disobedience. The apostle can say that there is even a sense in which our Lord Jesus is the Savior of all men.[21] This whole period of history, from Christ's first to his second coming, is an age of grace and forbearance, and therefore God is committed to restraining sin[22] and to punishing disobedience even in the present, so that there is a testimony about the destructive nature of evil.[23] This moral rule of God is true for every person, both believer and unbeliever. No person in this world can do something evil and produce goodness, truth, and beauty as the fruit of such an act. As I pointed out in the preceding section, it is true that God is so gracious that he sometimes overrules the evil deeds of men and women to advance the gospel in the world; but that does not change the evil nature of the human acts, nor can we bring good out of evil we do. Judas's betrayal of Jesus was a wicked act, and he had to suffer the consequences, even though God brought about our salvation

---

[20] Matthew 28:18–20; Ephesians 1:20–23.
[21] 1 Timothy 2:3–6; 4:10; Titus 2:11.
[22] Romans 2:4; 2 Thessalonians 2:6–7; 2 Peter 3:8–9.
[23] Romans 1:18–28; Galatians 6:7–8.

through Jesus's death. Judas's act does not become virtuous because of the self-sacrifice of Jesus!

5. *Our race is not abandoned to utter depravity, for the image of God is not completely obliterated in those around us.* This upholding of the image of God in every person means that people are not as bad as they could be. Humans are not demons, for demons only lie, deceive, accuse, betray, and destroy life. People are certainly deeply sinful, but they cannot be described fully in terms of their sins. Rather, because of God's ongoing kindness to humanity, we may still observe that people bear God's image. There is no one so wicked in this life that the image of God is completely obliterated from him or her.[24]

People reflect the nature of God as love, for they continue to love their children and to love one another in marriage and friendship, even to the point of self-sacrifice.[25] Adam and Eve, and with them every member of our race, were called, as God's image bearers, to rule over this world and its creatures. People still exercise dominion and sometimes exercise it well with genuine respect for the natural world. Environmentalists, or those who simply care for the plot of land where they dwell, are not all necessarily Christians. In fact, far too few Christians care for this lovely earth which the Lord has entrusted to us. It is sad to say that it may more often be unbelievers who have a deep sense of responsibility for this earth and for the creatures that inhabit it along with us.

People still sometimes choose to honor others more highly than themselves, thus imitating the eternal mutual honor within the Trinity. When I was growing up, my parents were not yet committed Christians, yet my father and mother had one of the best marriages I have ever seen. I do not think I ever heard my father say an unkind, disrespectful, or dishonoring word to my mother; and we lived in a small home where every word spoken could be heard by everyone else.

Calvin often comments on this revelation of God's glory in humans. In a passage from the *Institutes* he calls man a "microcosm," that is, a little world in which God is made known (Calvin goes on to say) as in a "clear mirror":

---

[24] Genesis 5:1–3; 9:6; Psalm 8; James 3:9.
[25] Luke 6:32–33; 11:11–13; Romans 5:7.

Certain philosophers, accordingly, long ago not ineptly called man
a microcosm because he is a rare example of God's power, goodness,
and wisdom, and contains within himself enough miracles to oc-
cupy our minds, if only we are not irked at paying attention to them.
. . . For each one undoubtedly feels within the heavenly grace that
quickens him.[26]

6. *People still have the law of God written on their hearts.* In the latter
part of Romans 1 and the first half of chapter 2, Paul, writing about
people who do not have the written laws of God, insists that they have
a deep and abiding moral consciousness that is not erased in this life,
and he argues that this leads them to an acute awareness of what is
truly good and truly bad:

> For when Gentiles, who do not have the law, by nature do what the
> law requires, they are a law to themselves, even though they do not
> have the law. They show that the work of the law is written on their
> hearts, while their conscience also bears witness, and their conflicting
> thoughts accuse or even excuse them.[27]

There are no moral relativists, in reality. Everyone you or I will ever
meet is attracted to some aspect of the beauty of righteousness and
will be critical of particular areas of human wickedness. All people are
blessed for even a measure of obedience to God's commandments; and
all reap sorrow and destruction for disobedience to God's laws in this
life. This is true whether they are Christians or not.

7. *In addition to the law written on every person's heart, God also gives his
wisdom generously to people in every nation.*

> Does not wisdom call out?
>   Does not understanding raise her voice?
> On the heights along the way,
>   where the paths meet, she takes her stand;
> beside the gates leading into the city,
>   at the entrance, she cries aloud;
> "To you, O men, I call out;
>   I raise my voice to all mankind. . . .

---

[26] Calvin, *Institutes*, 1.5.3.
[27] Romans 2:14–15.

> "By me kings reign,
>   and rulers decree what is just;
> by me princes rule,
>   and nobles, all who govern justly."[28]

Because of this moral wisdom given to every nation, all societies have laws against theft, child abuse, murder, and so on. People in every human culture know that neither individual life nor the well-being of society can be maintained without some respect for law and moral virtues. So God challenged not only Israel, but also the nations around Israel to live by what is right—and he judged their practice of injustice.[29]

Scripture demands that Christians acknowledge that wisdom, truth, and beauty are found not only among those who worship the one true God, for God in his kindness has given these gifts to all peoples. So if we read the book of Proverbs carefully, we will discover that some of the proverbs in our canonical book come from non-Hebrew collections. In fact, all the wisdom literature reflects the forms of a much wider cultural setting. In the same way, the poetic structure of our psalms is not unique to the Old Testament but is part of a cultural tradition in the Semitic world. God was pleased to use these cultural forms for the communication of his message to us.

Calvin, recognizing this reality of God's particular kindness in giving wisdom to all people, speaks of God's "special graces," which the Lord has bestowed generously on unbelievers:

> Whenever we come upon these matters in secular writers, let that admirable light of truth shining in them teach us that the mind of man, though fallen and perverted from its wholeness, is nevertheless clothed and ornamented with God's excellent gifts. If we regard the Spirit of God as the sole fountain of truth, we shall neither reject the truth itself, nor despise it wherever it shall appear, unless we wish to dishonor the Spirit of God. For by holding the gifts of the Spirit in slight esteem, we contemn and reproach the Spirit himself. What then? Shall we deny that the truth shone upon the ancient jurists who established civic order and discipline with such great equity? Shall we

---

[28] Proverbs 8:1–4 (NIV), 15–16 (ESV).
[29] See, for example, Psalm 82; Amos 1:3–2:3, Romans 13:1–7.

say that the philosophers were blind in their fine observation and art-
ful description of nature? Shall we say that they are insane who developed medicine, devoting their labor to our benefit? What shall we say
of all the mathematical sciences? Shall we consider them the ravings
of madmen? No, we cannot read the writings of the ancients on these
subjects without great admiration. We marvel at them because we are
compelled to recognize how preeminent they are. But shall we count
anything praiseworthy or noble without recognizing at the same time
that it comes from God? Let us be ashamed of such ingratitude, into
which not even the pagan poets fell, for they confessed that the gods
had invented philosophy, laws, and all useful arts.[30]

Two sections later, Calvin says:

To sum up: We see among all mankind that reason is proper to our
nature; it distinguishes us from brute beasts, just as they by possess-
ing feeling differ from inanimate things. Now, because some are born
fools or stupid, that defect does not obscure the general grace of God.[31]
Rather, we are warned by that spectacle that we ought to ascribe what
is left in us to God's kindness. For if he had not spared us, our fall
would have entailed the destruction of our whole nature. Some men
excel in keenness; others are superior in judgment; still others have
a readier wit to learn this or that art. In this variety God commends
his grace to us, lest anyone should claim as his own what flowed from
the sheer bounty of God. For why is one person more excellent than
another? Is it not to display in common nature God's special grace,[32]
which, in passing many by, declares itself bound to none? Besides this,
God inspires special activities, in accordance with each man's calling.[33]

8. *God has given to the human race the creation structures of marriage and
family.* Paul can say, "I bow my knees before the Father, from whom
every family in heaven and on earth is named."[34] Marriage and family
have been treasured by every people on the face of the earth throughout human history. This is true even where religions, philosophers,
state systems, and even our present idolatrous individualism have

---

[30] Calvin, *Institutes*, 2.2.15.
[31] The Latin is *generalem Dei gratiam*. In Calvin's French edition, he wrote *la gràce générale de Dieu*.
[32] The French here is *la grâce spéciale de Dieu*.
[33] Calvin, *Institutes*, 2.2.17.
[34] Ephesians 3:14–15.

sought to undermine these institutions. Studies have demonstrated that the health and endurance of all cultures are related to the degree to which marriage and family are honored in a society.[35]

9. *God has ordained the institution of government and the state to promote well-being and justice for human life in all nations.* The apostle Paul declares that those who rule over us are God's servants appointed for our good.[36] Because of this divine institution of government, and therefore for conscience' sake and for the Lord's sake, believers are to give honor to those in authority, and not just because of the fear of punishment. We should remember that Paul wrote these words about the pagan Roman authorities, and not about a modern democratically elected government. If Christians in the first century were required by the Lord to show respect to the brutal Roman government of their day, how much should we who live under government constrained by a constitution and laws respect those in authority over us. In addition, Paul commands us to pray for our rulers as a matter of first importance, and in our prayers we are to give thanks for them.[37]

In every society God has instituted governing authorities to rule wisely and justly. He calls them to account when they fail to be a terror to evil works and when they do not defend the cause of the poor, the oppressed, the widow, the orphan, and the alien.[38]

All these realities in which humans live give us a firm foundation for seeking to serve God in our secular societies. Indeed, it is a matter of obeying our Lord Jesus to do this. He gives every Christian the calling to be salt and light in society. This means that we are to seek to bring God's righteous laws to bear on our political, economic, judicial, educational, and cultural institutions. This will be the subject of our next chapter.

Questions for Personal Reflection and Group Discussion

1. I have tried to make a case that God is already at work in this world in many ways. As you read back over the series of points made in this chapter, which

---

[35] Olaf Raymond Johnston, *Who Needs the Family?* (Downers Grove, IL: InterVarsity, 1979), quotes from a study done by anthropologist J. D. Unwin, *Sex and Culture*, involving eighty societies, on the permanence and cultural power of monogamous marriage.
[36] Romans 13:1–7.
[37] 1 Timothy 2:1–3.
[38] See Psalm 82; Amos 1 and 2.

of these do you consider most significant as we think about seeking to have an impact on our secular society? (These points are summarized at the beginning of the next chapter.)

2. Do you think it is possible to convince unbelievers that certain kinds of behaviors are good and other kinds are bad? What approach would you use to convince unbelievers of the rightness of a particular moral virtue—such as chastity for singles or fidelity in marriage?

3. As you think about people you know who are not believers, where do you see them revealing a delight in creation?

4. Reflecting on non-Christians you know, what aspects of honoring goodness and moral beauty do you see in their lives?

5. Are you acquainted with non-Christians who have a deeper concern for the environment than many of the believers you know?

6. Who in public life seem to you to be examples of a passion for justice and mercy? Are they believers or unbelievers?

7. This question is preparatory for the next chapter. In Psalm 82 and in Amos 1 and 2, what are some of the moral issues and governmental obligations for which God calls pagan rulers and nations to account?

22

LIVING AS SALT AND LIGHT IN AND FOR THE WORLD

Our last chapter presented a theological framework for Christian engagement in unbelieving societies. We considered a series of biblical truths that describe the realities in which humans live.

God's Work in All the World

1. This is God's world, and all its peoples belong to him because he is the Creator.
2. God is not the distant God of deism, but rather continues to uphold this universe in existence.
3. God commits himself to care for and provide for all of created reality, for he has made a covenant with the human race and with the whole created order of this earth.
4. God rules the histories of every nation on this earth because all nations belong to him.
5. God upholds his image in every person so that all are crowned with that glory and honor.
6. People still have the law of God written on their hearts.
7. God generously gives his wisdom to people in every nation so that there is some justice and some wise rule in all nations.
8. God has given the human race the creation structures of marriage and family.
9. God has ordained the institution of government and the state to promote human welfare.

These realities give us a firm foundation for understanding Jesus's description of believers in the Sermon on the Mount:

> You are the salt of the earth. But if the salt loses its saltiness, how can it be made salty again? It is no longer good for anything, except to be thrown out and trampled by men.
>
> You are the light of the world. A city on a hill cannot be hidden. Neither do people light a lamp and put it under a bowl. Instead they put it on its stand, and it gives light to everyone in the house. In the same way, let your light shine before men, that they may see your good deeds and praise your Father in heaven.[1]

The Christian's calling is to be salt and light in the particular society in which we live at this point in history. This calling has many facets. We will look first at how we are called to think about the unbelievers around us, how we are to relate to them, how we are to speak to them and about them. What, in other words, is to be the Christian's fundamental posture toward the world of unbelief in which we live?

RELATING TO UNBELIEVERS AMID THE CULTURE WAR

Whether we live in the United States or elsewhere in the Western world, we live in a time of culture war. It is often described as a war about values: traditional values versus postmodern values, the past way of life versus the present way of life. Almost every politician on either side of the political spectrum addresses this issue of values, and almost all set themselves on the side of traditional values. We can listen to Democrat or Republican presidents or members of Congress or the Senate within the United States, or to Conservative or Labour Party leaders or members of Parliament within the United Kingdom, and we will hear them decrying the decline in values.

This was true for President Obama, who had much to say in defense of "traditional" values when he gave a speech in 2009 at Georgetown University on the problems in the economy. He criticized the greed, the risky financial strategies, the loss of responsibility to shareholders and to the public, and so on. He charged these immoral behaviors with causing the serious financial meltdown and the deep recession into

---
[1] Matthew 5:13–16, NIV.

which our economy and the economies of all nations have plunged over these past few years.

In October 2011 we listened to the young leader of the Labour Party in Britain making a very similar speech. He attacked the greed and folly of leading businesspeople and institutions. He challenged the irresponsibility of those who refused to work and who wanted to live off the welfare state. He spoke with horror about the riots that caused such damage to life and property in so many English cities in the summer of 2011. He praised those who resisted the rioters and who cleaned up after them. He honored hard work, responsibility, strong families, and the like. We can all remember politicians making such statements.

David Brooks, known as a moderately conservative columnist, commented on the above-mentioned speech of President Obama:

> When President Barack Obama summarized his economic policies in a speech at Georgetown last week, he departed from this story line and worldview [what Brooks sees as the typical Democratic Party line story and worldview]. Obama's chief concern was not inequality. It was irresponsibility. Obama didn't sound like an economic liberal at Georgetown. He sounded like a cultural conservative.
>
> America once had a responsible economic culture, Obama argued. People used to save their pennies to buy their dream houses. Banks used to lend by "traditional standards." Fannie Mae and Freddie Mac used to stick to their "traditional mandate." Companies like AIG used to limit themselves to the "traditional insurance business."
>
> But these traditions broke down, Obama continued. They were swamped by irresponsibility. Businesspeople chased "short-term profits" over long-term investments. Smart people spent more time manipulating numbers and symbols than actually making things. Americans consumed too much and saved too little. America became corrupted by "excessive debt," "reckless speculation" and "fleeting profits." Obama vowed to end this irresponsibility and the cycle of boom and bust. It's time to get back to basics, he said. He embraced tradition, order and authority. He quoted the New Testament and said that the U.S. built its economic house on rock and not sand.[2]

---

[2] David Brooks, "Big-Spending Conservative," the *New York Times* online, April 20, 2009, http://www.nytimes.com/2009/04/21/opinion/21brooks.html?_r=0.

As President Obama recognized in this speech about our economic problems, the culture war we face daily is a conflict about traditional values.

In the first few chapters of this book we saw that we might express the problem more accurately as a battle over the moral commandments given by God in his law versus the personal values the individual chooses for his or her own life. This battle touches issues of human life, of sexuality, of marriage and the family, of the stronger over the weaker, of respect for property, of business practice, of economic policy, of political corruption, and of personal responsibility and personal fulfillment.

Robert Bellah, one of the leading American sociologists, said that our two great goals as Americans are "vivid personal feelings and personal success."[3] Dorothy Sayers, the woman of letters and defender of the Christian faith, summed up the matter this way: "If you receive the pleasure-seasoned muse, pleasure and pain will be kings in your city instead of law and agreed principles."[4] This prophetic word of Sayers is now the sad reality almost everywhere in Europe; and it is increasingly the case in the United States.

This culture war is in itself an enormous challenge for the Christian, and indeed for everyone. Which side will we take? Will we, personally, be swept away by the pressures of a please-yourself culture and our own desire for personal freedom so that we too disobey the laws of God? Or will we devote ourselves to walking in obedience to his laws, regardless of the cost to us in terms of vivid personal feelings and personal success? This is the first and most significant battle of the culture war for each one of us.

In addition, the culture war raises another challenge to those of us who decide we must stand on the side of God's moral law: How do we fulfill our calling from Jesus Christ to go into the world with the good news of the Christian gospel while standing up for God's laws?

AN ESCALATING WAR OF WORDS

One of the obvious consequences of the loss of shared values is the breakdown of civil discourse in the public square. If we are simply

---

[3] See Robert Bellah et al., *The Habits of the Heart: Individualism and Commitment in American Life*, rev. ed. (Berkeley: University of California Press, 1996), 281.
[4] Dorothy Sayers, *The Whimsical Christian: 18 Essays* (New York: Macmillan, 1978), 81.

individuals pursuing our own personal vision of happiness, how can we treat others with honor and grace when they have a radically different vision? If we live in our isolated communities of belief (whether Christian, Muslim, secular humanist, liberal, or otherwise), how can we talk rationally to each other? How can we understand each other? How can we honor each other? We find that very few in the public square seek to understand others or to respect them or to speak across the barriers that divide us. People fight for access to media and political power—hence the culture wars—hurling abuse and passionate condemnation upon their adversaries.

Even Christians have taken up this battle of words and more. We readily develop a "we versus they" mentality and become drawn into the judgmental and abusive language that characterizes so much public discourse. Rather than being salt and light in this regard, Christians have sometimes been some of the worst offenders. Christian public discourse on radio and television and in the press is sometimes the most strident of any of the lobby groups jostling for political power and public influence. We have admired, listened to, and adopted the language of some of the most abusive radio and television talk shows. If the objection is made that such talk shows are a legitimate form of humor rather than serious public discourse—then we should just laugh at the humor and leave it at that. However, we all know that is not what happens.

Instead, there is the added problem that in our private conversation as well as our public discussion the abusive jokes and the bumper stickers become an open and scornful expression of this humor. Our public discourse readily becomes a self-condemning indictment of our failure to hear God's law; for God's law calls us to speech that is transformed by the Lord of mercy who dwells in our hearts. It is his kindness and grace toward us who were once his enemies that ought to be the motivating power and directing influence of our lives and of all our words.

On Judging and Being Judged

What does Scripture teach us about our manner of speech, and about when and how it is appropriate for us to judge? We can answer this question by asking whom Jesus judged. Perhaps to our surprise we find him judging those inside the religious establishment of his day, rather than those outside it. He cleansed the temple and he judged the religious people for having a zeal for God's law but missing its heart.[5] In our study of the parable of the good Samaritan we saw that Jesus judges the religious leaders of his time by using a priest and Levite as his examples of those who fail to obey God's laws about mercy and love.[6]

Jesus spent time, ate, and drank with the "sinners" and the untouchables of his time: prostitutes, tax collectors, and lepers.[7] He refused to judge the woman taken in adultery or the prostitute who washed his feet with her tears.[8] Jesus was, of course, criticized for this lack of condemnation of sinners, and also for the company he kept. However, his response was that he had come not to condemn but to save, not to judge but to serve, not to separate himself from sinners but to love them.[9]

These reflections on whom Christ judged raise the question, whom should we judge? As we have seen in Jesus's encounters with people, he teaches us that we should judge ourselves first of all, and that this judgment of ourselves is to be far more severe than any judgment of others. Jesus makes this demand emphatic with the use of a ludicrous image when he tells us that we are to take the logs out of our own eyes so that we can see to take specks out of the eyes of others.[10] In addition the Scriptures teach us that we are to deal with sin among those who claim to be Christians.[11] The church is called to judge itself. We should be regularly asking ourselves, How much of the present problems in our culture are caused by the failure of the church to be salt and light in the world?

It is also true that God's Word explicitly teaches us not to judge the world or to think of ourselves as better than the "sinners" around us.[12] Perhaps much to our surprise, Scripture turns this issue upside down and insists that the world judges us. Rather than giving us the

---

[5] Matthew 23:1–32; see especially verse 23.
[6] Luke 10:25–37.
[7] Matthew 9:9–13; 21:28–32; Luke 19:1–6.
[8] John 8:1–11; Luke 7:36–50.
[9] Matthew 11:19; Luke 15:1–7; 19:7–10; John 3:17; 12:47.
[10] Matthew 7:1–5.
[11] 1 Corinthians 5:9–13; 11:31; 1 Peter 4:17.
[12] Luke 18:9–14; 1 Corinthians 5:9–13.

calling to judge the world for its behavior and find it wanting, the Scriptures teach us that the world will judge Christians and the truth of our message by the way we live: our behavior and good deeds,[13] our love and unity,[14] and our work.[15] This is why Francis Schaeffer would often speak of the Christian living before the "watching world." We are to ask ourselves day by day, What conclusions are unbelievers drawing about the person of Jesus, about the Christian faith, about the church, and about me as they observe my life?

The world is the prosecutor of the church. Whether we like it or not, whether we acknowledge it or not, the truth is this. You and I are on trial before the world; our faith is on trial; God's Word is on trial; Jesus is on trial. We stand in the place of the accused with regard to each of these matters. Unbelievers draw their conclusions about Jesus, about the Bible, and about the church by looking at us. Are we making a good case for the defense?

As we reflect on the serious nature of this calling, we have to confess that we often fail to make a good case for the defense of the gospel in our words or in our lives. In making such a confession of our failure to be shaped in all we do by the good news we profess, we turn to Christ for mercy. Each moment he is living for us and speaking in our defense to his and to our heavenly Father. Even now he says, "Forgive them for they do not know what they do. I have taken their failures on myself." His life, full of mercy and kind deeds; his speech, anointed with gracious words; his death, given to replace ours; his present prayers—all these are offered to God the Father on our behalf that we might be forgiven and made clean. Every day, every hour, every minute we are received by God as those whose mouths and lives are pure. We have a Great High Priest, one who always lives to intercede for us.

PRIESTS FOR THE CHURCH AND THE WORLD

However, this is not all that Scripture has to say about priesthood. Yes, we have a High Priest, Jesus the Son of God; but we who have hoped

---

[13] Matthew 5:13–16; 1 Peter 2:12; 3:1–2.
[14] John 13:34–35; 17:23.
[15] Titus 2:9–10.

in him are also called to be priests.[16] As priests we are called to serve God and to serve one another. How do we exercise this calling to be priests? We are to offer ourselves to Jesus as those dedicated to live in his service. We are to be priests whose daily task is to pray for and to live for one another rather than to live solely for ourselves. We are to be imitators of the priesthood of Christ.

In addition to this priesthood toward our fellow Christians, we are also called to be priests for the world. We are to stand between the living and the dead as Moses and Aaron did when the people were dying of the plague that came on them because of their rebellion against God.[17] We are to stand between those who have been made alive in Christ and have thus escaped God's judgment, and those who do not yet know him and who remain in a state of death, subject to his judgment. Or to put it another way, we are called to stand in the gap between a holy and righteous God and a disobedient and rebellious world.

We may express this calling to priesthood in the following ways:

We Are to Be a Priesthood Active in Our Presence

In the weekly sacrifice of our worship we call on God to remember his covenant with the human race and with all creatures, among whom we live.[18] Think of the example of the Levites, who were commanded by the Lord to set their camps between the tabernacle and the people to protect the people from the holiness of God.[19] Every church all across the world is like this in its own community. We are camped between the heavenly temple of God and the sinful world around us. We are a line of defense between ungodliness and the wrath of God. And, we should take note, this is not because we are so righteous, as if we deserved mercy and the rest of the population does not. No, we have this calling to be God's line of defense simply because we have Jesus leading us in our worship, defending us from God's wrath by his righteousness. That righteousness of Jesus accounted to us makes us into God's protective system for the

---

[16] 1 Peter 2:9–10; Revelation 1:6.
[17] Numbers 16:47–48.
[18] Genesis 8:20–22; 9:8–17.
[19] Numbers 1:52–53.

unbelievers in our communities. This is why Jesus uses the image of salt of the earth for believers. We are the salt that preserves the world from corruption and judgment.[20]

We Are to Be a Priesthood Active in Prayer

We are to pray for the world rather than to hate, despise, abuse, or curse those who are not believers in Christ. This calling to be a praying priesthood includes the command to intercede for those who make themselves our enemies, or those who make themselves the enemies of God and of the gospel of Christ.[21] Think of the example of Abraham praying for the wicked cities of Sodom and Gomorrah.[22] Compare this with the response of many Christians to earthquakes in Los Angeles or hurricanes on the Gulf Coast. Whenever there is such tragedy, far too many preachers declare that our cities deserve the tribulations that have come upon them. They announce to the church and to the world that this particular trouble is a direct judgment of God for particular sins. Preachers do this even though Jesus challenges us instead to see all tribulation as a call to repentance because we are to recognize that we ourselves deserve judgment.[23]

Whenever we disobey Jesus by declaring that tsunamis, hurricanes, floods, tornadoes, and other disasters are God's direct judgment for particular sins, we also bring down on the church the scorn, abuse, and hatred of unbelievers, for we are perceived as self-righteous, and self-righteousness is one of the ugliest characteristics of those claiming to speak for God. When we make this serious error, we need to ask ourselves some tough questions: Are we more like Jonah than Abraham? Do we prefer to curse the unrighteous rather than pray for God to withhold his judgment? Do we desire that people should perish in their sins, or do we imitate the Lord and long for unbelievers to come to repentance?[24]

We can think also of the challenge that Jeremiah gave to the Jews in exile in Babylon. He urges them to pray for the peace and prosper-

---

[20] Matthew 5:13.
[21] Luke 6:27–28; Romans 12:14; 1 Timothy 2:1–6.
[22] Genesis 18:16–33.
[23] See Jesus's words in Luke 13:1–5, where he forbids us to imagine that those suffering tragedy are more worthy of judgment than we or others are.
[24] Jonah 4:1–4, 9–11.

ity of Babylon—even though the name Babylon was synonymous with idolatry and wickedness.[25] The apostle Paul charges us to pray for our rulers as a matter of first importance—both in our private devotion and in our public worship.[26] As you reflect on the public prayers in your church, would you say that prayer for our rulers and prayer for all sinners to come to repentance is indeed a matter of first importance?

We Are to Be a Priesthood Active in Proclamation

Peter calls us to make known the excellence and mercy of God who called us out of darkness into his marvelous light.[27] Paul tells us that it is his ambition to preach Christ where he is not yet known. His passionate desire is to offer the conversion of the nations as a pleasing sacrifice to the Lord.[28] Compare those words of Paul with the angry proclamation by Jonah to the people of Nineveh. Jonah was a most reluctant preacher. He denounced the people who lived in that great city, proclaiming the imminent judgment of God and calling them to repentance. Then he went outside the city to wait and watch for the judgment he believed it most richly deserved. When the people listened to his message and came to repentance, Jonah became angry and sulked. He told the Lord that this was exactly why he had been reluctant to come to Nineveh in the first place, despite the Lord's call. He knew that God was gracious and merciful and delighted to forgive transgression and sin. God rebuked him for his lack of grace.

How do our churches measure up? Are we like Paul with a passion to see people turning from their idolatry, their unbelief, and their sin and being saved? Or are we like Jonah, resenting the kindness of the Lord?

We Are to Be a Priesthood Active in Service

We are to give ourselves to the world in love, just as God has given himself in Christ.[29] Consider the example of Joseph serving Egypt in a time of famine, or of Daniel serving in Babylon: these two nations

---

25 Jeremiah 29:4–7.
26 1 Timothy 2:1–6.
27 1 Peter 2:9–10.
28 Romans 15:16, 20.
29 Matthew 5:43–48; Hebrews 13:15–16.

were the epitome of the spirit of idolatry and sin; yet God called his beloved children to serve in those nations. Or reflect on the challenges presented daily to Obadiah. He was called by the Lord to serve Ahab and Jezebel, two of the most wicked of all the rulers whose lives are recorded in the Old Testament.

I will conclude this chapter with a contemporary example, a local Christian believer named Ben Edwards, who died early in 2009. Our local paper, the *St. Louis Post Dispatch*, wrote this about him:

> Benjamin F. Edwards III, who helped build A.G. Edwards Inc. into the largest brokerage west of Wall Street, then watched appalled as it was sold by his successor, has died of prostate cancer at his home in Naples, Fla.
>
> In 1967, Mr. Edwards took the helm of a firm founded by his great-grandfather. At the time, A.G. Edwards had 300 brokers in 44 offices. When he retired as CEO in 2001, it had 7,000 brokers in 700 branches, as well as 5,000 workers at its sprawling headquarters complex on Jefferson Avenue. . . .
>
> Among his employees, Mr. Edwards was known as a gentle man with a sense of humor who made "having fun" one of the official corporate goals. Through 34 years at the company helm, family members say he never laid anyone off.
>
> On most days, he spent his first minutes chatting with the receptionist and security guard in the lobby. "He made a habit of walking through the building getting to know people. He had a view of employees that was pretty rare these days," Keller (one of the company's senior employees), said.
>
> Keller remembers a time, about two decades ago, when an employee's daughter needed a transplant to save her life, and the company's insurance wouldn't fully cover it.
>
> "Ben just made the decision, 'Oh, we'll pay for that.' That didn't surprise anybody," Keller said. "We had 10,000 employees in the firm. We all thought we worked for Ben."
>
> That was reflected in the company's unwritten policy of never laying anyone off. "A.G. Edwards did not lay off one soul for 115 years, even during the Great Depression," said his son, Benjamin F. "Tad" Edwards IV of Ladue. During a slump in the 1970s, better-paid employees took pay cuts to save jobs. The company's first layoff occurred after the senior Edwards left the firm.

"Down in the machinery, we thought of it as a social contract," said Keller, who now works at Confluence Investment Management in Webster Groves. "We could have got paid more at other places. There was a relationship that we all appreciated."

The company was on Fortune magazine's annual list of "100 Best Companies to Work for in America" for 10 straight years. . . .

"We thought we had built something special: a company that puts clients first, employees second and shareholders third," Mr. Edwards said. "Our theory was that if we did a good job for our clients and our employees, our shareholders would have maximum benefit in the long run. Our behavioral guideline was the 'Golden Rule.'

"I believed we had the people, the client base, the physical plant, the capital and the operating ethic to give us another exciting and enjoyable 120 years. We had no size or profit goals, but I was confident that our people did what each could to avoid waste and work together for the common good. This corporate philosophy worked successfully for the 45 years I was around."[30]

Ben Edwards was a servant of Christ who obeyed God's law in his own life. He served the church and the Christian community. He served his company and his employees. He served the world. He was an inspiring example of a Christian who truly was salt and light and a priest for the world.

Questions for Personal Reflection and Group Discussion

1. What has your attitude been toward your family members, neighbors, people at work, or others you know who are blasphemers, curse, are promiscuous, are adulterers, are gay, or are unethical in business dealings? Who, for you, are the "sinners" and "untouchables"? What have you done to seek to build a relationship with them?

2. Are there particular political leaders or other public figures, either local or national, about whom you have spoken abusively? Will you build prayer for them into your life whenever you hear about them or read about them? It does not take long to offer up a prayer for them as you listen to the radio, watch the news, read the paper, or participate in a conversation about them.

3. Are there people around you who judge Christianity unfavorably because of something in your life? What changes could you make with the Lord's help?

---

[30] Obituary, *St. Louis Post Dispatch*, April 22, 2009.

4. Is anyone attracted to Christianity because of your life? Do any unbelievers see your life closely enough to be drawn to God's truth by what they observe in you? If there is no one, will you start praying that the Lord will help you develop one or two relationships that make this possible?

5. Have you thought before about our responsibility to be priests for the world? (Read especially Jonah 4.) It is so easy for us to develop the kind of attitude that Jonah had, even though it is obviously wrong that he became angry when God was merciful to Nineveh.

6. As you reflect on the public prayers in your church and in your home, would you say that prayer for our rulers and prayer for all sinners to come to repentance is indeed a matter of first importance?

7. How does your church measure up in the priesthood of proclamation? Does your church imitate Paul with his passion to see people turning from their idolatry, their unbelief, and their sin and being saved?

8. In what ways does your church serve the community where it is based? If there are no ways that you can identify, ask the Lord and your fellow members how you could build some form of service into the life of your church.

9. In what ways do you and your family serve the society in which you live (not just the church, but the world)? If there are no ways that you can identify, ask the Lord and ask yourself how you could build some form of service into your life.

10. Would an obituary in your local paper praise you in the way Ben Edwards was praised?

23

OLD TESTAMENT LAW

How Should We View It?

In chapter 22 we considered the way in which Jesus described Christians as the salt and light of the world. We finished the chapter with the example of Ben Edwards, a believer in Christ who gave himself to live in obedience to the law of God, and who also sought to run the company of which he was president for many years by the principles taught in God's commandments. His story is inspiring to both Christians and non-Christians. The simple and profound reason for this admiration is that any true obedience to God's laws is seen to be wise, beautiful, merciful, just, and liberating. This is true in the life of an individual, in a marriage, in a family, or in a workplace.

This chapter asks, can we go one step further and take God's commandments into our wider society, into the life of our nation? Can we, and should we, work to have our local, state, and national laws shaped by the law of God? In chapter 21 I answered many of the fundamental issues that are important to this question. Here again is a summary of what God's Word teaches us about God's work in all the world:

1. This is God's world, and all its peoples belong to him because he is the Creator.
2. God is not the distant God of deism, but rather continues to uphold this universe in existence.
3. God commits himself to care for and provide for all of created reality, for he has made a covenant with the human race and with the whole created order of this earth.

4. God rules the histories of every nation on this earth because all nations belong to him.

5. God upholds his image in every person so that all are crowned with that glory and honor.

6. People still have the law of God written on their hearts.

7. God generously gives his wisdom to people in every nation so that there is some justice and some wise rule in all nations.

8. God has given the human race the creation structures of marriage and family.

9. God has ordained the institution of government and the state to promote human welfare.

These theological foundations put to rest most of the criticisms that can be raised—either by believers or by unbelievers—about the propriety of Christians engaging in our secular society with God's law as our guide. Christians should know that Christianity is the truth about the world in which we live and the truth about the human condition. This means that we can be confident that God's law is for Christian and non-Christian alike, for all persons are made in God's image. In this moral universe there are laws that govern everyone's life, and consequently there are blessings and penalties in our present experience for obedience and disobedience.

These basic principles also help us to see that we ought not to let the First Amendment "establishment" clause prevent us from entering into the public arena with God's law as a gift to our society; instead we ought to obey Jesus's description of believers and his command that all his people be salt and light in our society. The "establishment" clause of the First Amendment to the US Constitution says very simply, "Congress shall make no law respecting an establishment of religion, or prohibiting the free exercise thereof." The Supreme Court has interpreted this clause in the following manner in the case *Everson v. Board of Education* (1947). Writing for the majority in this 5–4 decision, Justice Hugo Black said:

> The "establishment of religion" clause of the First Amendment means at least this: neither a state nor the Federal Government can set up a church. Neither can pass laws which aid one religion, aid all religions, or prefer one religion over another. Neither can force nor influence

a person to go to or to remain away from church against his will or force him to profess a belief or disbelief in any religion. No person can be punished for entertaining or professing religious beliefs or disbeliefs, for church attendance or non-attendance. No tax in any amount, large or small, can be levied to support any religious activities or institutions, whatever they may be called, or whatever form they may adopt to teach or practice religion. Neither a state nor the Federal Government can, openly or secretly, participate in the affairs of any religious organizations or groups and vice versa. In the words of Jefferson, the clause against establishment of religion by law was intended to erect "a wall of separation between church and State."[1]

Many Americans, both Christians and non-Christian, understand Jefferson's "wall of separation between church and State" to mean that Christians have no business seeking to inform or influence the laws of the state because Christians come to the public square with religious convictions. However, this understanding is inaccurate. All people in any society have religious convictions. They have a view of the world that shapes what they believe about God, about human beings, about the universe, about the meaning of life in this world, about what is right and wrong, and about how people should live. The only thing unique about Christians is how we answer the questions about what we believe. A Hindu will answer these questions one way, a Muslim another way, a secular humanist another way, a postmodern relativist another way, and a Christian another way. No one comes to the public square with an empty head. Everyone comes with beliefs and convictions. Christians have just as much right as anyone else to bring their beliefs and convictions about what is right and wrong into the public square.

So, what are we as Christian believers to bring to the public square when we seek to fulfill Jesus's calling to be salt and light in the world? It is noteworthy that Jesus immediately draws our attention to the laws of the Old Testament after his words about salt and light.

> You are the salt of the earth. But if the salt loses its saltiness, how can it be made salty again? It is no longer good for anything, except to be thrown out and trampled by men.

---

[1] Accessed at http://www.law.cornell.edu/supct/html/historics/USSC_CR_0330_0001_ZO.html.

> You are the light of the world. A city on a hill cannot be hidden. Neither do people light a lamp and put it under a bowl. Instead they put it on its stand, and it gives light to everyone in the house. In the same way, let your light shine before men, that they may see your good deeds and praise your Father in heaven.
>
> Do not think that I have come to abolish the Law or the Prophets; I have not come to abolish them but to fulfill them. I tell you the truth, until heaven and earth disappear, not the smallest letter, not the least stroke of a pen, will by any means disappear from the Law until everything is accomplished. Anyone who breaks one of the least of these commandments and teaches others to do the same will be called least in the kingdom of heaven, but whoever practices and teaches these commands will be called great in the kingdom of heaven. For I tell you that unless your righteousness surpasses that of the Pharisees and the teachers of the law, you will certainly not enter the kingdom of heaven.[2]

Jesus insists that the law remains in force throughout this age and that even the tiniest part of the law must be fulfilled. This statement by Jesus about the permanence of the law raises many questions for us. Some of the most significant of these questions need to be set out here: How is the law to be fulfilled today? Just how does the Old Testament law apply to our lives? How much of the law remains in force? Should we commit ourselves to theonomy, which may be briefly stated as the conviction that the Old Testament laws should become the laws of the United States today? Should we take all the Old Testament commandments and simply apply them to our local, state, and national government and legal systems as if we were a contemporary version of Old Testament Israel? In answer to these questions there are widely differing views on offer in the church.

VIEWS ON OLD TESTAMENT LAW AND ITS APPLICATION TODAY

1. *Many churches and individual believers take the view that none of the Old Testament law should apply today.* Those who take this approach insist on a radical discontinuity between the Old and New Testaments. The most

---

[2] Matthew 5:13–20, NIV.

radical dispensationalists regard the Old Testament as an age of law in which the Israelites were saved by obedience to the law. We are in an age of grace, redeemed by Christ, and so the law no longer applies to us. In addition, most of those who hold this view insist that Christians should not be involved in trying to influence secular society. This position also holds that the church age is an interruption in God's purposes for Israel, and that once the church is raptured, God will get back to dealing with Israel, with the law as the means of their justification.

As we saw in an earlier chapter, many dispensationalists have now moderated these views and recognize that God's people are saved by grace in every age. In addition, many dispensationalists now see that at least some of the Old Testament laws have value both for the personal life of the believer and for our wider society.

2. *For many Christians our agenda for involvement is set by the culture and by our political allegiances rather than by Scripture, including Old Testament law*. This acquiescence to current cultural and political forces happens because most of us have never thought about developing a specifically biblical approach to politics, economics, and the laws of the land. The primary reason for this is the lack of teaching on such subjects in most of our churches. The consequence of this lack of teaching is that many of us think about political, economic, judicial, and social issues just as our parents did, or as our favorite radio, television, or newspaper commentator or college professor teaches us to think.

Despite this lack of a coherent biblical approach, almost all Christians, whether on the right or on the left of the political spectrum, will often use Scripture and God's commands to support their positions on political, economic, judicial, or social issues, but the Scriptures are appealed to and interpreted in a somewhat random manner.

If one's personal or family convictions are left-leaning, then the biblical appeal will be to laws about oppression of the poor, about the treatment of widows and orphans, about care for the environment, about mercy to aliens, and about other matters of social policy that are often considered liberal concerns. If one's personal or family convictions are right-leaning, then the biblical appeal will be to laws about work obligations, about responsibility, about economic opportunity, about sexual behavior, about human life, and about other matters of personal morality that are often considered conservative priorities.

But why should a Christian fit into either of these categories? Our desire ought to be faithfulness to God's Word in all of these matters, regardless of what the political right or left thinks at this moment of history. If I may give a personal example: I had been teaching a women's Bible study in a particular church in St. Louis for fifteen years. We covered Romans, Colossians, the life and letters of Peter, conversations with Jesus, women of the Word, Proverbs, Psalms, and the book of Revelation. When it was reported to me that some of the women were saying, "We cannot tell whether he is a liberal or a conservative," I was greatly encouraged by the comment!

3. *Many Christians hold to the view that out of the whole Old Testament law, only the Ten Commandments are still in force today, because they are so clearly a foundational part of God's Word.* Those who take this view usually see the Ten Commandments as primarily matters of personal obedience for the Christian and not as a means of serving the wider society. If this is our understanding of God's law, then we will likely resemble those in position 2 above. Our approach to political, economic, judicial, and social issues will be shaped primarily by our particular personal, family, educational, and social backgrounds.

4. *Another view of God's commandments is that only those laws repeated in the New Testament still apply to the believer at the present time.* Basically this view appears to be another version of the radical disjunction between the Old and New Testaments and of the very different callings of Israel and the church. Only when we have either Jesus or the apostles repeating a law is that law still in force for us. However, this understanding does not take seriously enough the words of Jesus in the Sermon on the Mount about the abiding nature of all God's law. Nor does this understanding reckon with the easy manner in which the New Testament quotes and alludes to many aspects of the Old Testament law. The New Testament writers seem to take it for granted that simply because the Old Testament is the Word of God, it is written for our instruction; indeed they explicitly teach as much.[3] Because this is the conviction of

---

[3] Romans 15:4.

the New Testament, we find that any commandment can be referred to as still having authority over the people of God.

5. *Other believers have held a view that Old Testament law can be neatly divided into ceremonial, civil, and moral, and that only the moral law still applies.* It is certainly true that many of the laws do fall into one of these three divisions (as the Westminster Confession acknowledges). However, these divisions are not hard and fast. For example, many of the ceremonial laws include moral and civil aspects. Many of the civil laws include moral aspects. A problematic consequence of this view, if it is held with systematic rigor, is that the beauties of the ceremonial and civil aspects of the law become lost to us during this present age.

6. *The law of Moses provides us with God's blueprint for every society in history. Therefore, Old Testament laws should be applied in totality to our society today.* This is the view of the theonomists, or Christian Reconstructionists. Such an approach to the law often stands together with postmillennial convictions about the future. Postmillennialists believe that by the proclamation of the gospel and the application of the law to our world, the nations will be transformed before the return of Christ. The gospel and the law will usher in the millennium toward the end of our present age, bringing long-term peace, social stability, and justice to our world.

I am not convinced that the Scriptures teach postmillennialism. However, I acknowledge gladly that the proclamation of the gospel and of God's commandments can indeed bring about change in a society. I see Scripture teaching that these changes are firstfruits of cultural transformation, but they are never a full realization of the kingdom. This partial transformation parallels our own growth and change as individual believers. In our own personal lives we see what Schaeffer called "supernaturally restored relationships" and "substantial healing"; but we do not see sinless perfection or anything even approaching it. To paraphrase Paul's words in Romans 7, "the good that we wish to do we do not do, and the evil that we do not want to do, that is what we do." This remains true of us throughout our lives and throughout this age. How much more is this true of the societies in which Christians live alongside unbelievers! In this age we never approach anything like the full coming of the kingdom, for there is always sin and idolatry in all our human institutions. These things are the reality of every human heart and of every human society throughout this age.

I am also convinced that the views of theonomy do not do justice to the distinction that the Scriptures do make between the calling of Israel in the Old Testament period and the calling of the church since the coming of Christ. I will address some aspects of this distinction in the next section. Here I will simply say that the Bible uses a series of comparisons and images to point to the relationship between the Testaments: promise and fulfillment; shadow and reality; preparation and coming, and so forth.

7. *The view I take is that the whole law provides us with principles for our personal lives and for serving the societies in which we live.* Below I will try to flesh out this idea for our reflection. Whichever of these seven views we are attracted to, we need to recognize that Jesus makes a very strong statement about the abiding nature of the law:

> Do not think that I have come to abolish the Law or the Prophets; I have not come to abolish them but to fulfill them. I tell you the truth, until heaven and earth disappear, not the smallest letter, not the least stroke of a pen, will by any means disappear from the Law until everything is accomplished.[4]

All Christians are to submit to Jesus's teaching; and so we all need to seek to understand how the law is to be fulfilled in our lives and in our societies.

THE LAW AS PRINCIPLES FOR LIFE AND SOCIETY

We will begin these reflections with a point I made earlier: when we look at the rest of the New Testament, we find that various Old Testament laws are repeated in the New Testament writings. Without having to think very hard, we remember the repetition of commandments such as "Do not kill," "Do not commit adultery," "Do not steal," and "Honor your father and mother."

In addition to these obvious examples, we find other laws readily referenced. Every Christian is familiar with Jesus's summary of the

[4] Matthew 5:17–18, NIV.

teaching of the Law and the Prophets: "You shall love the Lord your God with all your heart and with all your soul and with all your mind. This is the first and great commandment. And a second is like it: You shall love your neighbor as yourself."[5] What many Christians do not realize is that Jesus is not simply summarizing but is actually quoting the Old Testament law.[6]

Two other sample quotations of Old Testament laws appear in Paul's letters to the Corinthians and to Timothy: "You shall not muzzle an ox when it treads out the grain"; "The laborer deserves his wages."[7] In both cases Paul applies these laws to the financial support of teachers of God's Word. It is evident that Paul deems it appropriate to cite Old Testament laws about agriculture and then use them in an entirely different setting. Paul can do this because he sees these agricultural commandments as still in force and meant to be fulfilled in the Christian life.

In an earlier chapter we referred to Gordon Wenham's idea of the floor of the law. We saw that the believer's calling was to search for the moral principle, or the divine characteristic, at the heart of each law and then seek to apply this principle or imitate this characteristic in all of life. So Boaz, for example, understood that the laws that allowed aliens, widows, and orphans to glean required him to seek to imitate the kindness of God to his people. Paul has a similar attitude as he cites laws about letting animals feed as they work for their employer, or laws about fair pay for laborers. Paul realizes that these laws apply to any setting: a working animal, a human employee in any occupation, or a teacher of the gospel of Christ.

Another example comes from the very next verse in 1 Timothy, where we find Paul referencing another law, to which Jesus also appealed. Paul writes, "Do not admit a charge against an elder except on the evidence of two or three witnesses."[8]

Jesus quotes the law's requirement regarding witnesses in the context of church discipline of a fellow believer who is guilty of flagrant sin. Paul quotes this law about sufficient witnesses in the context of

---

[5] Matthew 22:37–39.
[6] See Leviticus 19:18; Deuteronomy 6:5.
[7] 1 Corinthians 9:7–9, particularly verse 9, and 1 Timothy 5:18, quoting Deuteronomy 24:14–15; 25:4; Leviticus 19:13.
[8] 1 Timothy 5:19; see also Matthew 18:16. Paul and Jesus are both citing Deuteronomy 17:6; 19:15.

serious problems in the conduct of church leaders. Both Jesus and Paul quote the law and then apply it to a very different situation than that originally envisioned. The original setting involved matters of civil justice and testimony sufficient to convict someone of a crime subject to punishment that might include the death penalty, such as willful murder. The law in its original setting also dealt with the problem of false testimony and the "purging" of that evil from Israel by making the penalty for false witness equivalent to the penalty for the crime about which the false testimony was given.

These examples, and we could find many more, teach us that the New Testament treats the law as principles to be fulfilled in a variety of ways. We are to ask ourselves what is the intent, what is at the heart, of every aspect of biblical law. Then we are to consider how we can apply these principles today in every part of our lives. We will consider some illustrations of this.

GETTING TO THE HEART OF PARTICULAR LAWS

Ceremonial Laws

Our first illustration comes from the ceremonial law and its commandments about the sacrifices, the priesthood, the tabernacle, and the temple.

1. *The laws about the ceremonies are never simply about the external observance of the different forms of worship that are prescribed, for the Old Testament itself applies all the language of the ceremonies to the hearts and lives of believers.* For example, God does not want merely the physical circumcision of male children. He desires circumcision of the hearts of all of his people, male and female.[9] God hates and despises sacrifices and ceremonies that are offered without faith or as a means to try to satisfy God with external obedience. The words of David in his psalm of confession and repentance after his sin are a very obvious illustration of this:

> For you will not delight in sacrifice, or I would give it;
>> you will not be pleased with a burnt offering.
> The sacrifices of God are a broken spirit;
>> a broken and a contrite heart, O God, you will not despise. . . .

---

[9] Deuteronomy 10:16–22. This passage about circumcision of the heart is addressed to the whole people of God.

> then you will delight in right sacrifices,
>> in burnt offerings and whole burnt offerings;
>> then bulls will be offered on your altar.[10]

One of the most striking illustrations of this principle is God's repudiation of the merely formal prayer and fasting of his people. This dramatic denunciation comes in the writing of the prophet Isaiah:

> Cry aloud; do not hold back;
>> lift up your voice like a trumpet;
> declare to my people their transgression,
>> to the house of Jacob their sins.
> Yet they seek me daily
>> and delight to know my ways,
> as if they were a nation that did righteousness
>> and did not forsake the judgment of their God;
> they ask of me righteous judgments;
>> they delight to draw near to God.
> "Why have we fasted, and you see it not?
>> Why have we humbled ourselves,
>>> and you take no knowledge of it?"
> Behold, in the day of your fast you seek your own pleasure,
>> and oppress all your workers.
> Behold, you fast only to quarrel and to fight
>> and to hit with a wicked fist.
> Fasting like yours this day
>> will not make your voice to be heard on high.
> Is such the fast that I choose,
>> a day for a person to humble himself?
> Is it to bow down his head like a reed,
>> and to spread sackcloth and ashes under him?
> Will you call this a fast,
>> and a day acceptable to the LORD?

> Is not this the fast that I choose:
>> to loose the bonds of wickedness,
>> to undo the straps of the yoke,
> to let the oppressed go free,
>> and to break every yoke?

---

[10] Psalm 51:16–19.

Is it not to share your bread with the hungry
    and bring the homeless poor into your house;
when you see the naked, to cover him,
    and not to hide yourself from your own flesh?
Then shall your light break forth like the dawn,
    and your healing shall spring up speedily;
your righteousness shall go before you;
    the glory of the LORD shall be your rear guard.
Then you shall call, and the LORD will answer;
    you shall cry, and he will say, "Here I am."
If you take away the yoke from your midst,
    the pointing of the finger, and speaking wickedness,
if you pour yourself out for the hungry
    and satisfy the desire of the afflicted,
then shall your light rise in the darkness
    and your gloom be as the noonday.
And the LORD will guide you continually
    and satisfy your desire in scorched places
    and make your bones strong;
and you shall be like a watered garden,
    like a spring of water,
    whose waters do not fail.
And your ancient ruins shall be rebuilt;
    you shall raise up the foundations of many generations;
you shall be called the repairer of the breach,
    the restorer of streets to dwell in.[11]

This beautiful passage from Isaiah makes it very clear that at the heart of all Old Testament laws about ritual, ceremony, devotion, and worship is the call to love God with heart, soul, mind, and strength, and to love one's neighbor as oneself. It would be easy to multiply such examples from every aspect of the religious life of God's people. The fundamental point here is this: the Lord despises religious devotion that is only external. Unless the worshipper comes to the Lord with his or her heart engaged, then the Lord rejects whatever is offered, no matter how costly, beautiful, time-consuming, or complex. The Lord receives only worship that comes from the whole person, body and spirit.

---

[11] Isaiah 58:1–12.

2. *All of these laws about worship and all the ceremonies associated with them picture the ministry of Jesus Christ and find their fulfillment in him.* Christ is the sacrifice, for he fulfills in his presentation of his perfect life and in the offering up of himself to death every aspect of the Old Testament sacrificial system. Christ is the Lamb of God who takes away the sins of the world. Christ is the Passover, who stays God's judgment. Christ is the Great High Priest, who stands between us and a holy God, interceding for us as one who shares our humanity, and yet is perfect. Christ is true God, who tabernacles among us. Christ is the temple, God's presence on earth. Christ is our Sabbath rest.

3. *The New Testament applies all the language of the ceremonies to believers.* We are to be living sacrifices, offering our praises and lives to God. We are God's priests on earth. We are the temple of the Holy Spirit, for the Spirit of God dwells in us individually and corporately. We are the firstfruits of the new creation. Thus Paul says, "I appeal to you therefore brothers [and sisters], by the mercies of God, to present your bodies as a living sacrifice, holy and acceptable to God, which is your spiritual worship."[12]

The New Testament has a great many such examples. Believers should have no hesitation in reading any part of these Old Testament laws and applying them to themselves, as my father-in-law did with the laws about offering his firstfruits to the Lord. Dad asked his heart: What is the intent of these ceremonial laws? How may I apply them in my own life? What will it mean for my life as a farmer in Central California to offer my firstfruits to the Lord? Dad was being obedient to the way the New Testament uses the Old Testament law, for he understood that the principles at the heart of these laws are still in effect. Jesus had taught him that not one iota or dot would pass away from the law until all is fulfilled. Dad believed that Jesus was the great firstfruits who offered himself to the Lord. Dad believed that his life was to be a daily presentation of firstfruits dedicated to the Lord. So Dad presented the firstfruits of his harvest to the Lord in a simple ceremony.

The calling of every believer is to read the ceremonial laws, to understand their original intent, to see how they are fulfilled in Jesus, and then to apply them to his or her daily life.

---

[12] Romans 12:1.

Laws and Penalties about False Teaching, False Worship, and the Like

The laws about false teaching, idolatry, false prophecy, blasphemy, witchcraft, and false worship give us another, very different and rather challenging example of the law's permanence.

In the Old Testament the truth of God's Word and the safeguarding of pure worship are upheld by the death penalty. Think, for example, of Elijah putting the prophets of Baal to death after his confrontation with them on Mount Carmel.[13] In subjecting these false prophets to the death penalty, Elijah was obeying the law. We should note that this penalty for false teaching and impure worship was to be applied by God's people only in Israel, and not in the nations round about Israel. The nation of Israel, as a nation called into being by God, had bound itself by a solemn covenant to worship the Lord and him only. Israel committed itself to the Lord with a declaration of the blessings that would come from obedience and the curses that would come from disobedience. In Deuteronomy 27–29 we read the account of the formal ceremony that was accompanied by these blessings and curses. Israel pronounced on itself and its people the penalty of death for false teaching, for idolatry, for disobedience to the laws about worship, and for the worship of other gods.

The United States has never had such a ceremony; nor has it ever made a commitment to worship the God and Father of our Lord Jesus Christ and no other god. Our Constitution declares that it is against the laws of the land to establish any religion. Church and state were bound together in Old Testament law for the people of Israel. In the United States church and state are bound apart by law.

This is one of the most obvious reasons why it is not appropriate to become a theonomist or simply declare America to be a New Israel that is bound to keep all God's laws—including the laws of the death penalty for false teaching. Our nation has never bound itself to abide by the covenant; nor has it formally committed itself to be a nation that worships the one true God alone. It has not called down the blessings and curses of the law in a formal ceremony.

However, we still need to ask what, if any, is the permanent appli-

---

[13]1 Kings 18.

cation or implication of these penalties for false teaching, for impure worship, and for idolatry. Israel and all other nations are taught by these severe penalties the importance of truth. False beliefs about God, about human life, about the world in which we live, and about how we ought to live bring destruction into the lives of individuals and nations. What we believe and what we teach are fundamental to our individual and national well-being.

Think, for example, of the consequence of the beliefs of Adolf Hitler: a war that led to the deaths of over fifty million people. Or consider the impact of the ideas of communism. Under Stalin more than sixty million people were put to death in the former Soviet Union. In an earlier chapter we saw what happened in Cambodia in the early 1970s with its attempt to have a "pure" Marxist revolution. Between one-third and one-half of the population was killed by the Red Army under Pol Pot's leadership. We all are aware of celebrities and we all know individuals personally whose lives are being wrecked by what they believe and by the idols they serve.

But at this time in history, neither Israel as a nation nor any other nation in the world can formally be identified as God's people. This is the time in history when the gospel of Christ is to go out to all the nations: into a world of Hinduism, Islam, Buddhism, and many other religions and philosophies. The gospel is coming from nations that have no formal covenant with God, and the gospel is going to nations that have no formal covenant with God. It would be completely inappropriate to apply the laws about the death penalty for false teaching and impure worship to Muslim imams, to Hindu priests, to teachers of atheism or Marxism, or to the teachers or practitioners of any other belief system or form of idolatry. It would be inappropriate to do so in nations that send many missionaries or in nations where Christians make up a significant proportion of the population, nations such as the United States, Brazil, Korea, or Ghana. Likewise, it would be inappropriate in nations that receive missionaries, nations where Christians are a tiny minority of the population, such as Japan, France, Saudi Arabia, or Ivory Coast.

Scripture teaches that in this age, the age of the gospel going to all peoples on earth, new weapons apply for upholding the truth and maintaining faithful worship. These weapons are prayer, righteousness, teaching, persuasion, the power of the Spirit, and church discipline; but the weapons for this age are not the death penalty or any other form of civil punishment, like imprisonment, beatings, or fines.

This change of weapons for preserving the truth does not change the permanent nature of the warnings of the law. Jesus himself reminds us that only truth, God's truth, can bring real freedom.[14] And Jesus's warnings against false teaching should strike terror in the hearts of those who communicate untruth. Consider what Jesus has to say about those who lead children astray: "Whoever causes one of these little ones who believe in me to sin, it would be better for him to have a great millstone fastened about his neck and to be drowned in the depth of the sea."[15] All who presume to teach in Christ's name need to heed his words against hypocrisy, falsehood, and ignoring God's commandments:

> Not everyone who says to me, "Lord, Lord," will enter the kingdom of heaven, but the one who does the will of my Father who is in heaven. On that day many will say to me, "Lord, Lord, did we not prophesy in your name, and cast out demons in your name, and do many mighty works in your name?" And then will I declare to them, "I never knew you; depart from me, you workers of lawlessness."[16]

The apostle Paul declares, "But even if we or an angel from heaven should preach to you a gospel contrary to the one we preached to you, let him be accursed."[17] Again, we observe that the intent of the laws about false teaching is still in effect. Denying the truth always destroys people and brings them to judgment.

Laws and Penalties about Human Life, Sexuality, and the Family

Another area where the question of the permanence of the law raises questions for us is the legislation about human life, sexuality, and the family—in particular, the penalties required for disobedience.

---

[14] John 8:32.
[15] Matthew 18:6.
[16] Matthew 7:21–23.
[17] Galatians 1:8. See also 2 Peter 2:1–10; Jude 8–14; Revelation 21:8 and many other passages that warn about the penalties for false teaching, idolatry, and disobeying the commands of the Lord.

In the Old Testament the death penalty is required both for those who wantonly take human life and for those who destroy the integrity of the family unit. Examples of situations where the death penalty was imposed are adultery, homosexual practice, rape, bestiality, and profoundly rebellious children. Lifelong monogamous heterosexual marriage is God's creation ordinance for the whole human race throughout this age. He has instituted the family to be earth's permanent reflection of the heavenly family of the Trinity.

Of course, the Old Testament law makes it clear that God is concerned both with outward obedience to the commands about sexuality, marriage, and family life, and with inward obedience to these commands. For example, the tenth commandment shows us that the aim of the law is the passions of the heart, and not just external behavior.

Jesus, in the Sermon on the Mount, reminds his hearers that this application to the heart is God's eternal standard and that, in God's eyes, lust is just as much a sin as is adultery or fornication. When we look at the New Testament epistles, we discover that church discipline is the penalty for such sins.[18] Yet the passages about church discipline make it very clear that these laws for the church are not to be applied to non-Christians. The church is not like Old Testament Israel, for we are not given the power of the sword to punish evil. The church is separated from the state in this age, according to Scripture as well as the US Constitution.

We may state it as a principle that all the areas of disobedience subject to the death penalty in the nation of Israel are now subject to church discipline for Christian believers where there is no repentance. In addition, the severity of Old Testament penalties for sins that dishonor God's intentions for human sexuality and family teaches us the permanent importance of these matters in the lives of individuals and nations. Honoring chastity, faithful marriage, and the family is basic to the welfare of all people and any human society.

Once more, however, just as with the truth of the gospel, the weapons given to the church have changed. Our calling is to use prayer, example, and teaching so that both believers and unbelievers will see the beauty and blessing that come from obedience to God's command-

---

[18] See, for example, 1 Corinthians 5:9–13; 6:9–11.

ments in these areas of life. Christians may use direct teaching, fiction, drama, movies, music, or whatever other means are consonant with this age to uphold sexual purity and fidelity, or the value of family life, or the protection of human life. We should be working in all appropriate ways to bring God's commands to bear on our society for the sake of the welfare of our fellow citizens. The central intent of these laws is still in effect.

It should be evident that the Old Testament law is a treasure store for helping us have God's agenda for our own lives and for the well-being of our societies. Were we to add chapters on each part of the law, we could begin as Jesus and the apostles did whenever they quoted from the law, by seeking to expose the central principles within the legislation. Then we could turn to the hard work necessary to consider how to apply God's laws about love, justice, mercy, and faithfulness. This application has to be made in a series of concentric circles: first to our own lives, then to our families, then to our churches, then to the areas of work in the world in which God has placed us (just as with Ben Edwards in financial management, or with my father-in-law as a farmer), then to the nation in which we live.

But we need to recognize that there will be no perfect application of the law in this present age. In the Old Testament setting, Moses had to take into account the hardness of people's hearts, and so some of the legislation acknowledges the imperfections of the people.[19] This principle of the hardness of the human heart requires us to recognize that we will often have a higher standard for Christians than we do for the secular society in which we live—for example, with regard to chastity and fidelity—for the New Testament charges us not to judge unbelievers in this area of life.[20]

This principle of the hardness of the human heart also means that we must acknowledge that it takes hard work and many years of effort to bring about changes in a whole society. It is not easy to change the laws of a land. The movie *Sophie Scholl: The Final Days* tells the story of a young Christian woman and her brother who tried to stand against the evils of Hitler's Nazi regime. In such a setting the believer may give

---

[19] Matthew 19:8. The setting of Jesus's words is a discussion about divorce.
[20] 1 Corinthians 5:9–13.

up life in a failed attempt to hold back a great tide of wickedness. In other times and places it may be possible, with the Lord's help, to bring about dramatic change. William Wilberforce worked for a lifetime to abolish the slave trade and slavery.[21]

What matters for each believer is faithfulness to the Lord and to his call to obedience in our particular place and moment of history.

Questions for Personal Reflection and Group Discussion

1. What has been your understanding of Jesus's words about the abiding nature of the law?

2. As you consider the seven different ways of thinking about the use of Old Testament laws today, which view has shaped your own approach?

3. Has the discussion of these seven different ways moved you in a new direction? Are you convinced by my arguments for number 7: all the Old Testament laws apply with regard to their internal focus?

4. Do you see the problems with the approach known as theonomy: seeing Old Testament law as a blueprint for our society today?

5. How would you express the differences between the nation of Israel as God's people and the church in your country today, whether in the United States or in some other nation?

6. Would you call your country a Christian nation, and if so, what would you mean by such a description? What are some of the problems with calling one's homeland a Christian nation?

7. Before reading this chapter, had you seen how clearly the Old Testament insists on internal obedience to the ceremonial laws?

8. Do you have a favorite example of a Christian, or group of Christians, who worked at bringing God's laws to bear on a society?

9. Which aspects of the law would you like to study to discover their inner meaning and then to apply in your own life and in your society?

---

[21] For an account of Wilberforce's life, see Eric Metaxas, *Amazing Grace: William Wilberforce and the Heroic Campaign to End Slavery* (New York: HarperSanFrancisco, 2007).

24

THE NEW COVENANT
AND THE LAW

Many lifetimes would be needed for Christians to explore the full treasury of God's law and then apply particular laws in their own personal lives and to the societies in which we live. Clearly this is a labor that will not cease until the end of this age, for God calls his people to live at different times and in different places across the face of this earth. Whatever geographical or cultural setting is ours, at whatever moment in history, we are called to a life of faithfulness: trusting the Lord, walking in his ways, and seeking to serve the people around us as the Lord's salt and light.

We know that until the Lord comes, our faith, our obedience, and our service will always be incomplete and imperfect, for we ourselves are incomplete and imperfect. Our faith is small and often wavers. Our hearts are prone to stray to idols, and so our obedience is wayward and poor. Our service in society is often hindered by our own selfishness, laziness, and unwillingness to love our neighbors as we love ourselves.

Yet the Lord is coming, and when he comes we will be made new, along with this whole earth. In this final chapter we will address, very briefly, the place of the law in the life to come. We will begin our reflections with a wonderful promise that the Lord made to Israel and Judah through the prophet Jeremiah:

> Behold, the days are coming, declares the LORD, when I will make a
> new covenant with the house of Israel and the house of Judah, not

328 DELIGHTING IN THE LAW OF THE LORD

like the covenant that I made with their fathers on the day when I took them by the hand to bring them out of the land of Egypt, my covenant that they broke, though I was their husband, declares the Lord. For this is the covenant that I will make with the house of Israel after those days, declares the Lord: I will put my law within them, and I will write it on their hearts. And I will be their God, and they shall be my people. And no longer shall each one teach his neighbor and each his brother, saying, "Know the Lord," for they shall all know me, from the least of them to the greatest, declares the Lord. For I will forgive their iniquity, and I will remember their sin no more.[1]

The writer of Hebrews quotes this promise of the new covenant and makes it clear that this is a covenant for God's people today.[2] All believers in Jesus are the recipients of the blessings of this new covenant. (The rest of the New Testament teaches explicitly that the new covenant includes not only Jews, but also Gentiles, as heirs of the promises to Abraham and his descendants, both literal and spiritual Israel.) God promises us that all of us as God's people, from the least to the greatest, will have the law written on our hearts. The time is coming when we will obey the commandments cheerfully, spontaneously, and freely, without effort, without struggle, and without resistance from a sinful nature. There will be no need for sermons to teach us how we are to serve the Lord, no need for personal advice or for warnings and rebukes about our behavior, no need for discipline, no need for confession and repentance, no need for wrestling with our consciences about the choices that need to be made.

Jesus fulfilled the law in his own life gladly, freely, and perfectly. His constant desire was to be obedient to his Father, to do his will, to reflect his character in every thought, word, and act every moment of his days. Paul writes that "Christ is the end of the law for righteousness to everyone who believes."[3] Jesus fulfilled the law for us, presenting his perfect righteousness to God the Father in place of our unrighteousness. Jesus bore the sanctions of the law in his death on the cross, removing from us the penalty of death that we deserve. Every day Jesus

---

[1] Jeremiah 31:31–34.
[2] Hebrews 8:8–13.
[3] Romans 10:4.

stands before the Father, offering to the Father his perfect obedience as ours. Every day Jesus is working in us through his love and by the power of the Spirit, enabling us to begin to love the law and to walk in its ways.

Let us love the law. Let us make it our prayer that we might walk in the ways of the Lord. Let us humble ourselves so that we might be instructed by God's Word and by his Spirit. Let us turn more often to the help that Scripture gives us in the prayers of David. For example, in Psalm 119 David writes about his gratitude for the law of God. He sets out these prayers and praises as completely as he can, virtually from A to Z. Here are two brief sections from that lengthy psalm:

> Teach me, O LORD, the way of your statutes;
>> and I will keep it to the end.
> Give me understanding, that I may keep your law
>> and observe it with my whole heart.
> Lead me in the path of your commandments,
>> for I delight in it. . . .
>
> Your testimonies are my heritage forever,
>> for they are the joy of my heart.
> I incline my heart to perform your statutes
>> forever.[4]

In truth we will treasure the heritage of the commandments forever. The day is most certainly coming when Jesus will make our wills completely new, when the law will be written on our hearts, when we will love the Lord our God with heart and soul and mind and strength, when we will love every neighbor as we love ourselves.

Already, as those who belong to Jesus, we see, as through a glass darkly, the beginnings and outlines of this new life of full and perfect obedience. Our confident prayer is to be, "Lord, write your law on our hearts, we beseech you." Already Jesus is beginning this work, for we are the inheritors of the promises of the new covenant. He will surely complete this work on the day we stand before him and see him face to face.

---

[4] Psalm 119:33–35, 111–12.

A Poem or Hymn for Confession
My sin, Lord Christ, oppresses me,
Betrays my body and my soul,
Corrupts my will and mind and heart;
Forgive me, Lord, and make me whole.

But you, Lord God, remembered me,
Disdained your glory and your throne,
Embodied will and mind and heart;
Praise you who made our life your own.

Then you, dear Lord, replaced me,
Received in death my guilt and shame,
Redeemed my will and mind and heart;
When you, my God, to judgment came.

Your love, Lord Jesus, strengthens me,
To battle sin and self with grace;
Renews my will and mind and heart;
Help me endure to see your face.

My hope, dear Lord, refreshes me
To wait your kingdom and the crown;
Perfect my will and mind and heart;
Oh risen Christ, to earth come down.

General Index

abortion, 17, 30, 45, 47
Abraham
　covenant with, 73–75, 82
　prayer for Sodom and Gomor-
　　rah, 303
absolute truth, 22, 30
Adam and Eve, rebellion of,
　137–38
adultery, 233, 323
Afghanistan, 61
agriculture laws, 103, 114, 116
Aikman, David, 49–50
alienation
　from bodies, 143
　from creation, 141–42
　from God, 139, 152, 157
　from others, 140–41, 152–53
　from self, 139–40, 152–53
aliens, 103, 104–5, 108, 114, 216,
　222, 245, 312
Allen, Woody, 22
Alzheimer's disease, 166–67
America, not in covenant with
　God, 321
Amin, Idi, 47–48
angel of death, 78
animism, 51
anorexia, 139
Antonioni, Michelangelo, 55
Apocalypse Now (film), 22
assurance, 163–64
atheism, 21, 27, 322
atonement, 84
Augustine, 268

Austen, Jane, 278
authority
　loss of respect for, 24
　undermined by legalism, 206

Babylon, peace and prosperity of,
　303–4
Barna, George, 29, 40
beauty, 50
Beckett, Samuel, 55
Bellah, Robert, 298
Bergman, Ingmar, 55
Berry, Wendell, 137
bestiality, 324
Bhagavad-Gita, 55
binding the conscience, 221
Black, Hugo, 309–10
Blade Runner (film), 22
Boaz, 106–11, 115, 216, 222, 278
bodies, resurrection of, 155–57
Brooks, David, 297
Buddhism, 322
bulimia, 139
Burnett, Frances Hodgson, 278–79
business ethics, 46
business laws, 103

call, self-centered, 102–3
Calvin, John, 163, 179, 260, 284,
　289–90, 291–92
　on image of God, 94
　on the law, 180–81
Cambodia, 49–50, 61, 322
Campbell, Joseph, 56

Camus, Albert, 55
Canaan, 76–77
capitalism, 37–38
Carmichael, Amy, 250
carnal Christians, 173
celebrity culture, 191
ceremonial law, 83–84, 88, 103,
    314, 317–20
ceremonial washing, 188–90
champion, 64
childbearing, 143
Child, Lee, 35n9, 109n11
child molestation, 31, 35
children, 164–65
    keeping separate from sinners,
        273
    rebellion of, 224
    rules for, 226
    teaching law to, 278–79
China, 288
choice, 44–46
Christian life
    "how-tos" in, 190–92
    and the law, 173
Christian Reconstructionists, 314
Christian schools, rules for, 218,
    221, 223
Christmas story, 137
church and state, 321
church discipline, 323, 324
circumcision of the heart, 194,
    202, 317
civil discourse, breakdown in,
    298–99
civil law, 314
clean and unclean, 188–90, 192,
    200, 202–3
commandments, inner intent of,
    228
common grace, 284
common law, 35–36
communication and language,
    92–93
communism, 322
conservatism, 313
Corban, 197
Cornelius, 202–3, 215, 245

covenant, 73–75, 85, 87, 321–22
    with creation, 283–85
    of grace, 76
Covenant Theological Seminary,
    278–79
Cowper, William, 165–66
creation, 51–52, 88, 141–42
    renewal of, 157, 160
    subjected to futility, 144
creation structures, 292–93
crime, 30–31, 40
cultural barriers, 256–57
cultural mandate, 90–91
cultural practices, 204, 206
cultural transformation, 314
culture, sets agenda for Christians,
    312
culture war, 23, 277, 296–98
curse, 162, 172
    overcome by Jesus Christ, 151
    removed from creation, 160–61
cynicism, 23–25

Daniel, serving Babylon, 304
Darby, John Nelson, 176–77
David
    acknowledges his sinfulness, 70,
        184
    delight in the law, 11–13, 182–84,
        329
Dead Man Walking (film), 257
death, 143
death penalty, 323–24
Deer Hunter, The (film), 22
defilement, from the heart,
    200–201, 212–13
deism, 18–20, 27, 31, 283
delight, in law, 69, 70
democracy, 47
depression, 165–66
"deserving poor," 105, 114–15
disasters, as God's judgment for
    particular sins, 303
discipline, 223
discrimination, 169
diseases, 172
dispensationalism, 176–78, 186, 312

dominion, 90–91, 144, 289
  loss of, 142–43
  restoration of, 154–55, 168–69
Dylan, Bob, 55
Dyson, Hugo, 95n14

Ecclesiastes, 57–58
Eden, 76–77, 85
Edwards, Ben, 305–6, 308, 325
Egyptians, 77–78
Eliezer, Rabbi, 213
Elijah, 321
elites, power of, 48
Elohim, 66
embryo experimentation, 47
employees, treatment of, 118–19,
  125
environment, 144, 312
environmentalists, 289
eternal life, 126–28, 229
ethnic cleansing, 47
euthanasia, 47
evangelicals
  appeal to rules, 190–92, 204
  on requirements of God's law,
    276
Everson v. Board of Education, 309–10
evolution, 20
existentialism, 21, 44
exodus, 75, 77–78
expert in the law, 125–26, 248–49,
  254, 262–63
external religious devotion, 318–19
extraordinary generosity, 120, 125
Ezekiel, 246

faith, as imperfect, 163
faithfulness, 106, 110, 115, 205, 221,
  313, 325, 326
fall, 93–95, 138–44, 282
false teaching, 321–23
false testimony, 233
false worship, 321–23
families, rules for, 218, 221–23
farming, 104–5, 142
farm subsidies, 48–49
fear of the Lord, 68, 82, 87, 183

Fellini, Federico, 55
fellowship with God, 77, 156
financial crimes, 46
First Amendment, 309
firstfruits, 116–19, 122, 158, 162,
  320
first table of the law, 234, 239
flood, 284
food laws, 201–3, 213
forgiveness, 70–71, 84–85, 184,
  233, 260, 264, 271–72
Formula of Concord, 174
frailties, 164–65
Franklin, Benjamin, 31, 33
fraud, 248–49, 255
freedom
  American understanding of, 103
  seen as opposed to morality, 37
freedom of choice, 44–46
fundamentalism, 178, 191

gardening, 142
gender barriers, 256–57
generosity, 103, 104–5, 107–8, 111,
  114, 119–20
Gentiles, 203–4, 213, 245, 250
gleaning, 107–8, 114
God
  character reflected in law, 13, 52,
    59, 62, 65–66, 68, 82–83, 88,
    99, 181, 220
  as consuming fire, 82
  Creator and sustainer of world,
    282–83, 286
  faithful to covenant, 66, 77, 87,
    100, 113
  as fountain of order and beauty,
    50–51
  generosity of, 108, 125
  glory of, 93
  goodness of, 183, 231–33, 239
  holiness of, 53–54, 58, 92, 261
  love of, 28, 92, 157, 283
  mercy in Christ, 124
  and morality, 42–43
  righteousness of, 84
  sovereignty of, 91, 164, 287–88

work in all the world, 295–96,
     308–9
Golding, William, 46–47
good and evil, 54, 58
good life, and law, 99, 102, 113
goodness, 231–34
good Samaritan, 129, 131–33, 136,
     228, 277, 300
government, 293
grace, 84, 87, 103, 105, 179, 228,
     240, 248–50, 252–55, 261–64
  of law, 127–28, 181–82
gratitude, 80, 82, 87, 184
Green, Michael, 156
guilt, 35, 39

happiness, 103
hardness of human heart, 325
Hardy, Thomas, 55
Harvard Business School, 46
healing, 156–58, 167–70
heart, 133, 194, 200–202, 204, 212,
     327
Hemingway, Ernest, 55
Herbert, Edward (Lord Herbert of
     Cherbury), 18–19
Hinduism, 51, 55, 322
Hindus, 310
Hitler, Adolf, 17, 48, 322
holiness, 70, 97–98, 189, 191, 261,
     274
holiness tradition, 173, 186
Holocaust, 17
Holy Spirit, 34
homosexual practice, 324
honoring parents, 233
hope, 24, 28, 29, 170, 172
hospitality, 120–22, 125, 156, 216,
     245–46, 271
human, meaning of, 54
human calling, 76, 87, 125
human dignity, 256–61
human flourishing, 102, 113, 220,
     226
humanity
  as finite and personal, 89
  limited sovereignty of, 91, 92

sinfulness of, 62
human nature
  modernism on, 20
  postmodernism on, 22
human rules, 190–92, 194–95, 199,
     204–11, 217–25, 226, 276
humility, 218
Hussein, Saddam, 48
hypocrisy, 193–94, 199, 212

Ibsen, Henrik, 55
ideology, 49–50, 60–61
idolatry, 321–23
image of God, 33, 88–93, 256–61
  after fall, 93–95, 289
  restoration of, 96–97, 101
imitation of God, 97, 99
immortality, 155
incarnation, 145
individual, autonomy of, 19, 44–46
individualism, 292
Ionesco, Eugene, 55
Isaiah, 318–19
Islam, 17, 49, 60–61, 288, 322
Israel
  and the church, 312, 313
  in covenant with God, 321
  disobedience and rebellion of,
     106

James, letter of, 174
Jefferson, Thomas, 31, 310
Jenkins, Jerry, 176
Jeremiah, 50
Jesus
  born under the law, 145–46, 148,
     151
  deity of, 241
  fulfilled law, 320, 328
  goodness of, 231–33
  as Great High Priest, 301
  on human rules, 192–98
  as image of God, 96–97
  kept company with sinners,
     246–47, 256, 300
  on the law, 79–80, 125–29,
     252–64

on legalism, 208–10
obedience of, 145, 148, 151–52, 179, 329
patience and kindness of, 254
as true Israel, 151
John Paul II, Pope, 16
Jonah, 304
Joseph, serving Egypt, 304
Jubilee, 103
Judaizers, on the law, 79–80
Judges, 106
judging others, 255, 274–75, 299–300
Julius Caesar, 244
justice, 205, 221, 325

Keller, Tim, 34
Khmer Rouge, 49, 61
Khomeini, Ayatollah, 288
kingdom of God, 236–37
kingdom of priests, 189–90
kneeling before Jesus, 262
knowing and doing the truth, 132–33
Kuyper, Abraham, 154

L'Abri, 120
LaHaye, Tim, 176
law, 30–31
additions to, 187–92
beauty of, 66–68
and character of God, 13, 59, 62, 68, 82–83, 88, 99, 181, 220
and conviction of sin, 84, 175, 180, 232, 237, 240
as definition of humanness, 97, 99, 101
and ethics, 104
as floor, 109, 119, 316
and grace, 127–28, 178
inadequate views of, 173–79, 186
leads to Christ, 180, 181–82
not a means of earning merit, 85, 100–101
open to manipulation, 39
as pedagogue, 263
permanence of, 311, 321, 323

principles of, 125, 315
righteousness of, 231–37
universality of, 34
written on hearts, 290, 329
lawlessness, 30–31
legalism, 39, 178–79, 187, 192, 199–200, 204–11, 217, 227–28
Levites, 302
Lewis, C. S., 23, 34, 40, 51, 62, 95
liberalism, 312–13
Liddell, Eric, 64, 155
light, 65–66, 68, 70
likeness of God, 89. *See also* image of God
Lindsay, Hal, 176
Lion, the Witch and the Wardrobe, The (Lewis), 279
litigation, 38
living sacrifices, 320
lobbying, 39
Lord's Supper, 163
Lou Gehrig's disease, 143
love, 28, 103, 205, 221–22, 325
for enemies, 154
for God, 104, 239, 263, 276, 315, 319
for law, 329
for neighbor, 104, 131–33, 152–53, 221, 232, 239, 263, 276, 316, 319
Luther, Martin, 174, 272
Lutheranism, on the law, 173, 174–76, 186

majority vote, 47
man, as "microcosm," 289–90
Mapplethorpe, Robert, 15
marriage and family, 90, 289, 292, 298, 324
Marriage Supper of the Lamb, 247
Mars Hill, 287
Marxism, 49–50, 60–61, 322
Mary of Bethany, 267–68
Matrix, The (film), 22
Matthew, 247
maturity, growth in, 222, 224, 227
melamine, 32

mercy, 84, 87, 103, 114, 205, 206, 221, 325
Messiah, prophecies of, 149–50
modernism, 17, 18–21
modesty in dress, 196
monastic movements, 191
money, 239
moral certainty, loss of, 24
moral education, 40
moralism, 178–79
morality, 313
    Christian view of, 42–43
    postmodernism on, 36–40, 42–43
moral law, 36, 288, 314
    Christian view of, 31–36
moral order, 30–36
mortality, 155
Moses, 79, 83
"mother promise" of Scripture, 148–49
motivation, for obeying the law, 78–80, 82, 87
murder, 233
Muslims, 49, 288, 310

naming of animals, 91
Naomi, 106–11
nations, belong to God, 287–88
Native Americans, 47
natural religion, 18
natural world, order and beauty of, 56–57
Nazi Germany, 17, 48
Nebuchadnezzar, 287
Nee, Watchman, 173
needy, 216, 247
neighbor, 129, 131–33
new covenant, 328–29
new creation, 76–77, 155
new heaven and new earth, 160
New Testament, quotation of Old Testament law, 315–17
Newton, John, 166
Nietzsche, Friedrich, 37
Nineveh, 304
Noah, covenant with, 283–85

nullifying God's commandments, 196–98, 199, 212

Obama, President, 296–98
obedience, 78–80, 82, 87, 223, 274, 326
objective truth, 22
oppressed, 293, 312
order, 50–52
original sin, 49, 61, 102
orphans, 103, 104–5, 108, 114, 222, 293, 312
outcasts, 245–46

parables, 129–30, 200–201, 278
Paradise Road (film), 257
parents, and church attendance, 34
Passover, 78, 84
Paul
    cites Old Testament laws, 316
    on false teachers, 208
    on government, 293
    on the law, 14, 79–80
    on Mars Hill, 287
    on preaching Christ, 304
pedophilia, 40
Pentecostal churches, 173
perfection, 314
personal truth, 22
Peter
    and Cornelius, 202–3, 215–16, 245
    on making known mercy of God, 304
Pharaoh, 77–78
Pharisees, 130
    additions to law, 187–90, 195, 200, 203, 214
    on obedience to law, 79–80
    pride of, 209–10
    on separation from sinners, 255, 273
Phelps, Michael, 64
physical death, 143
piety, 191
Pilate, 244
pluralism of belief, 23

Polanski, Roman, 55
political allegiances, 312
Pol Pot, 49–50, 322
poor, 48, 103, 104–5, 108, 114, 216, 234–37, 246, 312
postmillennialists, 314
postmodernism, 21–25, 27, 36–40, 42–43, 310
power, 47–49
practical wisdom, 227
prayer, 28–29, 303–4, 324
Presbyterian Church in America, 195, 221
pride, 208–10, 218, 277
Pride and Prejudice (Austen), 278
priesthood of believers, 301–6
proclamation, 304
prodigal son, parable of, 224, 228–29
Promised Land, 76
protoevangelium, 149
Proverbs, 227
providence, 107, 109–10
punishment, 40

racial barriers, 256–57
racism, 169
radiant, law as, 68, 183
Rahab, 111
Rand, Ayn, 37–38
rape, 167, 324
rationality, 92
reason, 20, 21
reconciliation, 153–54
Reformed churches, on the law, 173, 178–79
relationships, 90, 169
broken by sin, 140–41
relativism, 27, 30, 32, 36, 290, 310
religious barriers, 256–57
repentance, 248, 255
responsibility, 38, 298, 312
restitution, 248–49
resurrection, 157
revelation, in creation, 63–65
reviving, law as, 67, 182–83

rich young ruler, 229–37, 239–40, 248–49, 254, 262–63
righteous, law as, 68, 183
righteousness, 68, 98, 273
rights, 38
ritual washings, 200
Rolling Stones, 55
Roman Catholics, 16
Roman Empire, 244
rulers
obligations of, 103n6
prayer for, 304
rules. *See* human rules
Ruth, 106–11, 115, 216, 278

Sabbath, 76, 103
Sabbatical year, 103
sacred/secular distinction, 189
sacrifices, 83–84, 88
salt and light, 293, 296, 303, 306, 308, 310–11
salvation, 250
salvation by works, 85, 231
Samaritans, 213
Samaritan woman, 242–43
sanctification, 96, 178–79
Sanhedrin, 229
Sartre, Jean-Paul, 41, 44, 55, 58
Sayers, Dorothy, 298
Schaeffer, Edith, 162
Schaeffer, Francis, 34, 89, 95, 138n4, 155, 157–58, 161, 162, 178–79, 260, 301, 314
schizophrenia, 166
school of the law, 262–64, 265, 273, 275, 277
science, 20, 21
Scofield, Cyrus I., 177
"second blessing," 164
second table of the law, 232, 234, 235, 239–40
Secret Garden, The (Burnett), 278–79
secular culture, negative reactions to, 178, 191
secular humanism, 20–21, 27, 43–44, 310
secular society, laws for, 282–93

self, old and new, 153
self-alienation, 139–40
self-righteousness, 208, 217, 256, 303
  of Simon the Pharisee, 271–72
Sermon on the Mount, 217, 235, 296, 324
service, 304–6
sexual assault, 108–9
sexual intercourse, before marriage, 17
sexuality, 30, 32, 45, 277–78, 298, 324
Shakespeare, William, 95–96
shame, 139, 261
shared knowledge, 23
sicknesses, 172
Simon the Pharisee, 217, 265–66, 268, 270–72, 276
simul justus et peccator, 272
sin
  deep sense of, 253–54, 255
  sevenfold effects of, 138–44
Sinai, 53, 75–83
sinners
  association with, 255, 261, 273
  dismissal of, 255–61, 274
  kindness to, 216, 245
skepticism, 23–24, 27, 36
slavery, 35, 326
slavery prostitution, 35, 109n11
Sodom and Gomorrah, 303
Solzhenitsyn, Aleksandr, 38, 39
son of Abraham, 250
Sophie Scroll: The Final Days (film), 325
Soviet Union, 287, 322
spirit of the law, 109, 116
spiritual death, 143
spiritual disciplines, 191
spiritual poverty, 217
Stalin, Joseph, 322
state, 293
stealing, 114–15
stewardship, 124, 155, 223–24, 249
Stiles, Ezra, 33
stories, 135–37, 147

storm theophany, 53, 81
Strauss, Richard, 55
substantial healing, 157–58, 161–62, 314
suffering, 54, 161, 168
summary judgments, 255–56
sun, 64, 66, 68, 70
"supernaturally restored relationships," 314
Swinburne, Algernon Charles, 37

tabernacle, 85
Taliban, 61
Tamar, 167
tax collectors, 214–16, 243–44, 247, 248,
Ten Commandments, 67, 313
terrorism, 17
theft, 233, 248, 255
theonomy, 311, 314–15, 321
third use of the law, 174, 180–81
Tindal, Matthew, 19
tithing, 119
Tolkien, J. R. R., 95, 260
Torah, 67
Tower of Babel, 287
traditional values, 296–98
traditions of men, 188–89, 193, 200, 214, 245
treasure in heaven, 235
treasure on earth, 235, 239
Trinity, 90
trustworthy, law as, 67–68, 183
truth, 27, 29–30, 32
  as personal, 45
  postmodernism on, 22, 24
two great commandments, 127–28, 136
2 Live Crew, 15–16

unbelievers, 301
  and law, 282
  special graces of, 291–92
unclean, 213, 214, 245–46

violence toward women, 46

war of words, 298–99
Washington, George, 31
wealth, 234–37, 249–50
wedding feast, 156
Wenham, Gordon, 104, 316
Wesley, John, 173
Wesleyan movement, 173
"we versus they" mentality, 299
widows, 103, 104–5, 108, 114, 222, 293, 312
Wilberforce, William, 326
Wilder, Laura Ingalls, 279
Williams, Michael, 91, 148
wisdom, 34, 222, 227, 290–92
Witherspoon, John, 31
woman at the well, 213–14

woman who washed Jesus's feet, 216–17
works-righteousness, 207
world, as prosecutor of church, 301
worldly, 206
worldly religion, 207–8
worship, 81–82, 87, 206
wrath of God, 138, 151, 302

Yahweh, 66, 246
youth ministry
    rules for, 218, 220, 223
    and separation from sinners, 273

Zacchaeus, 214–16, 240–50, 252–55, 261, 262, 263, 265

Scripture Index

Genesis

1	88
1:20	89n2
1:24	89n2
1:26	90
1:26–27	89n1
1:26–28	88, 93
1:27	88, 90
1:28	90n4
2	91
2:7	89n2
3	139, 143, 149
3:1–20	149
3:15	148n
5:1–3	289n24
8:16–17	284n9
8:20–22	302n18
8:21–22	284n9
9:1–3	284n9
9:6	93, 289n24
9:7–17	284n9
9:8–17	283n6, 302n18
11	287n18
12:1–3	74n2
15	74n2
17	74n2
17:7	75n5
17:7–8	85n24
18:16–33	303n22
22:1–18	149
22:15–18	74n2
48:15–16	149
49:8–10	149

Exodus

1	77
3:6	74n3
3:15	74n3
14:30–31	78n10
15:2–3	78n11
19	53
19:4	77n9
19:5	75n4, 178
19:6	189n
19:11	81n16
19:16–19	53n19, 81n17
20	76
20:2	67n5, 77n8
20:8–11	76n6
20:18	53n19, 81n17
22:1–5	248n14
23:4–5	132n
24:4–8	84n22
30:17–21	188n2
40:30–32	188n2

Leviticus

book of	116
6:5	248n13
8:5–6	188
19	83, 97, 99
19:1–2	83, 97n21, 99n
19:9–10	104n
19:13	316n7
19:18	316n6
23:9–14	116n
23:15–21	116n

26:11–13	85n25

Numbers

1:52–53	302n19
5:6–7	248n14
16:47–48	302n17
23:18–24	149
24:3–9	149
24:15–19	149

Deuteronomy

4:1–8	97n23
4:5–8	83n20
4:37–40	79n12
6:5	316n6
10:12–13	97n23
10:16	202n4
10:16–22	317n
14:28–29	105n9
17:6	316n8
18:14–22	149
19:15	316n8
22:1–4	132n
24:14–15	316n7
24:19–22	105n8
25:4	316n7
27	151n
27–29	321
28	151n
28:1–6	178

Judges

book of	106
19	109
21:25	45n, 106n

Ruth

1:19	108
2:3	108
2:4	108
2:7	108
2:8–9	108
2:9	109
2:11–12	110
2:14–16	109
2:19–22	110
2:22	108

3:10	110

2 Samuel

7:1–17	149
12:6	248n14

1 Kings

18	321n

Job

19:23–27	150
38–41	51

Psalms

1	187
1:1–4	101n
2	150
8	94, 98, 259, 289n24
8:3–4	94n8
8:3–6	260n4
8:5–6	94n10
16	150
19	51, 57, 66, 71, 73, 182, 187
19:1–4	52n17, 57n29
19:1–6	62–63
19:2	63
19:3–4	63
19:4	71, 184, 282n3
19:4–6	64
19:7	67
19:7–8	281n
19:7–9	66, 182
19:7–11	65, 66, 182
19:10–11	69, 183
19:11	69, 183
19:12	70
19:12–14	69, 184n
19:13	70
19:14	70, 71
22	150
23	67, 183
24:1	282n2
25	12, 18, 25, 100, 113
25:4	113n
25:4–11	12n, 25, 100n3
25:4–14	97

25:8	97n22, 100n2
36:1	275n
49:7–9	270n5
51	202
51:16–19	318n
51:17	202n5
72	150
82	94n9, 291n29, 293n37, 294
82:1–4	103n
104	51, 283n5, 285
104:14–15	285n11
107	28–29
107:4–20	29n2
107:43	29n3
110	150
115:16	91n5, 144n12
119	187
119:18	35
119:33–35	329n
119:97	73n1
119:111–12	329n
145	285
145:9	285n10
145:14	285n12
145:15–17	285n10
148	51
148:3–6	51n15

Proverbs
book of	227
4:18	158n
8:1–4	34n7, 291n28
8:15–16	34n7, 291n28
31:8–9	103n

Ecclesiastes
1–2	57
1:2	57n30

Isaiah
6:3	52n18, 82n19
7:14	150
9:1–7	150
11:1–9	157n14
11:1–10	150
42:1–10	150

49:1–7	150
50:4–11	150
52:13–53:12	150
58:1–12	319n
59:2	138n5

Jeremiah
2:13	50n8
23:1–6	150
29:4–7	304n25
31:31–34	328n1
33:14–18	150

Ezekiel
34	246
34:1–31	150
34:11–16	246n8

Daniel
4	287n19
7:9–14	150
7:14	246n9

Hosea
6:7	284n8

Amos
1	293n37, 294
1:3–2:3	291n29
2	293n37, 294

Jonah
4	307
4:1–4	303n24
4:9–11	303n24

Micah
5:2–5a	150

Zechariah
9:9–10	150
12:10–13:1	150

Malachi
3:1–4	150
4:1–6	150

Matthew
1:18–25	150
2:1–12	150

4:4   69n6
5:3   217n
5:13   303n20
5:13–16   205n10, 296n,
               301n13
5:13–20   311n
5:17–18   137n2, 315n
5:43–48   304n29
5:44–45   286n14
6:1–18   217n
6:19–21   235n12
6:26–29   286n13
7:1–5   300n10
7:21–23   323n16
9:9–10   247n10
9:9–13   205n11, 247n11,
               300n7
9:12–13   261n
11:19   205n11, 261n,
               300n9
13:9–17   129n4
13:34–35   129n4
15   187, 200, 209
18:6   323n15
18:16   316n8
19:8   325n19
19:22   229n3
21:28–32   300n7
22:34–40   94n9
22:37–39   316n5
22:37–40   13n2
23   209, 228
23:1–32   300n5
23:15   207n13
23:23   205n9, 221n10,
               300n5
23:37   209n17
25:21   123n
25:23   123n
26:6–13   136n
28:18–20   288n20

Mark
4:9–13   129n4
6:53   187

7   187, 200, 203, 204,
               209, 228
7:1–5   188n1
7:6–13   193n
7:8   195
7:9   195
7:13   195
7:14–16   200n
7:17–23   201n2
10:17   229n4n, 230n7
10:21   230n8
12:28–34   127n2

Luke
1:1–4   240n
1:5–38   150
1:39–80   150
2:1–20   150
2:52   241n3
5:8   241n4
6:27–28   303n21
6:27–36   286n15
6:32–33   289n25
6:35–36   286n15
7:36–50   216n, 266n, 300n8
7:39   205n11
7:47   271n
8:8–10   129n4
8:41   229n5
10:25–29   125
10:25–37   228n, 300n6
10:27   127n1
10:30–35   129n3
11:11–13   289n25
12:37   156n12, 247n12
13   244
13:1   244n
13:1–5   303n23
14:12–24   247n12
15   261n
15:1–7   300n9
15:11–32   224n14
18:9–14   79n13, 205n8,
               300n12
18:18   80n14, 229n2
18:18–23   230n6

18:18–27	229
18:22	234n
19:1–6	300n7
19:1–7	215n4
19:1–10	214n, 241n2
19:7	205n11
19:7–10	300n9
19:8	252n
19:10	269n3

John

1:1–14	150
1:8–2:2	225n
1:17	177, 178, 178n
1:18	153n5
3:13	53n21
3:17	300n9
4	213, 251
4:7	213
4:9	213n1
4:20–24	201n3
4:27	214
4:34	145n13
8:1–11	300n8
8:29	145n15
8:32	323n14
9:41	209n16
10:34	94n9
12:47	300n9
12:49–50	145n16
13:1–20	270n6
13:23	153n5
13:34–35	205n10, 301n14
14:15	223n12
14:31	145n14
17:15–19	196n
17:20–21	205n10
17:23	205n10, 301n14

Acts

book of	203n7, 209
10	202
10:28	203n6, 215n5, 245n
14:15–17	287n16
14:17	34n6
14:22	170n6

17:24–28	287n17

Romans

1	290
1:18–21	282n3
1:18–28	288n23
1:18–32	138n6
1:20	63n4
2	290
2:4	288n22
2:14–15	34n7, 290n27
3	93
3:19–20	138n6
3:21	178
3:22	178
3:23	93n, 232n
4:4	178
4:5	178
5:7	289n25
7	80, 168, 173, 314
7:7–25	153n3
7:8–11	207n12
7:14–24	44n3
7:24	139n
8	144
8:4	178
8:20–23	144n11
10:4	80n15, 328n3
10:4–10	176
12:1	320n
12:1–2	14n
12:14	303n21
13:1–7	291n29, 293n36
13:8–10	222n
13:10	13n3
15:4	117n, 313n
15:16	304n28
15:20	304n28

1 Corinthians

4:8–13	170n5
5:9–13	300nn11–12, 324n, 325n20
6:9–11	324n
6:13	155n10
9:7–9	316n7

9:9	316n7
11:31	300n11
14:40	218n
15:19–26	170n7

2 Corinthians

3:18	96n20
5:10	138n7
5:17–20	77n7

Galatians

book of	203n7
1:6–9	208n
1:8	323n17
2:11–16	203n6
3:24	263n
4:4–5	137n3
5:1	210n, 224n15
5:6	269n4
5:17	168n
5:18	80n15
6:7–8	288n23

Ephesians

1:20–23	288n20
2:1–9	178
2:3	138n6
2:8	178
2:11–22	154n6
3:1–10	154n8
3:14–15	90n3, 153n4, 292n34
4:20–24	96n18
4:28	114n
6:4	141n

Colossians

book of	203n7
1:16–17	51n11, 283n4
2:8	207n14
2:9	241n5
2:16–17	84n23
2:20	207n14
2:23	195n
3:9–11	96n19
3:19	140n
3:21	141n

4:6	258n3

2 Thessalonians

1:7–8	54n27
2:6–7	288n22

1 Timothy

book of	203n7
1:8–9	80n15
1:16	274n
2:1–3	293n37
2:1–6	304n26
2:3–6	288n21
3:1–6	303n21
4:10	288n21
5:8	198n
5:18	316n7
5:19	316n8

2 Timothy

book of	203n7

Titus

2:9–10	301n15
2:11	288n21

Philemon

1:3	178
1:9	178

Hebrews

1:3	51n12, 283n5
8:8–13	328n2
11	162
12:5–11	223n13
12:18–29	53n21, 81n18
12:28–29	53n22
13:8	50n9
13:15–16	304n29

James

1:17	51n10, 58n31
1:18	77n7
1:22–25	174n
1:25	102n
2:10	268n
3:1	133n
3:9	289n24
3:9–10	94n11, 360n5

5:13–16   156n13

1 Peter
2:9–10   302n16, 304n27
2:12   301n13
3:1–2   301n13
3:15   258n2
4:17   300n11

2 Peter
2:1–10   323n17
3:8–9   288n22
3:13   157n15

1 John
3:2   169n
3:16–18   235n11

Jude
8–14   323n17

Revelation
book of   53
1:6   302n16
4:5   53n23
8:5   53n24
11:19   53n25
16:17–18   53n26
19:9   247n12
21:1–5   157n15, 167n
21:3   85n26
21:8   323n17
21:9   156n12

Seeing Women through God's Eyes

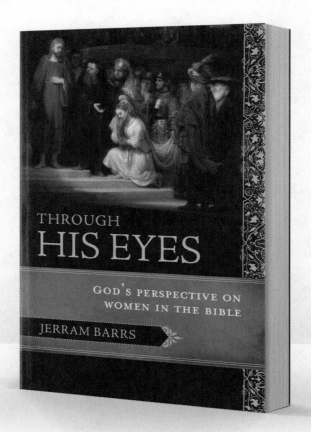

Few teachings have been as misunderstood and muddled as the Bible's instruction concerning women. *Through His Eyes* answers the question **"What does God think about women, and how does he treat them?"** by walking readers through several biblical case studies.

Jerram Barrs writes of the dignity and glory the Lord showers on women. He encourages women to delight in their creation and calling and challenges men to honor women as does the Lord himself.